YOU'RE FIRED

THE PERFECT GUIDE TO
BEATING DONALD TRUMP

PAUL BEGALA

Simon & Schuster

NEW YORK · LONDON · TORONTO
SYDNEY · NEW DELHI

Simon & Schuster
1230 Avenue of the Americas
New York, NY 10020

First Simon & Schuster hardcover edition July 2020

SIMON & SCHUSTER and colophon are registered trademarks
of Simon & Schuster, Inc.

For information about special discounts for bulk purchases,
please contact Simon & Schuster Special Sales at 1-866-506-1949
or business@simonandschuster.com.

The Simon & Schuster Speakers Bureau can bring authors to your
live event. For more information or to book an event, contact
the Simon & Schuster Speakers Bureau at 1-866-248-3049
or visit our website at www.simonspeakers.com.

Manufactured in the United States of America

3   5   7   9   10   8   6   4   2

Library of Congress Control Number: 2020937995

ISBN 978-1-9821-6004-3
ISBN 978-1-9821-6006-7 (ebook)

For Diane: my love, my life.

And for our sons: John, Billy, Charlie, and Patrick—
you give my life meaning. Your activism, your patriotism,
your idealism, your enthusiasm, your brilliance—
and that of your generation—will save us.

CONTENTS

YOU'RE
FIRED

MEA CULPA

What I Got Wrong in 2016

Everyone got 2016 wrong, so I am in good company. But that is small consolation. Here's what I got wrong the last time, and how to avoid repeating this fatal mistake in 2020.

I forgot Bill Clinton's First Law of Politics, taught to me a quarter-century ago by the smartest political mind I've ever known: elections are about the lives of the voters, not the candidates' lives. When we were mired in scandal—either real or manufactured—Clinton would inevitably look at me and say, "If we make this about the voters' lives instead of mine, we will both be better off."

I knew this in 2012. I was an adviser to the pro-Obama super PAC Priorities USA. We had voluminous research on Romney, and one thing was clear from the jump: he is a man of good character. Fine. (Also, great hair, which sent Carville and me into jealous fits.) We weren't interested in attacking his character. My experience in campaigns against people like George H. W. Bush (another man of upstanding character with whom I had important political and policy disagreements) had taught me that attacks on issues are far more effective than personal attacks.

With character attacks ruled out, we decided to define Romney as a rapacious financier who had gotten wealthy in part through business deals that sometimes hurt the middle class. As the top man in the private equity firm Bain Capital, Romney played a role in scores of deals. Some of them, truth be told, were terrific. Great companies like Staples owe their existence in part to Romney and his firm. But this was a campaign and he was the opponent. We didn't mention Romney's good deals. We figured he'd do that.

But there were other deals, like the paper plant in Marion, Indiana. Bain had bought a paper plant, loaded it with debt, drove it into bankruptcy, then laid off all the employees, canceled their health care and pensions, and left the town a desiccated shell. We sent a camera crew to Marion. We interviewed a carpenter from the plant named Mike Earnest. (I know: somewhere Charles Dickens is smiling.) Mike told his story: one day the boss told him to build a stage on the shop floor; the new owners were coming to town and wanted a team meeting. So, Mike and the boys built that stage, and Romney's suits stood on that stage, closed the company, and laid off every worker. Mike, who truly was earnest, looked in the camera and said, "I didn't know it at the time, but when I was building that stage, I was really building my coffin." GOP strategist Frank Luntz called it the most effective ad of 2012. Barack Obama won a second term. (In truth, he would have won without me or our ad; he is that talented. But I am proud to have played a small role in his winning a second term.)

But when 2016 came around, I took my eye off the ball. This time around, our super PAC took as its mission electing Hillary Rodham Clinton, someone I have known and loved for more than a quarter century. And her Republican opponent, Donald Trump: well, I could not stand him.

I was so shocked by Donald Trump's sewer-level character that I could not avert my eyes. Look! He's saying POW John McCain (R-AZ) was not a hero, because he was captured. Look! He's mocking a reporter's physical disability. Look! He's bragging about grabbing women by the . . . well, you know.

We made ads about those outrages. Our first ad—I loved it—

featured people, mostly women, wearing T-shirts bearing various pictures of Trump, unsmiling, often mid-shout. They lip-synced while the audio track repeated some of Trump's most odious vulgar comments: "There was blood coming out of her eyes, there was blood coming out of her . . . wherever." A man has his arm around a woman (presumably his partner) and looks on in astonishment as she mouths these words of Trump's: "Does she have a good body? No. Does she have a fat ass? Absolutely." A young father stands with his daughter and lip-syncs as Trump's distinctive voice says, "If Ivanka weren't my daughter, perhaps I'd be dating her." A white-haired woman throws her hands up in anger as Trump's bellow comes out of her mouth: "And you can tell them to go [BLEEP] themselves!"

We ran another ad, designed to shock the conscience of the electorate—especially Christians. The ad featured a girl in Columbus, Ohio, named Grace, who was born with spina bifida. We see a photo of her as a newborn, with tubes coming out of her. Then as an infant, sleeping peacefully, with a simple wooden cross next to her in her crib. Finally, we see her as a child, shooting hoops from her wheelchair. The ad then shows Trump mocking the physical disability of a journalist. Even years later, it is appalling. Grace's mother says, "The children at Grace's school know never to mock her. And so for an adult to mock someone with a disability is shocking." Grace's father, his eyes heavy with disappointment, says, "When I saw Donald Trump mocking someone with a disability, it showed me his soul, it showed me his heart. And I didn't like what I saw."

Spoiler alert: Trump won white evangelicals by an astonishing 80–16 margin, narrowly breaking the record held by George W. Bush, who is an actual, honest-to-goodness born-again Christian.

We attacked Trump for paying zero dollars in federal taxes. Trump's response, "That makes me smart." He also did better than Romney with voters making less than $50,000.

We attacked his racist rhetoric about immigrants: "They're bringing drugs, they're bringing crime, they're rapists." "We're going to have a deportation force." Trump got 1 percent more of the Latino vote than Mitt Romney had in 2012.

We attacked his misogynistic comments, including his infamous *Access Hollywood* remarks. "She ate like a pig." "When I come home and dinner's not ready, I go through the roof." "I moved on her like a b—h." Trump won just 3 percent fewer female voters than Romney.

We attacked his racist remarks, including his refusal to disavow former KKK leader David Duke: "I know nothing about David Duke, I know nothing about white supremacists." "Oh! Look at my African American over here!" "You're living in poverty, your schools are no good, you have no jobs." Trump exceeded Romney's percentage of the African American vote, albeit by a measly 2 percent.

In a particularly poignant ad, we featured former Indiana governor Joe Kernan, who, like John McCain, was a POW in Vietnam. The ad featured Trump denigrating McCain: "He's a war hero because he was captured. I like people that weren't captured." In a soft but steely voice, Kernan says, "What Donald Trump said about members of our military who have been captured is a disgrace," and as he shakes his head, the war hero Kernan says, "He's unfit to be president." Trump defeated Hillary by 27 percent among veterans, surpassing Romney's 20-point margin from 2012.

I admit it: I didn't get Trump. Didn't see the appeal. And I usually have a pretty good eye for political talent. From the first time I saw him in my home state of Texas, I always knew George W. Bush was enormously likable. And everyone who ever met the young Bill Clinton and Barack Obama came away predicting they'd be president. But I did not appreciate Trump's greatest gift—the ability to slip a punch; to avoid the collapse that any other politician would have suffered if they'd done and said half of the vicious, foul things Trump has. In short, I didn't realize he was Teflon Don.

I came to understand why only after the election. I was riding around Houston with my brother David. He's spent his career in construction, where he's built a successful business. He's my big brother, so I've always known that David was smarter than me, but I'd deluded myself into thinking I knew more about politics. As we sat in traffic on Loop 610, he gave me this epiphany about the election: "You treated Trump like a politician. He's not. He's a reality TV star. So when he got caught lying, it wasn't because he's a lying politician; he's just a bullshit artist on TV. When he said outrageous things, he was just being provocative for ratings."

Dear God, David was right.

I saw Trump as a politician: a candidate, a nominee, a potential president. Much of America saw him as a swaggering CEO, even if his boardroom was a cardboard set. His many outrageous statements were met with eye rolls or even laughter. Much of America was shocked and repulsed, to be sure. But a significant percentage of Americans just thought, *There he goes again! I wonder what The Donald is gonna say on the show next week?*

My Hollywood friends have a name for this: they call it a Pre-Aware Title. A pre-aware title is something the audience is already familiar with. Think of the Lego movie. Even if you've never seen it, you know what Legos are. Or *Iron Man XII*: you know what you're getting there. But a movie called *Harold and Maude*, well, we have no idea what that is when we first hear the title. Hollywood is replete with pre-aware titles because they sell. And the studio doesn't have to pay tens of millions of dollars to introduce the audience to the lead character. It is only a matter of time before we get a Play-Doh movie.

A great many of Trump's savage, obscene character flaws were already known to the audience. Or at least they were assessed less critically because they came from a man whose flamboyance earned him a place in your living room every Thursday night for fourteen years.

Boy, that was a depressing recap.

But I go through all of that not to depress you—although if right now you want to set this book aside for a long, tall glass of Zoloft, I understand. And lest you get too bummed out—or think I'm a total idiot—allow me to remind you of a very important number: 2,864,974. That's how many more votes Hillary received than Trump. If We, the People actually got to pick our president, my friend Hillary would be ramping up for her reelection campaign right now. As you'll see in chapter 7, I hate the Electoral College, and I have some thoughts on how to put the people in charge of picking the president. But for now, rather than complain to each other about how unfair the system is, let's focus on how to win.

I want us to learn from this dreary history—to ensure we are not doomed to repeat it. What should we have done? Well, I had a revelation, much like the one I had listening to my brother. It was a revelation about what really matters to voters, and why Trump won.

About three sleepless weeks after the election, it came to me. I thought about a farm family in Wisconsin, where my wife was born. They work their hearts out, rising before dawn to milk the cows, repair the tractor, clear the snow, or harvest the corn. Wisconsin being a swing state, they would have certainly seen our ads. I can imagine the family's matriarch (let's call her Esther) being shocked and turning to her husband (call him Ralph) and saying, "Well, Ralph, we can't have a man like that as our president!" The God-fearing, patriotic, kind, generous people of the rural Midwest could never countenance such a thoroughly awful person.

But then, in my imagination, a day before the election, Ralph sees Trump on TV shouting about ending unfair trade deals and saving manufacturing. He promises to take care of farmers and veterans. Esther is skeptical, but Ralph turns to her and says, "Well, ya know dear, he's not gonna grab YOU by the privates. But he just might reopen that factory that laid off our boy Harold."

Here's what I got wrong: I made it about Trump's life instead of Ralph and Esther's. We should have made ads like the ones we made against Romney. Mitt is a fundamentally good person who had some business deals that hurt him politically; Trump is an awful person of the lowest character. And he had a lot more business deals that screwed working people. We should have filmed the plumbing contractors he drove out of business when he wouldn't pay his bills. The housekeepers and cooks and blackjack dealers who lost their jobs when his casinos went bankrupt. The undocumented workers he used and abused at his golf courses. The veterans who lost tens of thousands of dollars on a worthless "degree" from Trump University. We should have shown how Trump has hurt people like you.

I focused too much on Trump and too little on voters. I fell into the Trump Trap.

CHAPTER 2

CORONAVIRUS

Now Elections Are a Life-and-Death Decision

As we saw in the previous chapter, I lost focus in 2016. For strategists like me, the campaign against Trump was focused on Trump's flaws, not on voters' lives. I did not connect them for folks; failed to show how Trump's personal failings could harm you.

The COVID-19 pandemic did just that. More than any message or strategy, the deadly virus exposed the spectacular risk of having an inexperienced, stupid liar in the White House. The coronavirus has changed our politics fundamentally. Not a single one of the ways it has changed our politics is to Trump's benefit. It's as if all his chickens have come home to roost at once.

Let me put it bluntly: more Americans are getting sick, and more Americans will die, because of Donald Trump's ignorance, arrogance, and incompetence. Let me count the ways things have changed.

Politics Is No Longer Merely a Spectacle

I'm the guy who coined the phrase "Politics is show business for ugly people." It stuck because it's somewhat funny, and also more than a little bit true. No more. The days of Donald Trump entertaining 40 percent of the country and enraging 60 percent with his florid histrionics, his open racism, and his insulting lies are over. They ended on January 19, 2020, when a thirty-five-year old man walked into an urgent care clinic in Snohomish County, Washington. He had just returned from visiting family in Wuhan, China. He had a fever, cough, fatigue. This was the first reported case of the coronavirus, or COVID-19, in the United States.

Back at his Mar-a-Lago resort, Donald Jumbo Trump spent the morning playing golf. He then flew to Austin, Texas, where he addressed the American Farm Bureau Federation. He gave a typically meandering, narcissistic speech and concluded by saying, "We're the greatest country anywhere in the world, and we're taking care of you." *We're taking care of you.* Right. At that moment, the Trump administration was doing anything but taking care of us.

We don't know whether Trump was briefed on that first US coronavirus case. But he and his administration had already done a lot on the issue of pandemic response. A lot of damage.

In April 2018, Trump fired Tom Bossert, his White House adviser for homeland security. Bossert had held a similar post in the George W. Bush administration and was known to be especially concerned with emerging threats—like pandemics. One assumes that's because he did not want America to suffer a sneak attack from a virus the way we had from terrorists when Bush was president.

A month later, Trump fired the pandemic response team that President Obama had created at the White House's National Security Council. Fired 'em all. These were not political hacks. Led by Rear Admiral Tim Ziemer, they were professionals who knew how to protect America. On the day Admiral Ziemer and his team were canned, Ron Klain, Obama's Ebola czar and an absolute genius, tried to warn us. Klain told the *Huffington Post* that the firing was occurring even as Ebola was flaring up again in Congo—and that in addition to firing the NSC pandemic team, Trump had sacked other pandemic experts and was trying to cut funding for pandemic defense. "Proposing a rescission of Ebola contingency funds on the very day that a new Ebola outbreak is announced is badly misguided," he said, with characteristic Klain prescience. "Forcing out the two top officials in charge of pandemic response at the White House—Tom Bossert and Tim Ziemer—is even worse. Doing it all at the same time shows a reckless disregard for the dangers we face." "Reckless disregard." That should be Trump's Secret Service code name.

The woman who'd held the NSC pandemic response post under Obama, Beth Cameron, called Adm. Ziemer's firing "a major loss for health security, biodefense, and pandemic preparedness. It is unclear in his absence who at the White House would be in charge of a pandemic." This, she said, is "a situation that should be immediately rectified."

But Trump was not through disarming America's pandemic response capabilities. He cut the pandemic prevention budget of the Centers for Disease Control and Prevention by 80 percent in 2018. One of the reasons the 2014 Ebola outbreak in West Africa did not become a global pandemic is because, through Ron Klain and others, President Obama decided to fight the virus over there so we would not have to fight it over here. Trump inherited a CDC that was forward-deployed in forty-nine countries. That funding was essential for training health care workers, improving labs, expanding emergency care—all the things you'd want to be doing to keep a virus from going viral. Trump's draconian budget cuts forced the CDC to abandon or drastically reduce efforts in thirty-nine of those forty-nine countries. One of the countries where we dramatically scaled back our efforts was China. And the virus came.

Experience Matters

Instead of highly trained, experienced medical and scientific SWAT teams protecting us, we were left with Pres. Trump and Vice President Mike Pence. Turns out you can't lie away a virus any more than you can pray away the gay. But you gotta hand it to Trump, he sure tried. (Not on the gay-pray thing, just lying about coronavirus.) On February 26, with the official count at just fifteen US cases but global health officials already warning of a worldwide pandemic, Trump said that in a few days the US number of cases would be zero. He should have understood the geometric progression a virus would have when no human being has immunity against it. He should have sprung into action. He should have followed the Obama-Biden-Klain Ebola playbook. He should have protected us. He did not.

By March 2020, the stock market had tanked, layoffs had skyrocketed, grocery shelves had been emptied, schools had been closed, bars and restaurants had been closed to in-house customers, hospitals were at risk of being overrun, and medical professionals were already running out of personal protective equipment—the exact things that happen in a pandemic. Trump blabbered one of his patented falsehoods, saying that the pandemic "just surprised the whole world." A few weeks earlier, he had said that the virus was "an unforeseen problem. What a problem. Came out of nowhere."

No, Mr. Trump, it did not come out of nowhere. It came out of China. One of the thirty-nine countries the CDC had to pull back from because of your budget cuts.

Donald Trump is the first president in all of American history with no prior experience in government or the military. For many of his supporters, that lack of experience was a blessing. Now it looks like a curse. Perhaps if, like Ron Klain, Trump had helped prevent a pandemic, or if, like Hillary Clinton, he'd had vast experience in government, he might have seen this coming. But here's the thing about being president: you don't have to know everything, because you have access to the world's foremost experts on everything. I saw Bill Clinton gorge himself on this intellectual feast on a daily basis. You want to know everything about how many bananas Europeans buy from Ecuador each year? We can get you a briefing on that. (That was actually a thing in the nineties. Clinton became an expert in the banana wars.)

So even if Trump did not have personal knowledge of how to prevent pandemics, he had experts who did. But he fired them. Or, at
least, a lot of them. This went beyond the normal turnover of political appointees that happens with every change of presidents. Trump,
as we have seen, shuttered entire programs designed to protect us
from pandemics. Why didn't any of his senior advisers or cabinet
officials warn him? In fairness, we don't yet know whether they tried.
I suspect when this god-awful presidency is over there is going to be
a spate of books from former Trump officials trying to whitewash
their legacy. There will be entire libraries of books, all with the title *I
Tried to Warn Him*.

The Obama team, pros to the end, did try to warn him. Or at least
his top people. In order to bring the new Trump team up to speed
on the threat of a pandemic, Lisa Monaco, Obama's top homeland
security adviser, organized a remarkably thorough and prescient
simulation of what a pandemic would look like. It is stunning how
accurately Monaco's war game anticipated the real thing. "We modeled a new strain of flu in the exercise," she told the *New York Times*,
"precisely because it's so communicable. There is no vaccine, and you
would get issues like nursing homes being particularly vulnerable,
shortages of ventilators," and more. The exercise, dubbed Crimson
Contagion, included twelve states, as well as the federal government.
It was a big deal. And it quickly demonstrated the chaos to come.
Federal officials didn't know who was in charge. Localities didn't
know whether to cancel school. Hospitals didn't know how much
equipment they would need or where they could obtain it. By the
end, 110 million Americans had, in the exercise, fallen ill; 7.7 million
were hospitalized; 586,000 were dead.

I have participated in a war-game simulation. It scared the crap
out of me. But few war games end with nearly 600,000 Americans
dead—a total that dwarfs US deaths in World War II. We have not
seen that level of mass death in America since the Civil War. Monaco
told the *Times* she was impressed by how seriously Bossert took the

exercise. But he was gone by the time the coronavirus struck. So were most of the other Trump officials who had participated. Gen. John F. Kelly, Trump's first secretary of Homeland Security and second chief of staff: gone. Rex Tillerson, Trump's first secretary of state: gone. Rick Perry, Trump's first energy secretary: also gone. Oops. In fact, the *Times* reported, "by the time the current crisis hit, almost all of the leaders at the table—Mr. Tillerson, Mr. Kelly and Mr. Perry among them—had been fired or moved on."

If Trump himself had been more experienced at governing, or if he'd kept some senior officials longer than one or two Scaramuccis, or if he'd surrounded himself with true pros, not sycophants and sons-in-law, things might have been different.

Honesty Matters

The truth hurts, they say. But lies hurt more. I call it Trump Respiration: he inhales oxygen and exhales lies. That is infuriating on a day-to-day basis. It is alarming in a crisis. Every crisis communications professional will tell you that credibility is the coin of the realm. You fight fear with facts, and facts should be sacred in a crisis. The credibility of the White House—and especially of the president of the United States of America—is a precious national resource. Trump has squandered it with an almost diseased disregard for the truth.

Some of his lies are simply self-justifying: "Nobody knew there would be a pandemic or epidemic of this proportion." Others, however, are dangerous. Consider these lies—total fabrications that people may have relied on, to their detriment:

- "Anybody who wants a test gets a test." Trump said this the day after Vice President Mike Pence had admitted, "We don't have enough tests today to meet what we anticipate will be the demand going forward."

- The coronavirus is "a problem that's going to go away." He said that while in India, as the contagion was spreading rapidly in the United States.

- The United States, he said, is "rapidly developing a vaccine." And we would "essentially have a flu shot for this in a fairly quick manner." False. No sooner was that lie out of Trump's mouth than Dr. Anthony Fauci, the director of the National Institute of Allergy and Infectious Diseases, corrected him, patiently explaining that a vaccine was twelve to eighteen months away, at best.

- "Ebola, you disintegrated, especially at the beginning. You got Ebola, that was it. This one is different, much different. This is a flu. This is like the flu." A lie stacked on another lie. Ebola did not cause people to disintegrate. That's from *Star Wars*, which is (and some of you are gonna hate me for saying this) not real life. Although Ebola is more lethal than coronavirus, it is also much less communicable, as transmission only takes place through bodily fluids. More important, coronavirus is not like a flu. Coronavirus is novel; it's new. No human has had it before this outbreak. Flu has been around in many forms for many decades. We have a vaccine for flu. We do not for coronavirus. (See the previous lie.) We have antiviral treatments for flu. We do not for coronavirus. And it appears the mortality rate for coronavirus is significantly higher.

- "The Democrats are politicizing the coronavirus. They're politicizing it . . . And this is their new hoax." Golly. This is so offensive. Democrats' deep and desperate concern about the coronavirus is not a "hoax." It is prudent public health policy. In fact, I was agitated at the Democrats for *not* telling people about Trump's complicity in the escalation of the pandemic due to his incompetence, dishonesty, firings, and budget cuts.

- By the time 100 Americans had been diagnosed and 12 had died, Trump said the number of cases "within a couple of days is going to be down close to zero. That's a pretty good job we've done. We're going very substantially down, not up." Do I even have to fact-check that? No, the number of cases did not go down. They went up catastrophically. Because that's what happens in pandemics.

- After the World Health Organization reported that "globally, about 3.4 percent of reported COVID-19 cases have died," Trump told Fox News's Sean Hannity, "I think the 3.4 percent is really a false number—and this is just my hunch." Of course, death rates vary greatly from one country to another. There are a lot of variables. But Trump's "hunch" is not one of the factors that epidemiologists consider.

- Trump suggested people who are infected by the virus might benefit from going to work. "If we have thousands or hundreds of thousands of people that get better just by, you know, sitting around and even going to work—some of them go to work, but they get better." This is dangerous. The CDC says people should do the exact opposite: "People who are mildly ill with COVID-19 are able to isolate at home during their illness. You should restrict activities outside your home, except for getting medical care. Do not go to work, school, or public areas. Avoid using public transportation, ride-sharing, or taxis."

- "There is a theory that, in April, when it gets warm—historically, that has been able to kill the virus." A lie. First, there is no evidence the virus dies out when the weather gets warm. In fact, numerous cases appeared in the Southern Hemisphere, where it was considerably warmer than in the United States or China. Second, there is no "history" to refer to. It is called a *novel* coronavirus not because it's a work of fiction but because it is new, unprecedented, without any history. *Grrr.*

- "It's going to disappear. One day, it's like a miracle, it will disappear." I cannot peer into Mr. Trump's soul. I have no idea how deep his faith is, or if he is a person of faith at all. But predicting the miraculous disappearance of the virus does little to help those infected, or those whose lives are upended by the threat.

- "Not only the vaccines, but the therapies. Therapies is sort of another word for cure." Nope. No effective therapies existed for the coronavirus at that time.

- On March 19, 2020, Trump claimed that two antimalaria drugs, chloroquine and hydroxychloroquine, would be available to coronavirus patients "almost immediately." He claimed that the drugs had been approved by the Food and Drug Administration for such treatment. Dr. Stephen Hahn, commissioner of the FDA, speaking after Trump at the same White House news conference, said no—that patients might be eligible for those medicines under the FDA's "compassionate use" program—which allows patients to use an unapproved drug if they are seriously ill and no other treatment is available—but that the drugs have *not* been approved by the FDA and would not be available by prescription.

- The next day, Dr. Fauci was asked about the malaria drugs Trump had claimed showed "very encouraging early results." Dr. Fauci did not mince words. "The answer is no," he told Fox News's John Roberts. "And the evidence that you're talking about is anecdotal evidence . . . it was not done in a controlled clinical trial, so you really can't make any definitive statement about it." As soon as Dr. Fauci finished killing the canard, Trump walked up to the podium and resurrected it. "I'm probably more of a fan of that [chloroquine] maybe than anybody, but I'm a big fan, and we'll see what happens. We all understand that the doctor is 100 percent correct, it's early. But I've seen things that are impressive . . . Let's see if it works. It might and it might not. I happen to feel good about it, but who knows? I've been right a lot." No, you haven't, you liar. In fact, the next time you are right about this pandemic will be the first. A chimp throwing darts at a wall of statements would hit something honest more often than you do.

- It is hard to describe how dangerous it is for a nincompoop like Trump to say things like that, or how courageous it is for a man of science like Dr. Fauci to stand in front of him and tell the world the emperor has no clothes.

- According to a count from CNN, Trump made thirty-three false claims about coronavirus between March 2 and March 15, a crucial time when Americans were seeking accurate information and making critical decisions about how seriously to take the virus. Alarmingly, even when he read a prepared script from the Oval Office, speaking from behind the historic Resolute desk, he was still misleading, telling Americans he was banning trade from Europe ("these prohibitions will not only apply to the tremendous amount of trade and cargo, but various other things as we get approval"). That was not accurate. Having helped write a great many presidential addresses, I know that when a president speaks from the Oval, the sanctum sanctorum of our democracy, every assertion must be 100 percent accurate. Not for Trump. Even in the most formal, official, staff-supervised settings, he misleads.

- He claimed he had not shaken hands with anyone on his recent trip to India: false.

- He blamed Obama for the delay in testing, saying, "The Obama administration made a decision on testing that turned out to be very detrimental to what we're doing. And we undid that decision a few days ago so that the testing can take place in a much more accurate and rapid fashion." False. Experts contacted by CNN could not even imagine what Trump was referring to. Peter Kyriacopoulos, chief policy officer of the Association of Public Health Laboratories, told CNN, "We aren't sure what rule is being referenced."

- He told reporters on March 6, "I hear the numbers are getting much better in Italy." False. In the three days after Trump said that, the number of cases in Italy nearly doubled, and the number of deaths went up 100 percent.

Americans needed facts. Trump fed them fiction, falsehoods, and fibs. Many people may have relied on Trump's happy talk and misinformation. There are an awful lot of people, good people, for whom Trump is a trusted source of news and information. When he misleads people, or simply gets facts wrong innocently, there can be consequences.

Trump's Central Defense Is a Lie: His China Travel Ban Was Too Late

There is one action Trump points to as if it were decisive: his January 31 order banning foreigners from entering the United States if they had been in China the previous fourteen days. But the virus was already here by January 31; the first US case was on January 19. Plus his travel ban only applied to foreigners; Americans who had been in Wuhan could come home without testing, quarantine, anything. In fact, as the *New York Times* has reported, nearly forty thousand people came to the United States from China after Trump's supposed travel ban.

Perhaps most important, *Trump's order banned flights that were already canceled.* By the time he issued his Swiss-cheese ban (remember, it only applied to non–US citizens, as if only foreigners could carry the contagion into the United States), the major airlines— Delta, American, United—had already halted service from China to the United States.

Bizarrely, Trump claims Democrats attacked him for barring foreigners from China from entering our country. Another lie. He even went so far as to claim that Senate Minority Leader Chuck Schumer

(D-NY) "didn't like my early travel closings. I was right. He is incompetent!" It is a fib, a myth, a fabrication. A lie. Schumer said nothing of the kind. Aaron Blake of the *Washington Post* ran it to ground, surmising that Trump fell for a falsehood posted on conservative websites.

Instead of banning foreigners from getting on flights that had already been canceled, it would have been a good time to apply the lessons of Crimson Contagion: institute massive testing; ban public gatherings; distribute millions of masks, gowns, gloves, and other personal protective equipment; coordinate the federal, state, and local responses; order the navy to prepare their two world-famous hospital ships, the USNS *Comfort* and the USNS *Mercy*, for the pandemic. He could have ordered the US Department of Veterans Affairs to spring into action, the Army Corps of Engineers and the Seabees to plan for field hospitals. He could have gathered congressional leaders, business leaders, labor leaders, and academics to begin to project the economic and fiscal costs and prepare a plan. He could have used the power of the Defense Production Act to order factories to make more ventilators and other lifesaving supplies. But he didn't. Instead, a week after the China travel ban he now touts, he was telling the American people, "I think the virus is going to be—it's going to be fine."

It was not fine.

As if that wasn't bad enough, in February the Trump administration boasted about sending 17.8 tons of personal protective equipment—*our* American PPE—to China. He sent them our masks, our respirators, our gowns. When he tries to bash China now, keep in mind China didn't steal our protective gear—Trump gave it to them.

The Trump Administration Was Warned

Worst of all, the US intelligence community specifically warned that the coronavirus posed a grave danger. The *Washington Post* described the early warnings as "ominous." But, the *Post* said, at the very time the intelligence professionals were issuing those ominous warnings, Trump was downplaying the threat.

The intelligence reports described how the coronavirus could affect the entire planet, something that would require immediate and drastic action to prevent. But despite what the *Post* calls a "constant flow of reporting" about the threat from American intelligence, "Trump continued publicly and privately to play down the threat the virus posed to Americans."

The timeline is crucial. If, as the *Post* reports, the warnings came in January, Trump did little to protect the public in that crucial first month. Fortunately, by the third week of January, diplomats were pulled out of Wuhan, China, where the contagion began. But otherwise, officials found it difficult to reach and engage Trump. Secretary of Health and Human Services Alex Azar had been briefed on discussions between Chinese and American health officials but could not get through to Trump for days or weeks. The *Post* further reported that Joe Grogan, the head of Trump's Domestic Policy Council, sounded the alarm to acting chief of staff Mick Mulvaney in a January 27 meeting. Mulvaney then began convening meetings on the virus, but "officials said Trump was dismissive because he did not believe that the virus had spread widely throughout the United States."

On February 19—more than a month after the system began, in the words of one official, "blinking red"—Trump was giving the American people happy talk. "I think it's going to work out fine," he said. "I think when we get into April, in the warmer weather, that has a very negative effect on that and that type of a virus." On February 24, he tweeted, "The Coronavirus is very much under control in the USA."

Who knows why? It could be that, as a salesman, Trump reflexively wanted to put a positive face on the news. It could be that he was worried about spooking the markets. It could be that, as the owner of golf resorts and other hospitality businesses, he did not want people to self-isolate, as it would hurt his bottom line. It could be, as some of Trump's advisers told the *Post,* that Trump had too much faith in the honesty and accuracy of reports the world was receiving from China. Trump did vouch for the Chinese government and President Xi Jinping, tweeting on January 24:

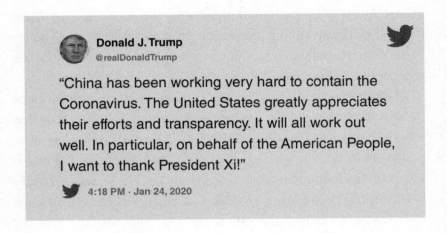

Donald J. Trump
@realDonaldTrump

"China has been working very hard to contain the Coronavirus. The United States greatly appreciates their efforts and transparency. It will all work out well. In particular, on behalf of the American People, I want to thank President Xi!"

4:18 PM · Jan 24, 2020

Bailouts "R" Us

The pandemic, predictably, spurred an economic crash. Within weeks, stocks had lost all the gains they had made during the Trump presidency and then some. It was one of those situations where you can't win for losing: the steps needed to protect public health—shutting down businesses, canceling travel, shuttering bars and restaurants—helped propel us into a recession. And vice versa: the more economic activity, the more the virus would be transmitted. No sensible person blames Trump for this conundrum. It is what he did, and failed to do, before and after the economic collapse that merits attention.

As we shall see in chapter 10, the Trump tax cut transferred $1.9 trillion of projected federal revenue into the pockets of corporate America. Before the coronavirus pandemic and attendant crash, while we thought we were still in a boom, Trump's federal budget had a $1 trillion deficit. That's the annual operating deficit, and that was when things were good. It was unconscionable for Trump to run those kinds of crushing deficits when the economy was strong, because it severely weakened our ability to respond to the crisis. John Maynard Keynes was right: deficits are good when times are bad; but they are bad when times are good. The countercyclical effect of federal deficits has been understood for a very long time, believe me. I helped President Clinton balance the budget in the late nineties. We did it knowing that while times were flush, we should pay down our debt so that we would have the option of relatively painless deficit spending when a crisis hit. Trump had the opposite view. Senate Majority Leader Mitch McConnell (R-Russia) told Trump that no one ever lost an election for spending too much. So Trump spent, mostly on corporate tax giveaways. We go into greater detail in chapter 10, but for now it is enough to note that Trump's deficits meant that the radical spending needed once the pandemic struck would come at a much higher cost.

The reaction of the two parties was instructive. Republicans became socialists: calling for a half-trillion-dollar fund to bail out corporations. Democrats expressed dismay at the lack of transparency and lack of guarantees that corporations would not use taxpayer funds to enrich their shareholders and executives at the cost of their employees.

Trump is a Republican, but he is a Trump first, last, and always. And the Trump business empire (such as it is) is built on hospitality: hotels, resorts, golf courses. (Now that his casinos have gone bankrupt.) Before bailout legislation was even drafted, Trump was calling for federal assistance to hotels. "We're also talking to the hotel industry," he told reporters on March 9, 2020. "And some places, actually, will do well, and some places probably won't do well at all. But we're working also with the hotel industry."

Now, I'm no expert, and it may well be that the hotel industry (a personal favorite of mine) needed a bailout. But how the heck does a president who is a hotel magnate promote bailing out, potentially, his own properties? By being shameless. Fortunately for the American people, Democrats were on guard. Sen. Chuck Schumer inserted a provision into the bailout bill that would bar Trump, other senior administration officials, and their families from benefiting from the bailout. Amazingly, the last minute before the vote, Schumer realized the provision he'd insisted on was missing. Just an oversight, he was assured. Right. Schumer held firm. For two hours he and his fellow Democrats refused to let the bill come up for a vote until their anticorruption (aka, anti-Trump) provision was put back in.

In Trump's defense, if you can call it that, he also called for bailing out the oil and gas industry, where he has no known investments. But, still, it shows his priorities. When the elderly are at special risk, when vulnerable people are facing a potentially deadly virus, when doctors and nurses lack gowns and masks, his focus turned to the oil and gas industry? Really?

Yep. According to the *Washington Post*, which based its reporting on four people privy to internal Trump White House discussions, oil and gas were targeted for support. Perhaps coincidentally, the *Post* also reported, "One of the companies hardest hit was Continental Resources, founded by Harold Hamm, a Trump supporter and an adviser to the president on energy issues."

Again, the conflicts and potential conflicts of interest are glaring. Apparently for Trump, even a pandemic, combined with an economic meltdown, are opportunities to feather your own nest, or the nests of your buddies.

Democrats had a different approach. They wanted federal aid to target health care workers especially, and working men and women generally. Rarely has the difference in the two parties' priorities been more apparent. The taxpayers had already given corporations almost $2 trillion, thanks to the Republicans, who controlled the House, Senate, and White House in 2017. Corporations did not use the bulk of that money to invest in their people—to extend, for example, paid sick leave, or to subsidize child care for their employees. Nor did they set it aside in a rainy-day fund, as many well-run states do when they have a surplus. In just the first three quarters of 2018, corporations bought back a staggering $583.4 billion of their own stock—a 52.6 percent jump from the previous year, before the Trump tax cut. Democrats stood strong against subsidizing more stock repurchases, and insisted that the economic lifeline be extended to those most at risk of sinking: working people.

The final $2.2 trillion coronavirus rescue package bore the unmistakable stamp of the Democrats, who used their leverage to fight for people rather than lobbyists. Speaker Nancy Pelosi, who personally negotiated the bill with Trump treasury secretary Steve Mnuchin (R-Very Fine People), made sure that relief targeted those who were most affected: working families and the poor. She included a $260 billion investment in unemployment benefits, extending the lifeline for an additional thirteen weeks. She also beat back a coldhearted effort by Republicans to, as Pelosi put it, "claw back the $600 per week in added benefits . . . to the record number of Americans losing their jobs." That's right. Even as they were throwing hundreds of billions of your dollars at corporations, Republicans were trying to take back $600 a week from working people.

Pelosi pushed hard for—and won—a $200 billion emergency injection of funds into our besieged health system: rescuing hospitals, research facilities, health centers. She also secured $150 billion for state and local governments. Not enough, to be sure, but all she could get, given the GOP's dominance of the Senate and the White House.

While Republicans focused on big business, Pelosi and the Democrats went all-in for small businesses, with a $377 billion relief package for the little guys and gals, along with expanded loan relief from the Small Business Administration. Pelosi also insisted that education get a $30 billion lifeline, and eliminated the tax on student loan repayment assistance by employers.

Perhaps most important, Schumer in the Senate and Pelosi in the House—with the unwavering support of their fellow Democrats—insisted on oversight, accountability, and transparency, especially in the half-trillion corporate bailout, which is controlled by the treasury secretary. Republicans caved. Taxpayer protections were included.

When Trump signed the $2.2 trillion bailout bill, he refused to invite Democrats. Typical Trump pettiness. Then, hours after signing the bill into law, he issued a statement proclaiming that he would not obey some of the provisions designed to protect taxpayers and prevent corruption. Typical Trump crookedness. Understandably concerned about the potential for waste, at the very least, or abuse, at worst, Congress had created a special inspector general to police the treasury secretary as he doles out a half-trillion dollars of our money. In his statement, Trump objected to the transparency and accountability provisions. "These provisions," the statement said, are impermissible forms of congressional aggrandizement with respect to the execution of the laws." First, let's note that those are awfully big words for Donny, which means that someone wrote them for him. More important, those are a declaration of war against Congress's authority to protect the taxpayers' money. Why is he so afraid of oversight? Why would he block transparency? Why does he so bitterly oppose accountability?

The late William Goldman, who wrote the screenplay for *All the President's Men*, penned these deathless words for Deep Throat: "Follow the money." Following the money was the key to Carl Bernstein and Bob Woodward's uncovering the corruption of Watergate. All of us who pay taxes have a right to follow the money we are entrusting to Trump to use to save our economy from the pandemic he failed to save us from.

The H-E-B Grocery Chain Took Early Action. Why Didn't Trump?

H-E-B is a Texas-based grocery chain that anticipated and responded to the coronavirus plague faster, more effectively, and more humanely than Trump's administration. As *Texas Monthly* reported,

H-E-B has a full-time, year-round emergency preparedness director, since Texas gets hurricanes, tornadoes, and, yes, viruses. The folks at H-E-B were in touch with their supply chain partners in China as early as January 15, when the first reports of COVID-19 in Wuhan came to light. On that very day, as H-E-B was beginning to prepare for the pandemic, Trump was—amazingly—meeting with the Chinese. He hosted Vice Premier Liu He at the White House, where the two signed a trade deal and slobbered all over Chinese president Xi Jinping ("a very, very good friend of mine"), who didn't even bother to attend.

Meanwhile, as the virus was spreading, someone was tracking it carefully. No, not the National Security Council's pandemic response unit; Trump had fired them. Rather, the people tracking it included H-E-B, which has its headquarters in San Antonio. Justen Noakes, H-E-B's emergency preparedness director, told *Texas Monthly*, "We modeled what had been taking place in China from a transmission perspective, as well as impact. As the number of illnesses and the number of deaths were increasing, obviously the Chinese government was taking some steps to protect their citizens, so we basically mirrored what that might look like [in Texas]."

Meanwhile, Trump careened wildly from denial through "hunches," ran aground in grievances, contradicted scientists, berated journalists, and had a daily meltdown in the White House press room on live TV.

As he was lying and denying, H-E-B was planning and prepping; anticipating and responding. H-E-B activated its Emergency Operations Center in San Antonio, set up clear lines of authority, delegated responsibilities, and empowered employees. H-E-B knew that emergencies were inevitable, so they prepared. And when the coronavirus emerged, they quickly identified the threat. They trusted experts. They supported their people on the front lines. They adapted to changing exigencies. They built a spirit of camaraderie and cooperation on their team. They communicated with their suppliers, employees, customers, and communities.

H-E-B kept stores stocked and customers happy. They cared for their employees, and even pasted footprints on the floor to space their customers six feet apart in the checkout lines. Craig Boyan, H-E-B's president, summed up his company's grace under pressure and the effect it has had on his customers and neighbors: "The spirit of Texans and their treating H-E-B partners with the respect and pride that they do makes us feel fantastic. I drove by a church the other day in San Antonio that had a sign out front that said, 'Thank an H-E-B checker.' We've seen an outpouring of support for our partners and truck drivers that gives us a great sense of pride."

In a crisis, as in combat, three Cs are essential: Command, Control, and Communications. H-E-B mastered all three. Trump instead demonstrated complete incompetence, total dishonesty, and chaotic management. He could never make it as a store manager for H-E-B. And your life is in his hands.

How Democrats Should Run on This

After a long time in Washington, I have learned this: anyone who says "Don't play the blame game" is trying to avoid responsibility. Play the blame game. Demand accountability.

No, obviously, the virus was not caused by Trump; nor was Hurricane Katrina caused by President George W. Bush. But Trump's response showed how unfit he is to lead a great nation. Heck of a job, Trumpy. When there is a market crisis, experts say, investors pursue a "flight to quality"; they move from riskier investments to safer ones. I think voters do the same. Democrats need to be the safer investment.

Joe Biden has emerged as the presumptive Democratic nominee because he is everything Trump is not: he is empathetic; Trump is narcissistic. He is unifying; Trump is divisive. He is experienced; Trump is a rookie. He believes in science; Trump trusts his "hunches."

The coronavirus crisis is testing the central theme of this book:

that the way to beat Trump is to focus less on Trump and more on the people who are hurt by his policies. One of the key lessons of the Trump presidency is, if you vote to tear down the system, it just might come crashing down on you.

It is essential for Democrats to show the American people that voting for Trump is not cost-free. It's not a protest vote. You're not sending a message. You're hiring a commander in chief. Your job, your health, and your life will be fundamentally affected by who is elected president in 2020. It was deeply affected by the last election, and Democrats should explain how. Every voter should know that Trump fired the National Security Council's pandemic response team. Every voter should know that he slashed the Centers for Disease Control and Prevention's pandemic response budget by 80 percent. Every voter should know that he downplayed the threat, and botched the response. Every voter should know that his fig leaf about banning flights from China is a fib. Every voter should know that his dishonest, incompetent response to this crisis has had disastrous consequences.

Raise the stakes, Democrats. Tell folks this is not a reality show. This is not a spectator sport. This is not a spectacle. This is real and this is serious. Deadly serious.

CHAPTER 3

BUT TRUMP *IS* DIFFERENT

The Unique Challenges of Running Against Donald Trump

A central thesis of this book is that it is a trap to fixate too much on Trump. He is a narcissist. As such, he craves attention and will say or do anything to grab it. (And, according to his boasts, he will grab anything.) His actual policies have done very little to help the country: our water is dirtier, our air more polluted; our farmers are hurting, our working people dying before their time; our health care is costlier, our medicines out of reach; our leaders are more corrupt and our citizens are more divided. But the Trump Trap lures us into talking about him, not us.

This chapter outlines how he does it and how Democrats should counter it. Diversion is Trump's superpower. This chapter is his kryptonite.

It's Damned Difficult to Defeat an Incumbent President

First thing first. Trump loves the letter *I*. He uses the first person pronoun in nearly every sentence. I bet his favorite song is George

Harrison's "I, Me, Mine." Of course, there are other *I*-words that come to mind: Incompetent. Indictable. Ineffective. Impeached.

But like it or not, Donald Jackalope Trump is also one other *I*-word: Incumbent. That status confers huge advantages. Like Air Force One and Marine One. Like the ability to stride the world stage. Like gathering people in the Rose Garden to sign legislation while the cameras carry it live. Like greeting the latest championship sports team, ensuring you lead the local news in that TV market.

In the last hundred years, incumbent presidents have faced the voters sixteen times. They have won twelve times. An incumbent president starts out, historically, with a 75 percent likelihood of winning. Here are the four who lost: Herbert Hoover, Gerald Ford, Jimmy Carter, George H. W. Bush. Notice anything? They each presided over a bad economy. Recession, depression, inflation, stagflation, unemployment: these are the incumbent's enemy. Before the crash, the macroeconomy seemed strong: low unemployment, low inflation, steady growth, a roaring stock market. These conditions allowed presidents like Ronald Reagan and Bill Clinton to cruise to reelection. It does not look like Trump will have the economic winds at his back, to say the least. A depressed economy is bad for us all, of course, but it is especially bad for a president seeking reelection.

How important? Well, the last incumbent president with a strong economy to lose was William Howard Taft, in 1912. Poor Taft. He was Teddy Roosevelt's handpicked successor, but TR couldn't bear to be out of the White House. His daughter Alice Roosevelt Longworth said of Teddy, "My father always wanted to be the corpse at every funeral, the bride at every wedding, and the baby at every christening." (Sound familiar?) Unable to bear seeing anyone else in the White House, Teddy started his own party, the Progressive (or Bull Moose) Party, and ran against both Taft and Democrat Woodrow Wilson. Teddy carried six states with 88 electoral votes, enough to outpace Taft, who only carried two states, but both men lost to Wilson in an Electoral College landslide. I don't exactly see former Massachusetts governor Bill Weld, who is challenging Trump for the GOP nomination, playing the role TR did in 1912. Democrats are going to have to win on their own.

Even more remarkable, given the country's appetite for change, we have had three two-term presidencies in a row. That has not happened since the founding generation, when Jefferson, Madison, and Monroe each served for two terms. Perhaps voters at the dawn of the nineteenth century wanted to cling to the founders as long as they were around. Perhaps they were satisfied with the direction of their new nation—after all, Monroe's presidency began at the outset of a period that came to be called the "Era of Good Feelings." I don't think historians will hang a similar moniker on the period during which Trump was president.

I'm not sure what to make of today's string of two-termers. But there it is. Both George W. Bush and Barack Obama were re-elected despite having approval ratings that hovered just below the all-important 50 percent mark, which suggests that an endangered incumbent who runs an aggressive, negative campaign can win in an era of bad feelings.

Negative Partisanship

If you ask any of my sons what time it is, they'll say, "It's eleven fifty-five and OU sucks." It's not enough that they love my Texas Longhorns; in fact, it's more important that they repeat that the University of Oklahoma sucks. That's negative partisanship.

Many observers have described our politics as driven by hyperpartisanship. I think it's worse than that. We are not merely hyperpartisan, we are consumed with negative partisanship. Negative partisanship is important. So important that I save it for what matters most in life: Texas Longhorn football. The problem comes when negative partisanship bleeds into other, less important facets of life. Like politics.

For too many of us, it is more important that the other party loses than that our party wins. Indeed, the majority of the people who voted for Trump in 2016 (53 percent) did so more because they were rejecting Hillary; and the precise same percentage of Hillary voters said that their vote was more against Trump than for Hillary. This is unusual. In 2008, 68 percent of the people who voted for Obama said it was because they believed in him, and 59 percent of McCain voters said the same about their candidate.

Incumbency, the economy, partisanship—all these fundamentals would apply no matter who the president was. But Trump brings attributes that are unique. Democrats are going to have to deal with them.

"I'm a Ratings Machine!" Just as Democrats maligned Ronald Reagan for being a movie star, they underestimated the advantages Donald Trump gained from being a reality TV star. I know I did. He understands how to grab an audience and how to hold it. He knows the power of simple story lines with cartoon villains and overdrawn heroes. He knows the need for drama, conflict, comic relief, and resolution. And he knows that in our short-attention-span media environment, subtlety and nuance are the enemy. From the get-go, his outrageous schtick drew the cameras and allowed him to dominate a field of sixteen others. By March 16, 2016, more than thirty states and territories had had their primaries or caucuses. Trump by then had won 1,448 delegates—comfortably past the 1,237 required to be the GOP nominee. Yet he had spent only $10 million on television advertising. (Jeb Bush had spent $82 million on advertising alone. By the time he was done, he and his allied super PAC had spent a whopping $130 million.) How can anyone run in thirty contests—and win—by only spending $10 million on advertising?

It's the Earned Media, Stupid. By the time he'd locked up the nomination in March, Trump had received $1.9 billion in earned media.

No one else was even close to half that amount. (Hillary was a very distant second, with $746 million.)

And on it went. By November, Trump was the beneficiary of $4.96 billion in earned media—more coverage than any politician in history. To be sure, much of that coverage was negative, some of it savagely so. But Trump lived by the adage—often attributed to P. T. Barnum—"There's no such thing as bad publicity."

Attack, Attack, Attack. The late Roger Ailes used to say to politicians, "There are only four stories the media will cover in a campaign: polls, scandals, gaffes, and attacks. Only one of them is under your control. So, get your ass on the attack." Trump understands this. The more outrageous, the more outlandish the attack, the better. He attacked a war hero for being a POW, he attacked a Gold Star family, he mocked a journalist's physical disability, Marco Rubio's height, Jeb Bush's stamina. He never stopped attacking, and the strategy never stopped working.

Trump Wins a Race to the Bottom. This is important. The relentlessly negative tone set by Trump drove both candidates' negative ratings through the roof. By Election Day, Donald Trump and Hillary Clinton were the two least-liked presidential candidates in history—and it wasn't even close. In the exit polls, Hillary's unfavorable rating was a whopping 55 percent. Trump's was 60 percent. But wait. How can a guy who's disliked by 60 percent of the voters get 46 percent of the vote? Because, crucially for Trump, nearly one in five voters hated them both. And Trump won those voters by a crushing 17-point margin (47–30).

Lie, Lie, Lie. Never in presidential history have we had a person so unmoored to factual accuracy. The *Washington Post's* Glenn Kessler, in his Fact Checker column, and other accuracy cops, including CNN's Daniel Dale, must feel like Lucille Ball in the chocolate factory. The lies from Trump come faster than they can document them. Trump is the biggest, fattest liar in recorded history.

Take one, just one, of the thousands and thousands of lies. He implied the father of his GOP primary rival, Ted Cruz, was complicit in the assassination of President John F. Kennedy, telling his pals at *Fox & Friends*: "His father was with Lee Harvey Oswald prior to Oswald's being—you know, shot . . . I mean, what was he doing—what was he doing with Lee Harvey Oswald shortly before the death? Before the shooting? It's horrible." Yes, it is horrible. Think about that. I know we've become inured to his mendacity, but stop for a minute and ponder the fact that a leading candidate for president accused his opponent's father of complicity in the most notorious assassination of the twentieth century. *And he got away with it.* It worked. Journalists rushed to Cruz and his father, an evangelical preacher, who decried the attack. But some number of people undoubtedly thought, *Well, they would deny it if it were true, wouldn't they? I mean they're not going to admit to being part of a plot to kill JFK.*

And yet if you ask Trump supporters why they like him, one of the first things you're likely to hear is, "Because he tells it like it is. He's a truth-teller." Whiskey Tango Foxtrot? For his supporters, Trump has redefined truth. For most of us, truth is fidelity to facts; to some Trump fans, truth is reflecting what they believe in their bones but cannot state without fear of repercussions in our "politically correct" world: Mexicans are rapists. Black people are stupid. Puerto Ricans are lazy. African countries are "s—hole countries." Trump supporters do not give a ripsnort whether he accurately counted the number of people at his inauguration, so long as he gives voice to their deepest biases—the ones they feel in their bones but dare not state lest they be ostracized.

Showmanship, Salesmanship. The man makes carnival barkers seem shy. Trump once called a press conference surrounded by raw meat. He understands how to hype, tease, and promote. And as president, he has nearly limitless tools to seize the spotlight, as he demonstrated when he took the spotlight off allegations that Brett Kavanaugh had committed sexual assault: he distracted his audience by threatening to fire Deputy Attorney General Rod Rosenstein. He has even used his powers as commander in chief to divert the media spotlight. He ordered the deployment of thousands of troops to the US-Mexico border to heighten the saliency of the migrant caravan in the days before the midterm elections. And he did that for congressional Republicans. There is no telling how far he will go when his own job is on the line.

Trump's Core Supporters Are Insanely Loyal. Most politicians seek to broaden their support. Trump seeks only to deepen his. In a vast and heterogeneous nation (and, no, Mike Pence, "heterogeneous" is not a sex term), deepening is easier than broadening. Most presidents have rejected that strategy, however, as it often leads to an electoral cul-de-sac. Trump does not care. He doubles and triples and quadruples down on his base. His fanatics fuel his rallies, and his rallies in turn fuel Trump's fanaticism. It's a closed loop. Public Policy Polling (a Democratic firm) decided to put Trump's infamous maxim about his voters' loyalty to the test. Turns out 45 percent of Trump voters would *approve* of him shooting someone on Fifth Avenue. (Just 29 percent would disapprove.) This is why it's a fool's errand to try to talk diehard supporters off the Trump train. Indeed, in one CNN focus group, a Trump supporter actually said, "If Jesus Christ gets down off the cross and told me Trump is with Russia, I would tell him, 'Hold on a second. I need to check with the President if it's true.'"

Trump's Mastery of Fear. When I was a freshman at the University of Texas, the Greatest University in the World, I came home from Austin one weekend. My older brother, who went to the University of Houston, lived at our home, in Missouri City, about twenty-five miles from U of H. He didn't know I was coming, so when I was fumbling with the front door at midnight on a Friday night, he thought our house was being robbed. I walked into the house and was greeted by my brother with a shotgun. Now, Missouri City, Texas, was not exactly a hotbed of home invasions. But the sound of someone banging around in the middle of the night scared my brother, and out of fear he reached for a gun. What was he thinking? That's the point: he wasn't thinking. Neuroscience teaches us that fear shuts down thought. The amygdala overwhelms the hippocampus and the frontal cortex. (I'll pause here while those of you who went to Texas A&M google those words.) This is why simply telling someone "Don't be afraid" rarely works. Replacing fear with thought and action is critical.

Another example: a dear friend of mine had open-heart surgery. Soon his house was full of flowers and notes and prayer cards. When I called to check on him, he said, "I love that people care, and I appreciate the prayers. But what has given me confidence is when the doctor came in and walked me through the whole procedure. I asked a million questions, and he answered them all. You fight fear with facts."

You fight fear with facts.

The Special Weapons and Tactics Required to Run Against Trump

- **Contextualize, Objectify the Attack.** Rather than respond literally—"I really am part Cherokee!"—it's better to step outside the attack, hold it up for folks to look at, and analyze it, the way an adult would take off a scary Halloween mask and show a child it's just Uncle Bob behind it. In terms of Trump, that means explaining the tactic behind the lie or attack: "Trump doesn't really care about my heritage. He cares about stacking the economic deck against you. So, he's using this to distract you in the hopes you don't notice that he's cut his own taxes by hundreds of millions of dollars."

"Ridicule is man's most potent weapon." So said activist Saul Alinsky. He was right. Ridicule, rather than outrage, should be our response to Trump's attacks, his fear, his bigotry. I would have loved it if Sen. Elizabeth Warren had said she would release her DNA test . . . when Trump releases his tax returns. *"And I bet you a dollar I'm more of a Cherokee than he is a taxpayer."* Never answer his attacks. Always contextualize, ridicule, and counter. Gen. George Patton is often quoted as saying, "The object of war is not to die for your country. It's to make the other son of a bitch die for his country." The object of a campaign is not to answer the other candidate's attacks; it's to make him answer yours.

- **Shift the Attack to Favorable Terrain.** Too many Democrats are too literal—maybe because so many of our politicians are lawyers. A political campaign is not a high school debate: you don't win by answering arguments seriatim. You win by shifting the entire debate to a topic that's favorable to you. Hence, rather than walk people through the complexities of his marital issues, in 1992 Bill Clinton simply said, "The Republicans want to make this election about my past; I want to make it about your future."

  I cannot stress enough how important it is not to let Trump dictate the topic. Sen. Brian Schatz (D-HI) has a Twitter feed that is a model of how to maintain political focus. When the media is fixating on the latest Trump outrage, he can be relied on to tweet something like this, when Trump was fulminating about light bulbs: "The thing about this tweet is that they are in federal court trying to take your healthcare away." Brilliant. Sen. Schatz doesn't take the bait. Although he is a self-described "climate hawk," he doesn't waste time engaging in a debate about why LED lights are better than incandescent bulbs—he knows that is largely irrelevant to voters' choice. Instead, he replies to a light bulb attack with a health care counterattack. More Democrats should emulate Sen. Schatz.

Whose campaign is this, anyway? Trump is a narcissist. Duh. So he loves when the conversation revolves around him. My bet is voters are tiring of this. They are tired of endless arguments over whether Trump is a hero or Trump is a villain; whether Trump is a racist or Trump is a victim of the PC police. I believe they hunger for a politics that revolves around them, not Trump—or his opponents. I think we should state it openly. "Donald Trump wants this election to be about one person: Donald Trump. And I want it to be about one person: you."

You Can't Beat Trump by Trying to Be Trump

"The pendulum of the mind oscillates between sense and nonsense," Carl Jung said, "not between right and wrong." I am terribly worried that some Democrats will swing from sense—which Hillary embodied—to nonsense, which Trump epitomizes. Trying to answer Trump's division with our division, his vulgarity with our vulgarity, his hate with our hate, his lies with our lies—therein lies the path to defeat. If we try to out-Trump Trump, we will not only lose the election, we will deserve to.

*"When we replace a president, the American
people want the remedy, not the replica."*

—David Axelrod

After Nixon's criminality and deceit, Jimmy Carter promised "a government that is as honest and decent and fair and competent and truthful and idealistic as are the American people." But after Carter was seen as folksy but hapless, we turned to the majesty and confidence of Reagan. After eight years of Reagan, Americans responded to Bush's call for "a kinder, gentler nation." But when Bush was seen as out of touch with the middle class during a recession, Clinton pledged that he would "put people first." Although Gore won the popular vote in 2000, there was great appeal in George W. Bush's essential argument that he wasn't slick. When it came time to replace Bush, Americans were tired of W's swagger and stupidity, so they elected the supremely elegant and erudite Barack Obama. And then, tragically, Obama's cool intellect was replaced by Trump's wrecking ball.

It seems to me Americans in 2020 may well be looking for the opposite of Trump: in both substance and style; in tone and temperament. In fact, they're already telling us that. Look who has succeeded since Trump was elected:

- Ralph Northam, a pediatric neurologist, swept into office in a landslide one year after Trump won, Northam ran as a soft-spoken candidate for governor who would bring Virginians together. Northam trounced Ed Gillespie, who ran fear-mongering, racist Trumpian ads about MS-13.

- Conor Lamb, a moderate and a former marine, won the sixth-whitest congressional district in America—a district Trump won by about 20 percent.

- Doug Jones won his Alabama senate seat by emphasizing "kitchen table" issues like health care and the economy, and by calling for bipartisanship and common ground.

- Nearly all of the 41 House challengers who flipped GOP districts ran on health care. In fact only one newly elected Democrat that I know of, Rep. Rashida Tlaib of Michigan, called for impeaching Trump during the 2018 campaign—and her district is solidly Democratic. Nor did many Democrats feature Trump in their ads, the way the Tea Party class of 2010 ran against Obama.

The Maya Angelou Test. The great poet reportedly said: "I've learned that people will forget what you said, people will forget what you did, but people will never forget how you made them feel." How does Donald Trump make his voters feel?

Fearful. Aggrieved. Angry. But also, part of a tribe, respected, valuable. Even patriotic.

I don't believe the Democrats can or should compete with Trump on anger, fear, or grievance. We should capitalize on Trump's weakness: he can't write a song except in the Key of Fear. We should heed the prayer of St. Francis: "Where there is hatred, let me sow love. Where there is injury, pardon. Where there is doubt, faith. Where there is darkness, light. And where there is sadness, joy."

Too often, Democrats appeal to the head, not the heart. We focus on policy, not feelings. Position papers will not defeat Trump. Nor will trying to match him hate for hate. We need to tell folks how we feel, not what we think. Any Democratic message must begin by asking how we want people to feel.

CHAPTER 4

THE LESSONS OF 2018 AND 2019

If November 8, 2016, was the worst election night of my life—and it was—November 6, 2018, was one of the best. Right up there with the day Diane and I were married, the birth of our kids, and the Longhorns winning the 2005 national championship. Don't ask me if that's the right order.

The Democrats won their biggest midterm landslide since Watergate. They needed to pick up 23 seats to take back the House—a daunting task when you realize that even with Barack Obama on the ballot in 2012, they only gained 8. The Democrats didn't just win the 23 they'd needed; they flipped 41. They won Republican-held seats in places where they used to hunt Democrats down with dogs: Utah and South Carolina; Georgia and Oklahoma; Kansas and Texas. Perhaps most exciting, the 2018 midterms saw the largest turnout of any midterm election since 1914—before women had the right to vote. This is a complete turnaround from the catastrophic midterms of 2010 and 2014, where turnout dropped dramatically and Democrats lost, bigly. Important lesson here: when more Americans vote, more Democrats win. It kinda goes with being the party of the people.

Nancy Pelosi asked me to introduce her and other Democratic leaders at their victory party on election night. What an honor. I have known Speaker Pelosi for a very long time, and I have said for years that if there were a Mount Rushmore for Speakers, she would be on it. (The president of the Hair Club for Men has a better chance of being added to the real Mount Rushmore than Donald "Jazz Hands" Trump.)

A few days before the election, she called me and walked me through the House races all across the country. Her knowledge was encyclopedic. She began on the East Coast and did not stop until she assured me that Ed Case would win the open seat in Hawaii's First Congressional District. It was a tour de force, and I say this as someone who has spent thirty-five years running and analyzing elections. Nancy Pelosi is a political genius. The Democratic Party is blessed to have her. Like Hillary Clinton, Pelosi has been a lightning rod for the kook right. But unlike Hillary, Nancy did not have to contend with the Electoral College. In the People's House, the candidate who gets the most votes actually wins—and Pelosi helped her Democratic House candidates get more votes in more places than any Democratic congressional leader in memory. Numbers guru Nate Silver called it a "crazy number of votes." That crazy number was 60 million—nearly matching the 62 million votes Trump got in the presidential year of 2016. For the opposition party—in a midterm election where turnout is usually down—to essentially match the total number of votes received by the president in the previous election is remarkable and unprecedented.

After the heartbreak of 2016, and the nightmare of Trump's inauguration, Democrats were desperate and despairing. Pelosi got to work. Her task was daunting. Donald Trump is a prodigious fund-raiser and a vicious, demagogic campaigner. The economy was strong, which usually favors the party in power. The districts—most of them, anyway—had been drawn by hyperpartisan Republicans after the GOP's midterm landslide of 2010. From Fox News to Rush Limbaugh to Breitbart and Donald Trump's Twitter feed, a right-wing noise machine was doing all it could to destroy Pelosi and her party.

Pelosi didn't flinch. True to form, she put on her heels and went to work. She named New Mexico congressman Ben Ray Luján chairman of the Democratic Congressional Campaign Committee. Luján is soft-spoken but strong. With Pelosi and Luján working nonstop, the DCCC raised a record-shattering $296,422,428 for the 2018 elections. Its competition, the National Republican Congressional Committee, had all the advantages: the majority, and with it the Speakership, every chair of every committee, the power to pass or kill any legislation in the House, and, of course, the GOP's longtime love affair with Big Money. But a funny thing happened on the way to the election: the DCCC outraised the NRCC by more than $90 million.

Money, as the late, legendary Jesse "Big Daddy" Unruh used to say, is the mother's milk of politics. Unruh was state treasurer of California, and a Democrat. I think he would be proud of how his fellow Californian Nancy Pelosi crushed the GOP in fund-raising. But money is not always outcome-determinative. Pelosi knew how to deploy those resources strategically. Her strategy, it seems to me, had four elements: diversity, moderation, message discipline, and organization. Let's walk through them.

Diversity. Democrats recruited the most diverse class of candidates ever, loaded with women and people of color. According to an analysis by the Reflective Democracy Campaign, the number of women of color nominated by Democrats to run in the general election increased 75 percent over 2012 levels. The number of white women nominated by Democrats had jumped 36 percent, and men of color were up 8 percent. For the first time in history, Democrats nominated more women and people of color than they did white men.

This is critically important. The Democratic Party cannot expect to earn the votes of women and people of color in overwhelming numbers if it shuts the door to diversity. Come to think of it, I have not voted for a white man for president, either in the primary or the general election, in sixteen years. In 2008, 2012, and 2016, I voted either for Barack Obama or Hillary Clinton. Like most Americans, I did not vote for them simply because of their race and gender. We Americans voted for them because we believed that they would be the best president. This is not political correctness, people, and Democrats should never allow the GOP to attack us for seeking out women and people of color to run. Greater diversity brings in greater talent.

Pelosi's Democratic candidates were also diverse in life experience. In addition to the usual lawyers and politicians, Democrats recruited people with backgrounds in national security, law enforcement, and other fields—even an NFL linebacker and a former mixed martial arts fighter.

Moderation. Democrats ran moderate candidates in moderate districts. More to the point, they fielded candidates who reflected the ideological composition of their districts. Some of my Republican friends don't get this. When I say we need more women and people of color as candidates, they hear "liberal." Sure, some are liberal. Others are moderate. Unlike our GOP rivals, Democrats believe in ideological diversity as well as other kinds of diversity.

There is no question that one of the massive stars of the 2018 election was Alexandria Ocasio-Cortez, and for good reason. She knocked off Rep. Joe Crowley, who as chair of the House Democratic Caucus was the fourth-ranking member of the House Democratic leadership. AOC is a rare and remarkable talent, the sort of new blood a centuries-old political party needs. Like Hillary and Pelosi before her, she has already become a favorite target of the right-wing attack machine. It's because they fear AOC. At thirty, she and Iowa freshman representative Abby Finkenauer are the youngest women ever elected to Congress.

AOC represents parts of the Bronx and Queens, where her fearless and fiery advocacy of sweeping economic change, from Medicare for All to the Green New Deal to free college, has made her a rock star.

But it is Rep. Finkenauer, from Sherill, Iowa (population 177), whose politics typify the new Democrats elected in 2018. Finkenauer is focused on the needs and concerns of her eastern Iowa constituents: welders like her father, secretaries like her mother, farmers like her neighbors. Her district, which voted for Barack Obama in 2012 and Donald Trump in 2016, is precisely the kind of place Democrats need to win back if they are to defeat Trump. Rather than radical, sweeping, costly programs, Finkenauer is fighting for rural broadband, biodiesel, and farm programs. Even before she had hired all her staff and settled into her new congressional office in Washington, she introduced legislation and—are you ready for this?—cosponsored it with a Republican. Rep. John Curtis (R-UT) and Finkenauer teamed up on legislation to help small businesses apply for government grants and contracts. It was the first bill sponsored by a freshman to pass the House, clearing it just eleven days after Finkenauer was sworn in. "She came here to get things done. It's far more important to her to get things done than to get on the national news," her Republican colleague Curtis told *USA Today*.

Message Discipline. This is absolutely critical. The party that defines the terms of the debate wins the debate. The biggest issue Democrats ran on was not Russia or special counsel Robert S. Mueller III. No one won a red district promising to impeach Trump. Nor did they promise a socialist revolution. Instead, the Democrats wanted the 2018 midterm election to be about health care. Republicans wanted it to be about immigration. The Democrats won. By an overwhelming margin, they said that health care was their top concern. In the exit polls, immigration lagged far behind.

Rather than run on a grandiose pledge to remake one-seventh of the US economy, Democrats said that they would protect people with preexisting conditions. Rather than pledge to eliminate all private insurance, they pledged to take on Big Pharma to lower the cost of prescription medications. Instead of nationalizing the race, the Democrats localized it and, better still, personalized it. Republican districts switched to Democrats because, in the main, voters saw Democrats as practical problem-solvers, not radical revolutionaries.

Organize, Organize, Organize. Every election, it seems, the story pretty much writes itself: Dems in disarray. Not in 2018. In 2018 Democrats were in array, splendid array. Grizzled warhorses who'd been Democratic leaders for decades worked shoulder to shoulder with newly radicalized activists. Leftists knocked on doors to elect moderates, and moderates listened to and learned from younger progressives.

Take the example of The Last Weekend initiative. A coalition of two dozen progressive organizations, including Swing Left, MoveOn, Indivisible, and the Working Families Party, came together to invest one million hours in phone-banking, door-knocking, block-walking—all in the final seventy-two hours of the campaign. It did this knowing that the vast majority of the Democrats it was helping to elect was probably somewhat less progressive than it was. That kind of bighearted commitment is both selfless and strategic. Liberal groups earned themselves a seat at the table through their sweat equity. At the same time, the more traditional arms of the movement, like the Democratic National Committee, were hitting the streets as well. Under chairman Tom Perez, former labor secretary under President Obama, the DNC reached a staggering 50 million voters.

This Is What Victory Looks Like

Pelosi's strategy worked. In addition to driving turnout to a record high, Democrats earned the votes of 90 percent of African Americans, 68 percent of Hispanics, and 67 percent of young voters, and beat the GOP among women by a 20-point margin. Most exciting, while firing up the Democratic base, Pelosi's candidates simultaneously won the middle, crushing Republicans in the crucial independent vote by a 14-point margin. Democrats cut into traditional Republican demographic groups, outperforming the Clinton-Kaine campaign by 4 percent among voters over sixty-five and by 8 percent among white women without a college degree, and increasing their 2016 support among white men without a college degree by a striking 9 points and among white evangelical Christians by 6 points. White men without a college degree and white Christian evangelicals are the heart of the Trump base. Democrats did dramatically better among them, not by calling them racists and not, tellingly, by simply bashing Donald Trump. They gained 9 points among the most loyal Trump voters by talking about voters' lives, voters' health, voters' future—not about Trump. Democrats avoided the Trump Trap, and they won.

The election of 2018 changed the geography of American politics. Across the country, Democrats won in suburban communities where they had not won in decades. Like these:

- In the suburbs of Atlanta, Lucy McBath, an African American, now holds Newt Gingrich's old House seat.

- In suburban Houston, Lizzie Pannill Fletcher now occupies the House seat that had been Republican since George H. W. Bush won it in 1967.

- In suburban Dallas, Rep. Colin Allred, a former linebacker for the Tennessee Titans and an attorney in the Obama Department of Housing and Urban Development, represents the Thirty-second District, which includes the George W. Bush Presidential Library at Southern Methodist University; the former president is one of Allred's constituents.

- In the suburbs of Kansas City, Sharice Davids, a Native American LGBTQ lawyer and former professional mixed martial arts fighter, became only the second Democrat to represent the Third Congressional District in the last fifty-seven years. She narrowly defeated a Bernie Sanders–endorsed candidate in the primary and yet had strong progressive support in her general election victory.

- Orange County, California, south of Los Angeles, was once a hot-bed of the ultraconservative John Birch Society. Democrats swept all seven House seats there. It's hard to imagine that a community that named its airport after John Wayne, where Richard Nixon was born, and where Ronald Reagan is revered is now wholly in the hands of Democrats. Orange (County) is the new blue.

This did not happen by accident. It took grassroots heroes: volunteers devoted hundreds of millions of hours to the hard work of democracy. On that wonderful election night, I told the crowd in a packed ballroom at the Hyatt Regency on Capitol Hill about a very different hill: Missionary Ridge. In November 1863, the Union was on the march, but Confederate resistance was fierce. Fifteen thousand Union troops were pinned down at the base of Missionary Ridge in Tennessee. From five hundred feet above, Confederate cannons and rifles pummeled them. General Ulysses Grant wanted them to hunker down. The soldiers decided otherwise. Without an order, they charged, climbing up the ridge directly into rebel fire. Many troops fell, but their brothers pressed on. It was audacious, spontaneous, and successful. The Confederate line broke. The Union had prevailed.

Although Grant was a military mastermind, that battle was won when ordinary troops, thousands of them, decided not to hold, not to seek shelter, but to advance together, fight together, live or die together. Without waiting for orders, they charged. They took on an entrenched opponent, one that had all the advantages, fearlessly. And they won.

Leaders matter, and there are none more effective than Nancy

Pelosi. But at the end of the day, the victory of 2018 belongs to the grassroots activists who did not wait for orders from headquarters but simply charged, attacked, and prevailed.

2019: Another Year, Another Democratic Victory

There weren't a lot of elections in 2019, but the elections we had brought more good news for the Democrats. After taking control of the House, the Democrats went to work. By the end of 2019, they had passed almost six hundred bills and resolutions—an astonishingly productive year.

- Democrats began with H.R. 1, the For the People Act. It is a sweeping reform of our political system, expanding voter registration, making Election Day a holiday, reforming how our campaigns are financed, increasing disclosure in campaign ads, and much more. (For a full discussion of the kinds of reforms Democrats should run on in 2020, see chapter 13.)

- Democrats passed H.R. 3, to reduce the cost of prescription drugs.

- Democrats passed H.R. 5, the Equality Act, to protect the rights of LGBTQ+ Americans.

- Democrats passed H.R. 6, to protect Dreamers—hundreds of thousands of children who were brought to this country without papers by their parents and who have been living, studying, and working here for years.

- Democrats passed H.R. 7, guaranteeing fair pay to women.

- Democrats passed H.R. 8, expanding background checks for gun purchases.

- Democrats passed H.R. 9, putting America back into the Paris Climate Accords.

- Democrats passed H.R. 582, raising the minimum wage.

- Democrats passed H.R. 5377, restoring state and local tax deductibility.

- They even passed the United States-Mexico-Canada Agreement (USMCA)—one of Trump's top priorities.

Except for the US-Mexico-Canada trade deal, all of those bills, and hundreds more, are languishing on the desk of the Grim Reaper, Republican Senate leader Mitch McConnell (R-Crypt). His only legislative priority is to confirm Trump's right-wing judges. As former Kentucky Democratic secretary of state Alison Lundergan Grimes once said, "If the doctors told Senator McConnell that he had a kidney stone, he'd refuse to pass it."

Chances are, you had no idea that House Democrats had already passed all those bills. The news in 2019 was utterly dominated by Donald Trump: Mueller's investigation into the 2016 Trump campaign's Russian contacts, and Trump's attempts to cover it up; then the investigation and impeachment of Trump for abuse of office and obstruction of Congress.

I lived through the Clinton impeachment and am proud that, as counselor to the President, I defended our Constitution against Ken Starr, Newt Gingrich, and the rest of the right-wing sex police. The American people agreed with the president's defenders and sent President Clinton's approval rating soaring up to 73 percent. Republicans paid a political price for impeachment back then. The conventional wisdom was that the Democrats would pay one this time.

But this impeachment was different. It was not a violation of anyone's marital vows but rather a violation of the oath of office. A majority of Americans supported not only impeaching Trump but convicting him and removing him from office.

Still, Republicans believed that impeachment would hurt the Democrats. Here again, Speaker Pelosi saved her party. Her reluctance to impeach, and her reverence for the Constitution, made it difficult for Trump to caricature her party as a pack of rabid partisans. (Although Trump was helped when, hours after being sworn in, freshman Rep. Rashida Tlaib said, "We're going to go in there and we're gonna impeach this m——f——.") But Pelosi, as usual, got it right, saying, "We shouldn't be impeaching for a political reason, and we shouldn't avoid impeachment for political reasons." Perfect balance.

When the story of Trump's attempt to solicit a bribe from the president of Ukraine came to light, Pelosi and other Democrats felt they had no choice. And Republicans thought that Democrats would be hurt politically the way Republicans had been in 1998. Thus the elections of 2019 would be the test. And the Democrats aced it, winning the governor's mansions in both Kentucky and Louisiana, two states that aren't on anyone's list of swing states.

Kentucky: Trump's Mini-Me Loses

In Kentucky, GOP governor Matt Bevin was a Bluegrass State Trump wannabe. He insulted teachers, tried to cut their pensions, undermined unions (which have more than a few Trump supporters in them), and dumped his own lieutenant governor. His reelection strategy was straight out of the Trump playbook. He ran a hysterical ad on immigration (Kentucky is 1,300 miles from the US-Mexico border), claiming that his Democratic opponent, Attorney General Andy Beshear, "would allow illegal immigrants to swarm our state . . . While President Trump and Governor Bevin crack down on illegal immigration, liberal Andy Beshear sides with illegal immigrants."

Beshear was too smart, too disciplined, to rise to the bait. He understood the Trump Trap and relentlessly stayed on message. He ran against Bevin's "name-calling and rancor," calling for "real solutions for our state." He focused on health care and protecting those with preexisting conditions (sound familiar?). He promised to secure pensions, "strengthen our public schools and build an economy that helps our local businesses flourish and workers get ahead."

The race was like a lab experiment: Could a Democrat focused on kitchen-table issues defeat a Trumper in a state The Donald won by 30 points? Trump himself weighed in heavily. He deployed his mighty Twitter account, flexing his short, pudgy thumbs as he banged out pro-Bevin, anti-Beshear messages. He fired up Air Force One and flew to Lexington, where—you know what he did—he made it all about Donald Trump. A Bevin loss, he told Kentuckians the day before the election, "'sends a really bad message . . . you can't let that happen to me!'"

The last poll before the election, by the Republican Trafalgar Group, showed Bevin leading by 5 points. Beshear won.

Even Donald Trump had fallen into the Trump Trap. He made it all about Trump. Voters wanted it to be all about them.

Louisiana: "You Gotta Give Me a Big Win, Please. Please!"

The story repeated itself in Louisiana, a state Trump carried by 20 points. This time the incumbent governor was a Democrat, John Bel Edwards. His Republican opponent, Eddie Rispone, sought to nationalize the race, hugging Donald Trump so close that it made Mike Pence uncomfortable. Trump traveled to Louisiana three times to campaign for Rispone. He attacked Edwards repeatedly on Twitter. The GOP tried to paint Edwards as, in the words of Edwards's campaign manager, "a radical liberal who's going to take away your guns." This was a tough sell against Edwards, a former Army Ranger and West Point grad who is pro-gun and pro-life.

Edwards, like Beshear, stayed on message. In a post-election discussion of the campaign, Edwards's campaign manager, Richard Carbo, said, "There's no competing with the leader of the free world when he comes and campaigns against you. Our strategy became

'Continue telling the story that we've been telling all along.'" When Trump came to attack him, Edwards simply decried partisanship and said that the election would turn on "Louisiana issues, not Washington, D.C. issues." While Rispone was hugging Trump, Edwards was hugging health care, reminding Louisianans that on his first day in office he signed an executive order expanding Medicaid, bringing health coverage to more than 450,000 Louisianans. He touted his bipartisan success in balancing the budget; the state was $2 billion in debt when he took office. He emphasized his commitment to protecting higher education, which had been devastated by budget cuts, boasted of the teacher pay raise he achieved, and highlighted his criminal justice reform.

Trump, here again, tried to make it about Trump—especially about impeachment. He charmingly called the process a "bulls—impeachment." He told a Lake Charles rally, "Nancy Pelosi hates the United States of America." In Bossier City a few weeks later, he changed his tune. He claimed that impeachment was helping him politically. "The people of this country aren't buying it—you see it because we're going up and they're going down," Trump said. "Let's keep it going for a while." Then, repeating the self-centered appeal he'd tried in Kentucky, Trump begged the crowd, "You gotta give me a big win, please. Please!"

Trump lost. Or, rather, Rispone lost and Edwards won. Once more, making it all about Trump proved to be a failed strategy. Focusing on voters' health care and education and on criminal justice reform was a winning strategy, even in a Deep South state that hasn't voted Democratic in a presidential election in a quarter century.

Virginia: A Blue Wave Flips Both Houses

Republicans had controlled the General Assembly for twenty-five years. They'd held the state senate for seven of the previous eight years. In 2019, Democrats, who held every statewide elected office, were determined to take back both houses. From Richard Nixon in 1968 to George W. Bush thirty-six years later, Virginia had voted for every Republican presidential candidate. But the Old Dominion has a new politics. Barack Obama won it twice, and Hillary did as well. Mark Warner and Tim Kaine are both popular Democratic senators. Democrats are ascendant. But in the early months of 2019, the Commonwealth's Democratic leaders were on the ropes. Governor Ralph Northam was caught up in a blackface scandal, and Attorney General Mark Herring confessed that he had worn blackface as well. Lieutenant Governor Justin Fairfax was accused of sexual assault.

Chaos reigned in Richmond. Democratic presidential candidates tripped over each other calling on Northam to resign. After a few shaky days, the governor righted the ship, ignored the calls for him to quit, and went back to work. Northam is living proof that tough times don't last but tough people do. Four hundred years after Africans were first brought to Virginia and enslaved, Northam pledged to confront the past and atone, both for his own history and the commonwealth's. He appointed the commonwealth's first diversity and inclusion officer. He named a commission to pore over Virginia's statutes and identify antiquated, racist language. He established a commission to propose a new curriculum for teaching black history. He expanded access to state contracts for minority- and women-owned businesses. His budget reflected the needs and priorities of the African American community: pre-K, reducing maternal mortality for African American women, free community college to low-income Virginians.

And then disaster struck. On May 31, a gunman murdered twelve innocent public servants in Building Two of the Virginia Beach Municipal Center. He was armed with two .45-caliber pistols, high-capacity ammunition magazines, and a sound suppressor. Northam, who had served as an army doctor, comforted the families of the dead. He visited the wounded in the hospital. He wept at the funerals. And then he acted. Standing in that shattered community, he said that while Virginians truly welcomed people's good wishes, what the people of his commonwealth needed was "votes and laws, not thoughts and prayers." He called the legislature back into a special session and said he would call on them to pass the package of gun safety laws he had introduced in the last session. Northam, a Virginia Military Institute graduate, grew up in a rural community and is a hunter himself. His gun safety package included a ban on silencers and high-capacity magazines, stronger background checks, and a "red flag" law that would allow a judge to order someone to surrender firearms if he is a threat to himself or others.

The Republicans, fully aware that Virginia is the home state of the National Rifle Association, gaveled the session closed in just ninety minutes. They didn't consider a single one of the governor's bills. It took many of the Republicans longer to drive to the session than to actually have one.

Northam, like most Virginians, was incensed. The arrogance and ignorance, the callousness and cowardice of the Republicans changed everything for his standing. Democrats who'd called for Northam's resignation were now praising his political courage. Northam's steady, strong leadership had a profound effect: it allowed his supporters to come back together and focus on booting out the recalcitrant Republicans.

Across the commonwealth but especially in the suburbs, activists, volunteers, and outraged citizens went to work. They registered voters, recruited candidates, raised money. Former governor Terry McAuliffe was all-in as well, frenetically raising funds and raising hell.

Although Virginia is just across the Potomac River from Washington, Democrats did not make Trump an issue. The impeachment investigation drew all the national attention, but Virginia Democrats ran on gun safety, women's rights, health care, and other Virginia issues. Panicked Virginia Republicans went full-Trump. They accused Democrats—Virginia Democrats—of being socialists. They ran ads featuring Alexandria Ocasio-Cortez and Bernie Sanders, neither of whom was on the Virginia ballot. In Virginia Beach, where the mass shooting was still fresh in people's minds, one Republican attacked her Democratic opponent, photoshopping a picture of her into a picture of MS-13 gang members.

On Election Day, Virginians gave both the General Assembly and the Senate to the Democrats. Today, for the first time in the four-hundred-year history of that body, the Virginia General Assembly has a woman speaker, Democrat Eileen Filler-Corn. For the first time in history, Virginia has an African American female majority leader, Charniele Herring. Suzette Denslow was unanimously elected the chamber's first female clerk. Across the capital, Senator Louise Lucas was named president pro tempore of the senate. So perhaps it shouldn't surprise you that Virginia in January 2020 became the thirty-eighth state to ratify the Equal Rights Amendment.

The Bottom Line

The lesson of nearly every election since Donald Trump took the oath of office is clear: if Democrats focus on voters, not the giant orange narcissist rage-tweeting and obstructing justice, they win. Even in places where voters overwhelmingly voted for Trump, Democrats can win.

Speaker Nancy Pelosi, Governor Andy Beshear, Governor John Bel Edwards, Speaker Eileen Filler-Corn, and Louise Lucas, senate president pro tempore. They all hold office because they made their election about their citizens. Giving the campaign back to the voters should be the Democrats' highest priority in 2020.

CHAPTER 5

BLUE-COLLAR
BETRAYAL

*How Trump Conned Working-Class Whites,
and What Democrats Can Do About It*

W e are in the middle of a fundamental realignment in American politics. It's been coming for a while, like a person bobbing along the Niagara River. On November 8, 2016, we went over the falls. I know a lot of my fellow progressives who wished they'd landed on the Canadian side.

I was on the set at CNN's Washington bureau, watching my colleague John King plot the election results on his Magic Wall. I love King, but I wasn't about to just sit there and passively watch him, so I started texting. After decades in politics, I am blessed to know some of the smartest operatives in America, women and men who know the most arcane and important details of the swingiest precinct in the bellwether counties of the decisive states. In Florida, that person is Steve Schale. He ran the state for Barack Obama, who defeated John McCain there by 3 percent in 2008 and edged out Mitt Romney in 2012 by a single, vital percentage point.

Florida, of course, is the largest swing state, with 29 electoral votes. I was as nervous as a porcupine in a balloon factory. More nervous, actually. As nervous as Donald Trump at a Weight Watchers meeting. Or Prince Andrew in a deposition. Anyway, I was nervous. I texted Schale manically. At first, he told me things seemed to be going according to plan. Trump was hitting his numbers in the northern, Republican parts of the state. Hillary was hitting her numbers in the South. (One of the clichés about Florida politics is that the farther South you get, the farther North you are, given Miami-Dade's transplanted Yankees and progressive voting habits.) If everyone performed as expected, Hillary would win narrowly, as Obama had.

Then, ominously, a one-word text: *Wait*.

Wait? What? Why?

Radio silence.

Then came a message that shattered me: *Volusia. Trump's burying her. It's over.*

I love Volusia County. Home of Daytona International Speedway, it's the kind of place where you can always find a cold beer and a warm greeting. As a White House official, I'd gone there in the summer of 1998 with President Bill Clinton, as he came to offer assistance and thanks to firefighters and National Guard troops who had been battling a catastrophic wildfire. Volusia County is filled with working-class white folks who enjoy the sea breeze on the Atlantic coast of central Florida. Bill Clinton carried Volusia County twice, Barack Obama carried Volusia County handily in 2008, but something happened in 2012. The Democrats' grip on the county was slipping. Obama lost Volusia County by 2,742 votes—less than 1 percent.

As I had gamed-out 2016, I figured Hillary would match or even exceed Obama's performance among working-class whites. After all, they'd been a strong constituency for her in her 2008 primary battle against Obama. And Hillary's story of her parents' rise from little or nothing to the comfortable middle class was a classic tale of the American Dream. I was wrong. Hillary did not match Obama's performance. Instead of losing the county by two or three thousand votes, as Obama had in 2012, she lost it by nearly 34,000 votes.

I was stunned. Schale stopped texting me. What do you say after "It's over"? Volusia County had ghosted Hillary. And that was just the beginning.

My eyes grew large and my chin nearly slumped to my chest as I stared at the reality of Hillary's collapse in Volusia and reflected on what it meant for the national election. Sitting next to me on the CNN election night set was my then-colleague and now White House press secretary Kayleigh McEnany. A native Floridian and Harvard Law grad, Kayleigh is as loyal to Trump as she is smart. And she is very smart. Sensing my shock, she leaned over and whispered, "What's going on?" I turned to her and said that Volusia County was a landslide for Trump. "It's over," I said. "You've won." "We won Florida?" she asked. "No, Kayleigh," I said. "You've won America."

I knew that if Hillary was collapsing in Volusia County, she would collapse in other, similar places. And she did. Take Luzerne County, Pennsylvania. Home of Wilkes-Barre, this northeast Pennsylvania county has long been a Democratic stronghold. Obama carried Luzerne by a solid 9 points in 2008 and by 5 percent in 2012—a far cry from the 14-point landslide Bill Clinton won there in 1996, but good enough to help Obama carry Pennsylvania twice.

Hillary Clinton has roots there. Her father grew up next door to Luzerne County, in neighboring Scranton. As a child, Hillary used to spend vacations at Lake Winola, just north of Luzerne County. She understood folks in northeast Pennsylvania. On one of her many visits to Scranton, where her parents are buried, one local voter said, "Every time that she comes back to run, she comes here as one of her main stomping grounds, so I think she has Scranton's back and hopefully we can have hers, so, I'm excited for today."

But Luzerne County did not have Hillary's back. She lost this formerly reliable Democratic county by a staggering 24,237 votes, helping to power Donald Trump to victory in the Keystone State by less than 1 percent.

This is how Trump broke down the Democrats' fabled Blue Wall:

he crushed us in formerly Democratic areas filled with high school–educated white people—places like Macomb County, Michigan, or any of the twenty-two counties in Wisconsin that flipped from Obama to Trump.

This is a sea change.

From FDR to Bill Clinton, the Democratic Party was a "black and blue" coalition: African Americans and white working-class voters. Clinton's strength with white working-class voters powered him to a landslide in West Virginia, for example. He carried Kentucky, Montana, Louisiana, Tennessee, Arkansas (natch), and Georgia in 1992. Imagine any Democrat carrying any of those states today—although Georgia will be in play, thanks in part to changing demographics (more on that in chapter 6).

The Canary in the Coal Mine

The former Democratic stronghold of West Virginia, chock-full of working-class white people, was the canary in the coal mine, if you'll pardon the cliché. There are fifty-five counties in West Virginia; in 1992, Bill Clinton carried forty-two of them, from the northern tip of Hancock County to the southern end of McDowell County. McDowell County is especially illustrative. President Kennedy traveled there at least three times to shine a light on rural poverty. McDowell County is coal country, and coal has long been a boom-or-bust business. Even in 1960, JFK saw the human cost of automation. The challenge, he said was "what to do with men when machines have thrown them out of work." Without a solution, he predicted, "what has happened here is going to happen across the country." Those impoverished, unemployed coal miners came to love the wealthy, aristocratic war hero. They gave him 74.8 percent of the vote against Richard Nixon.

The bond between working-class West Virginians and the Democratic Party endured. By the time 1992 rolled around, Bill Clinton, who famously shook JFK's hand in the Rose Garden, carried West Virginia in a landslide and carried McDowell County with 71.8 percent of the vote. Pretty impressive, considering H. Ross Perot was waging a fiery third-party candidacy.

By 2016 all that had changed. McDowell County, home to more than 70,000 people when JFK visited, and 35,000 when Clinton carried it, today has just 18,223 souls. Just 2,068 of them have a job. Of the 3,142 counties in America, McDowell is at or near the top in drug-related deaths, substance abuse, and self-harm, and at or near the bottom in life expectancy. Folks in McDowell County, West Virginia, are in desperate, dire pain. Jobs have left, drugs have flooded in, and death comes too often through diseases of despair: addiction, cirrhosis, depression, suicide.

In 2016, Donald J. Trump won 74.6 percent of the vote in McDowell County on his way to carrying every single county in the state, racking up 68.5 percent of the vote.

McDowell County is an especially heartbreaking example, but the truth is the movement of white working-class voters away from the Democrats had been going on for some time; Donald Trump just put it on steroids. His spectacular performance among white people with a high school education allowed him to win Michigan, Wisconsin, and Pennsylvania by a combined total of just 77,744 votes. Three Dog Night may think one is the loneliest number, but 77,744 is the most tragic number of all. That's the number by which Donald Trump became president. And 77,744 people would not sell out a football game at Penn State's Happy Valley, or the University of Michigan's Big House, or the University of Wisconsin's Camp Randall Stadium. Yet 77,744 voters swung all three of those states to Trump, giving him the White House.

Shelves groan under the weight of the books that have been written about the crisis facing the white working class. Good. There has been a quiet crisis going on for years, and too few members of the elite seem to give a damn. How can it be that the Democratic Party,

the party that created the weekend, the minimum wage, Social Security, and more, has lost the support of working-class whites? It's
because they think we Democrats don't care about anyone who's not
from Hollywood or Harvard. I know they're wrong, but we have to
show them that.

A Downside of the Meritocracy

Perhaps some of it is inherent in the move toward a meritocracy. I
believe in meritocracy. It allowed me, the grandson of an immigrant
housekeeper, to wind up an adviser to the president of the United
States and a cable news talking head. Meritocracy has been a boon
for America. Instead of the entitled kids of the gentry effortlessly
sitting atop the ruling class, meritocracy has thrown open the doors
of opportunity. Thrown them open so wide that the son of a Kenyan
villager who as a child herded goats can become the most powerful
person on the face of the earth. That is to be celebrated. America is
smarter, richer, and more just because of the meritocracy.

But there is no such thing as an unalloyed good. Every blessing
is mixed, at least a little. There is a downside to everything, even
expanding social and economic opportunity. It may well be that a
downside to meritocracy is an end to noblesse oblige. The inbred
progeny of the moneyed elite knew in their hearts that they didn't
really deserve their privilege. Their headmasters at their boarding
schools beat it into their heads that they had a duty, an obligation, to
give back.

There was much to loathe about the American aristocracy: the
lack of opportunity for women, people of color, the poor; the vast,
inherited (and thus unearned) wealth. But this sense of noblesse
oblige, that is to be admired. It took hold in the young son of a mil-
lionaire senator who prepped at Phillips Academy Andover, George
H. W. Bush. Bush, whose life circumstances were the very definition
of privilege in the first half of the twentieth century, heard a lec-

ture given by Establishment mandarin and former secretary of war Henry Stimson, himself an Andover man. The year was 1940. Hitler was on the march. Stimson had volunteered for the army at age fifty in World War I. His lecture, Bush said, shaped his life. Stimson described the age as "a dark hour for the civilized world." He saw the evil that Hitler represented and expressed it in the language of the eastern elite. Hitler was a bully, he said, with no "respect for justice and fair play." Today that choice of words seems archaic, if not tragically quaint. A genocidal maniac, a fascist animal, is simply a bad sport. Mass murder is not to be equated with cheating at golf.

But the larger message Stimson gave those entitled boys was this: there is good and evil in the world. You must stand for good, even at the risk of your life. In fact, for the children of privilege to march off to war is not merely a duty, it is an honor. "I wish to God," Stimson said, "that I were young enough to face it with you." George H. W. Bush heard Stimson's call. At age seventeen, preppy young Poppy risked his life as the youngest pilot in the navy. He was shot down over Chichijima and rescued by a nearby US submarine. I played a central role in Bush's defeat in 1992, and I'm proud I did. The country wanted change, and he was seen as the status quo. But in his commitment to serve, to give back, to take responsibility for those less fortunate, George H. W. Bush embodied the best of an unfair, antiquated system.

Perhaps other lucky products of the American meritocracy should adopt a bit of Bush's humility. Humility, of course, is essential when much of the blessings of your life are unearned. But we who have benefited from the meritocracy too rarely pay tribute to luck. The new elite often didn't have wealthy families—both Bill Clinton and Barack Obama were raised mostly by single mothers—but they had the unearned benefits of brains, of good schools and good looks, of teachers and preachers and mentors and coaches and teammates and roommates and neighbors who saw their potential and gave them a leg up. Of not being afflicted with addiction, of not being killed in combat. To make it in America, a million breaks have to go your way. Too many in the meritocracy look at their own success and think, "I did it all on my own." As my late friend and mentor Zell Miller, the former governor of Georgia, used to say, "If you ever see a turtle up on a fence post, you know one thing: he didn't get there on his own. Somebody had to put him there."

Perhaps those who made it to the top of the fence posts of government, business, and academia are today callous to those who have been left behind by the meritocracy. Obviously, the thinking goes, they lack merit. This makes it easier to turn a blind eye to the suffering of laid-off factory workers and struggling family farmers and office workers and families who live in coal-mining towns where opioids are laying waste to families and jobs, and a deaf ear to their pleas for help. And if not help, just a modicum of respect. *We built this country,* they say, *and now you're tossing us aside in the name of globalization and market efficiency and technology.*

Even worse than neglect, some elites treated the white working class with contempt; at best, they patronized them. "You go into these small towns in Pennsylvania," then-senator Obama said to a group of wealthy meritocrats in San Francisco, "and, like a lot of small towns in the Midwest, the jobs have gone now for 25 years and nothing's replaced them. And they fell through the Clinton administration, and the Bush administration, and each successive administration has said that somehow these communities are gonna regenerate and they have not. And it's not surprising then they get bitter, they cling to their guns or religion or antipathy toward people who aren't like them or anti-immigrant sentiment or anti-trade sentiment as a way to explain their frustrations."

Obama is a caring, decent man. But when he saw the pain of the white working class, he seemed to offer analysis rather than empathy. Whatever his intent, working-class whites took umbrage. Country singer Charlie Daniels penned a biting response: "My faith goes much deeper than his superficial explanation, and I love my guns even when I'm not frustrated." He went on to say, "To me this latest Obama blunder only helps reveal the depth of condescension the far left wing of the Democrat party has for the folks out here in flyover country."

Eight years later, my friend Hillary Clinton made a similar gaffe, also when speaking at a fund-raiser. Analyzing her campaign's priorities in terms of targeting voters, she pointed out that not every voter was open to supporting her—an obvious truth. "You know, to just be grossly generalistic, you could put half of Trump's supporters into what I call the basket of deplorables. Right? The racist, sexist, homophobic, xenophobic, Islamophobic—you name it. And unfortunately there are people like that. And he has lifted them up." Oops. She then went on to say that she felt the pain of other Trump voters, those who are not racist but "feel that the government has let them down" and who are "desperate for change. Those are people we have to understand and empathize with as well."

To this day, many Trump supporters proudly call themselves "Deplorables." There is no doubt that comment hurt Hillary. It wounded the pride of people in places like western Pennsylvania, the Upper Peninsula of Michigan, and northern Wisconsin. And they remembered in November.

In fairness to Hillary, some Trump supporters *are* racist. The problem is, when you say Trump supporters are racist, you tar a lot of good people with a lethal epithet. Democrats are never going back to being the party of the racists. Trump wants them; he can have them. We don't want them or need them. But we do need some of the Trump voters—some of the millions who voted for him who are not racist. Democrats would do well to keep in mind the fallacy of composition: all racists are Trump supporters, but not all Trump supporters are racists.

Trump Lights the Fuse

Trump did not create the conditions of despair and disillusionment in the hearts of so many white working-class Americans. But he knew, as all demagogues do, that he could exploit those conditions for his own ends.

Donald Jessica Trump (as Randy Rainbow hilariously dubbed him) is a most unlikely working-class hero. How a man whom Montana governor Steve Bullock describes as "a con man from New York with orange hair and a gold toilet" became the champion of farmers and factory workers is one of the great ironies of American history. Sure, everyday Americans have turned to wealthy leaders from time to time. George Washington comes to mind. Or Teddy and Franklin Roosevelt. JFK is another.

But Trump is not merely rich. Unlike Washington or the other wealthy presidents, his rhetoric is vulgar, vicious, even violent. Can you imagine FDR saying, "I grab 'em by the p—y"? Democrats need to understand that Trump's coarse, crass savagery is a feature, not a bug. Many Trump voters support him *because* of it, not in spite of it. As one strategist who played a central role in electing Trump said to me after the election: "What you guys never understood is that our people loved all that stuff. They were looking for a big, throbbing middle finger to the Establishment."

They wanted a middle finger, not a reformer. And so they sorted through sixteen other GOP candidates, who had combined governmental experience of more than two hundred years, and chose a man with no experience, one with no filter, and one with no scruples. The more the GOP Establishment howled, the better Trump's voters liked it. Just as suburbanites shook their heads and wondered why inner-city African Americans would burn their own neighborhoods in the sixties, comfortable members of the meritocratic elite today scratch their heads when working-class whites support Trump destroying the institutions that made this country great.

A lot of the Democrats' collapse among the white working class is economic. Much of it is cultural. But let's face it: race is a central part of it, too. I can't unpack how much is which, and I can't peer into people's souls. But Trump says racist things, and those things resonate. I believe it is because all of us have the capacity to hate; each of us can give in to prejudice.

This was explained to me best by a dear friend, the late trial lawyer Steve Mostyn. Mostyn had grown up in the East Texas town of Whitehouse (just off Farm to Market Road 346, in case you're wondering) and with his brilliant wife, Amber, had built an astonishingly successful practice. Like all great trial lawyers, he was a master of human psychology. I was pondering why good people in towns like the ones he and I had grown up in were so enamored with Trump; why they would support someone whose appeal was that he was so blatantly racist. Human nature, Mostyn said. Think about it: this is biological evolution. It's all about the amygdala, the two little glands in the brain that play a central role in our emotions, especially fear. Twenty thousand years ago, if you and your tribe were living on the plains, or in the mountains, or the desert, or wherever, and suddenly someone came into your camp who looked very different from you, it was a very good idea to kill him. He could be a threat, so why take a chance?

That worked twenty thousand years ago. But something happened. Something called civilization. With it came things like religion and philosophy. And one thing every decent religion or philosophy has in common: be good to people who are not like you.

Empathy is the soul of morality. In the Christian tradition we are taught the Golden Rule: do unto others as you would have them do unto you. In Judaism, Hillel teaches, "If I am not for myself, who will be for me? But if I am only for myself, what am I?" The Prophet Muhammad taught: "None of you have faith until you love for your neighbor what you love for yourself." Confucius said, "What I do not wish men to do to me, I also wish not to do to men." In Buddhism it is written: "Hurt not others in ways that you yourself would find hurtful."

Those religions call upon us to rise above human nature, even as our amygdala tells us to fear the Other. It is the eternal tension every human faces: the angel on one shoulder, the devil on the other. "Love Thy Neighbor" versus "Build a Wall."

Trump touches something very deep and very dark. Also very powerful. Strong enough to turn people who had voted for Barack Hussein Obama into people who will attend Trump rallies and chant, "Lock her up!" This is not new in American life. Alexander Stephens, the vice president of the Confederacy, said in his famous "Cornerstone Speech" of 1861 that he and his fellow Confederates explicitly rejected the notion that all men are created equal: "Our new government," he said, "is founded upon exactly the opposite idea; its foundations are laid, its corner-stone rests upon the great truth, that the negro is not equal to the white man; that slavery—subordination to the superior race—is his natural and normal condition." Strom Thurmond, who served in the Senate into the twenty-first century, ran for president on a racist platform. Of segregation, he famously said: "All the laws of Washington and all the bayonets of the Army cannot force the Negro into our homes, into our schools, our churches and our places of recreation and amusement."

Of course, the correct lesson from those men's lives is that racism is evil. It is despicable, immoral, unholy. But it has also been effective. Ol' Strom, as they called him in South Carolina, was the longest-serving United States senator in history. George Wallace is the only third-party candidate to win any states in the last fifty years—five, to be exact. And Donald J. Trump won thirty states and 306 electoral votes. As President Lyndon Baines Johnson, a son of the segregated South who committed his presidency to civil rights, said, "If you can convince the lowest white man he's better than the best colored man, he won't notice you're picking his pocket. Hell, give him somebody to look down on, and he'll empty his pockets for you."

This whole discussion is depressing as hell. But it is real. Countering Trump's racist appeals will require creativity and discipline, but it will also require empathy. It requires us to amplify the angel that sits on his voters' left shoulder. If all we do is shout "Shut up, racist" at his voters, they will only redouble their commitment to him. Instead, we should follow the lead of Barack Obama and Bill Clinton, and raise folks' sights, show how racist appeals only distract from our common humanity and our shared goals. President Clinton used to tell people that, as an Arkansan, he'd seen it all his life: demagogues who divide white working people from black working people so they can distract them from the fact they're both getting screwed economically. Instead of telling people they are evil racists for voting for Trump, tell them they've been duped. And show them how their interests are being betrayed by those who are preaching division.

The Political Imperative of Winning Some Rural States

We don't have a democracy; we have a Republic. And in our Republic, rural areas have an outsize influence. The Electoral College is, of course, how we actually choose our presidents. It is tilted toward small rural states. The Senate is even more unbalanced. Just 18 percent of Americans control fifty seats in the Senate, and a mere 7 percent of our citizens can save a president from impeachment by delivering a whopping thirty-four Senate votes. Think about that: Just 23 million people can block the other 308 million Americans from removing a corrupt president. Put another way, Wyoming, Alaska, and the Dakotas, with fewer than 3 million residents, can outvote California, New York, and Illinois, with almost 72 million residents.

There are some interesting proposals to work around the Electoral College (which I discuss in chapter 7). But there is no way to work around the fact that the Senate will always be a counter-majoritarian institution. What do we do? Well, we win some Senate seats in rural America, that's what.

In 1993, Clinton's economic plan received not a single GOP vote in the Senate, and passed by just one vote. In 2009, Obama's health care plan had the same result: no GOP votes, passed by just one. In both cases, the vote that pushed the president's most important legislative goal through the Senate came from a Democratic senator from Nebraska. In the case of the Clinton economic program, it was Bob Kerrey. In the case of Obamacare, Ben Nelson.

We can't change the Senate. But Democrats can win in rural states. Just ask Sen. Joe Manchin of West Virginia. Or Sen. Jon Tester of Montana. Or Sen. Doug Jones of Alabama.

Newton's Third Law Still Applies

If the 2016 election was about the Democrats' collapse among the white working class—and it was—the 2018 election was about Newton's third law: for every action there is an equal and opposite reaction. (I always knew that two courses of "Physics for Idiots" at the Greatest University in the World would come in handy.)

The Republican collapse among suburban voters—especially white women with a college degree—is spectacular. Just as Trump won counties where Democrats used to dominate, Democrats won in places where bluebloods always voted red. My friend and colleague Ron Brownstein, as insightful an observer of politics as there is, calls it "class inversion." As country music voters are moving from D to R, country club voters are moving the other way.

We political consultants used to have a name for college-educated white people. After all, the phrase "college-educated white people" is a bit clunky. So we came up with a shorthand term for them. Bear with me, because this is a bit technical. Political consultants used to call college-educated white people "Republicans." For most of my lifetime, college-educated whites voted Republican. Just as Volusia

County, Florida, and Luzerne County, Pennsylvania, were the heart of working-class Democrats, leafy, wealthy suburbs like Chesterfield County, Virginia, and Orange County, California, were where Republicans met, married, and raised little Republicans. Orange County, the heart of Reagan Country, voted Republican in presidential elections for eighty years before Hillary Clinton carried it in 2016.

Eighty years, people. That's not a trend; it's a lock. This is how life was. If your name was stitched above the pocket on your work shirt, you were a Democrat. If your initials were monogrammed on your French cuffs, you were a Republican.

But the suburbs are a-changin'. Two factors are driving this: the shifting political values of college-educated whites, and the increasing diversity of formerly lily-white suburbs.

Let's start with education. There is what's been called a diploma divide. As Brownstein has noted, from 1952, the advent of modern political polling, no Democrat has ever won college-educated white voters. Ever. Not the erudite Adlai Stevenson, nor landslide Lyndon Johnson, nor even the brilliant and urbane Barack Obama. If only college-educated white people could vote, the Democrats would be 0 for life. We would be the Cleveland Browns of politics.

Obama did better than most Democrats, losing college-educated white voters to Mitt Romney by 14 percent. Hillary only lost them by 3 percent. And she won college-educated white women by 7 percent. Her strategists hoped that she would win college-educated whites outright, which would offset the aforementioned collapse among working-class whites.

Close, but no Oval Office.

Hillary's increase in popularity among college-educated whites was stopped when, on October 28, 2016, then-FBI director James Comey sent a letter to Congress saying that he had reopened the investigation into her emails. Stated simply: James Comey cost Hillary Clinton the election, period.

Yes, I wish Hillary had run stronger among the white working class, and, yes, I wish her campaign had been able to motivate and mobilize communities of color like Barack Obama's did. But every campaign makes mistakes. No other campaign had the head of the FBI weigh in twice: once, in July, to trash the candidate publicly, even as he cleared her of any criminality. And then again ten days before the election. Comey's October surprise deflated Hillary's rising support among college-educated whites, costing her Michigan, Wisconsin, Pennsylvania, and maybe more states—and the White House.

Don't take my word for it. Here's what Nate Silver of FiveThirty-Eight wrote, in a piece entitled "The Comey Letter Probably Cost Clinton the Election." (Gotta hand it to Nate: he doesn't hide the ball.) "At a maximum, [Comey's letter] might have shifted the race by 3 or 4 percentage points toward Donald Trump, swinging Michigan, Pennsylvania, Wisconsin and Florida to him, perhaps along with North Carolina and Arizona. At a minimum, its impact might have been only a percentage point or so. Still, because Clinton lost Michigan, Pennsylvania and Wisconsin by less than 1 point, the letter was probably enough to change the outcome of the Electoral College."

I will never get over that, and neither should you. But we have to get past it. We have to become better, not bitter. Hillary's breakthrough with college-educated white women pointed the way to even more impressive gains in the next election. Under Nancy Pelosi's suburban strategy, Democratic House candidates improved upon Hillary's performance, winning an eye-popping 59 percent of white college-educated women, giving Democrats a 20-point victory in a demographic they had won only once before. The Pelosi Democrats lost college-educated white men by only 4 percent. In the end, this made the 2018 election the first in history in which the Democratic Party carried college-educated white people.

The problem for the Democrats is that only 33.4 percent of Americans have a college degree. The Democrats risk trading dominance among the majority of whites for dominance among a minority of them. Still, the number of Americans with a college degree is rising. In FDR's time, less than 5 percent of Americans had a college education. A decade ago, it was just 28 percent.

As much as I love my fellow college-educated white people, while they are necessary, they are not sufficient. For the Democratic Party to win, it has to energize a far broader, more diverse, and, frankly, more interesting electorate. I believe Democrats can appeal to both college-educated and working-class white people while also energizing our base of communities of color and young people. The key is to answer the Republicans' fabled "wedge issues" with what President Clinton used to call "web issues": ideas that stitch people together across the lines that divide them.

How to Drive a Pickup Between Trump and His Voters

A lot of good people voted for Donald Trump. I know that makes some people angry to read. They feel as if I'm saying, "A lot of good people torture puppies." But bear with me. I am a Catholic, and I am obligated to "love the sinner, hate the sin," as Nancy Pelosi reminds us. Yet the practical political strategist in me says, "Just win, baby." Eating into Trump's support, even a little bit, could win the election for the Democrats.

The first bite to take when you are trying to eat into that support is to analyze the disparity between Trump's populist supporters and his plutocratic policies. I have never seen a bigger mismatch between a politician's supporters and his policy priorities. Sure, in some ways they align logically: people who voted for Trump because they wanted the Supreme Court to reverse *Roe v. Wade* and gay rights rulings are going to be thrilled with his judicial nominations. But a whole lot of Trump voters were not right-wingers. At least not typical right-wingers. The key to Trump is that he harnessed economic populism and paired it with traditional right-wing conservatism. That's new, it's different, it's potent, and it's dangerous.

The heart of Trump's support is working-class whites. Yet as president he has abandoned them. This should not shock you. He's had three wives, four chiefs of staff, and three attorneys general, and he has been in three political parties. He abandons people quicker than Billy Zane getting into the lifeboat in *Titanic*.

Trump campaigns as a populist but governs as a plutocrat. Of all his thousands of lies, this one may be the most important, and the most evil. He hijacked the legitimate pain of millions of people and used it to make himself and his fellow robber barons even wealthier. He's Dooh Nibor; Robin Hood in reverse. It is an outrage. Rather than denigrate Trump's voters, Democrats should find solidarity with them. That begins by showing how Trump is betraying them.

Working-Class Americans Are Dying Before Their Time

There is perhaps no statistic more telling about a society's health than life expectancy. According to the CIA, the tiny principality of Monaco has the highest life expectancy worldwide, at 89.4 years. The central African nation of Chad has the lowest, at 50.6 years.

I have never been to either country, but I'm guessing things are going better for the average Joe or Jane in Monaco than in Chad. The United States, as the wealthiest nation in the world, is number forthy-three, with a life expectancy of eighty. I gotta tell you, not psyched to see my beloved country behind Greece and Germany and Ireland and South Korea.

Still, eighty years is better than the "threescore years and ten" that Psalm 90 promises us. ("And if by reason of strength they be fourscore . . .") I'll take it. But if you are a white man without a high school diploma—the heart of Trump's political base—it's just 67.5 years. For white women without a high school education, it is 73.5 years.

It is important to realize that for people of color in America life expectancy has always lagged behind that of whites. That is a tragic legacy of racism, affecting everything from infant and maternal health to victimization by violence. But as life expectancy fell by five years for white women without a high school diploma, and by three years for white men without a high school degree, life expectancy for African Americans without a high school diploma actually surpassed that of whites without a high school diploma. That's not because racism ended. Far from it. And it's not because America is doing all it can to address racial health disparities, crime, or all the other burdens it places on communities of color. It's because of the quiet crisis facing poorly educated white people.

As a matter of political analysis, it is striking that the voters who are most loyal to Donald Trump seem to be losing ground in the game of life itself. Why are they dying before their time? The causes, of course, predate Trump. According to a seminal 2015 study by Anne Case of Princeton and Angus Deaton of the University of Southern California, we are losing them in part to what the researchers called "diseases of despair": death by drug and alcohol abuse, and suicide. A paper from the Brookings Institution summarized it this way: "Case and Deaton document an accumulation of pain, distress, and social dysfunction in the lives of the white working class . . ."

Has President Trump felt their pain? Has he lightened their distress? Has he calmed the social dysfunction? Far from it. He has manipulated their pain for his personal and political benefit. He has added to their distress by using them as pawns in his trade war. He has manifestly worsened our social dysfunction by dividing Americans by race and gender and region and religion.

Nowhere is that neglect and manipulation more evident than in the opioid crisis.

Opioids: More Deaths in One Year Than We Suffered in Vietnam in Twenty

Addiction to pain killers is at epidemic levels. According to the Centers for Disease Control and Prevention, in 2018, 67,367 Americans died from drug overdoses, the vast majority of them—46,802—from opioids. That's slightly down from the peak of 2017, and yet in each of those years, we lost more people to drug overdoses than we lost in twenty years of fighting in Vietnam. From 1999 to 2017, more than 700,000 Americans died from drug overdoses—and 400,000 of the deaths were due to opioids. To put that into perspective, 405,000 Americans died in World War II. Opioids have killed as many Americans as did Nazi Germany and Imperial Japan combined.

No community has gone untouched, but rural America has been especially hard-hit. A study published by the *Journal of the American Medical Association* reported "a clear overlap between counties that had high opioid use . . . and the vote for Donald Trump," James S. Goodwin, of the University of Texas Medical Branch in Galveston, told NPR. Trump typically won 60 percent of the votes in counties with higher than average rates of chronic opioid prescriptions, the study found.

These folks are desperate. They are dying before their time. They may feel as if the system has abandoned them. Their economies are failing, their prospects are dimming. "People who reach for an opioid might also reach for . . . near-term fixes," Dr. Nancy E. Morden, of the Dartmouth Institute for Health Policy and Clinical Practice, said to NPR. "I think that Donald Trump's campaign was a promise for near-term relief."

Of course, there is no causal link between opioid abuse and support for Trump. But there damn sure ought to be a closer link between Trump's policy priorities and the epidemic that is savaging communities that supported him.

Trump did what Trump does best: he makes grandiose promises and then does little or nothing. In this case, he declared a public health emergency. Good. And then . . . and then . . . Well, not much. The Government Accountability Office found that Trump's declaration helped cut red tape. Okay. He allowed two states to proceed more quickly on their own opioid programs. Good. And he sped up some funding for research. Fine. But all in all, that's a pretty tepid response to this crisis. For example, the GAO report found that the Public Health Emergency Fund has a grand total of $57,000 in it. Fifty-seven grand can't save the lives of 70,000 people.

You want a crisis? It's not corporate profits. It's drug addiction, especially opioids. If corporate profits are worth spending $1.9 trillion on, how much is Trump willing to spend to combat an epidemic that's taking tens of thousands of lives each year? Eleven billion dollars. That's all. The Bipartisan Policy Center combed the federal budget and found fifty-seven different federal programs that work to curb the epidemic. All told, they spend $11 billion a year. At that rate, it will take well over a thousand years for Trump's opioid response to match his corporate tax giveaway. Corporate profits are literally a thousand times more important to Trump than are people dying from opioid addiction.

Democrats should be there. They should—and many do—feel the pain of people fighting addiction. They should propose more action—and more funding. Senators Patty Murray (D-WA) and Elizabeth Warren (D-MA) have been strong voices urging action, as has Massachusetts congressman Joe Kennedy III. Politicians like them can bring cameras, they can shine a spotlight on the fact that only one in ten addicts (and one in five opioid abusers) ever seeks specialty treatment. While Trump is barking at one of his carnival rallies, Democrats could go to a clinic and call attention to the fact that half of the patients don't have access to some of the most effective medications to counter opioid addiction.

The late Rep. Elijah Cummings (D-MD) was, as usual, on the side of the angels. His Care Act, cosponsored with Senator Warren, would have boosted federal spending on the opioid crisis by $100 billion over ten years. Cummings knew, as Scripture teaches: "Where your treasure is, there will your heart be also." Democrats' hearts—and their treasure—should be with every American struggling with addiction.

Farmers: Wake Up and Smell the Bull$#!+

Donald Trump has been the worst thing to hit farmers since the locust. How did Trump hurt farmers? Let me count the ways:

- **His Trade War Shut Farmers Out of the Chinese Market.** China, the second largest market for American farmers, punished farm country as part of Trump's trade war. After buying almost $20 billion of farm products in 2017, China cut back to $9 billion in purchases in 2018. Soybean purchases by China fell 75 percent in just nine months, from September 2018 to May 2019.

- **Farm Income Is Down.** Way down. From 2013 to 2018, farm income plunged 45 percent. Trump's welfare payments, which cost taxpayers $16 billion, have not made up the difference. One North Dakota farmer told CNBC he was losing $70 per acre on his 1,500-acre grain farm. The subsidies cover about $15 an acre, he said, leaving him $82,500 in the hole. Farmers feed the world and take pride in it. And they resent welfare, just as they resent being a pawn in Trump's trade war.

Donald Trump's idea of a good farm program
seems to be Hee Haw.

—Jim Hightower, former Texas Department of
Agriculture commissioner

- **Farm Bankruptcies and Farmer Suicides Are Up.** According to the US Department of Agriculture, even with Trump's farm welfare, net farm income in 2018 was the second lowest in a decade, and while 2019 was a little better, both years were in the bottom quarter of years for farmers since they started keeping the statistics ninety years ago.

The number of farmers who went bankrupt in 2019 jumped 20 percent over the previous year, making 2019 the year with the biggest spike in farm bankruptcies since 2010, as farmers were still reeling from the Great Recession. The highest number of farms went under in Wisconsin, which, of course, is a key swing state in 2020. Foreclosures were at or above a decade high in Iowa, Illinois, Kansas, Minnesota, South Dakota, South Carolina, Ohio, and Wisconsin. Now, bankruptcy may be no big deal to a flop artist like Donald Johnsongrass Trump. He has run businesses into bankruptcy six times: the Trump Taj Mahal, the Plaza Hotel, Trump Hotels and Casinos Resorts (twice), and two other Atlantic City casinos. If you can't make money running a casino, man, you suck at business. But farming, that's a horse of a different color. Farmers have always found it difficult to stay in the black—as the old saying goes, you can make a small fortune in farming, but you've got to start with a large fortune. Farmers have to deal with so many variables: rain (too much or too little), bugs, fluctuating commodity prices, soaring interest rates, and more. Not to mention having a knucklehead president—one you voted for—declaring a trade war with your biggest customer.

Bankruptcy, for farmers, is a catastrophe. Farming is often a family business, and an intergenerational one at that. To lose the farm is to lose more than a source of income; you lose a way of life. And sometimes it is more than a troubled farmer can bear. Ninety-one percent of farmers and farm workers say financial stress affects their mental health.

Statistics on farmer suicides are hard to come by. Families are private and communities protective. Beyond that, some farmers may disguise suicide as a farm accident. But Patty Edelburg, vice president of the National Farmers Union, told Fox News that the problem is serious. "It has been insane," she said. "We've had a lot of farmers—a lot more bankruptcies going on, a lot more farmer suicides."

Jennifer Fahy, communications director for Farm Aid, the wonderful pro–family farmer organization started by Willie Nelson, told the *St. Cloud Times*, in Minnesota, that when Willie and his friends started Farm Aid in 1985, "The farm crisis was so bad, there was a terrible outbreak of suicide and depression." But today, she says, "I think it's actually worse."

> This is a good time to remind folks about the website www.suicidepreventionlifeline.org and the National Suicide Prevention Lifeline, 1-800-273-8255. Please.

- **Tax Cuts for CEOs, Funding Cuts for Farmers.** In his 2020 budget proposal, Trump included a massive 15 percent cut in funding for the US Department of Agriculture—a reduction of $3.6 billion. Why? Well, programs that benefit farmers are "overly generous," the Trump budget said. This proposal came at a time when floods, drought, and Trump's trade war were all pressuring farmers, and while the opioid crisis was hammering farm country. Just so we get this straight: corporate profits are at an all-time high.

Farm incomes are at an all-time low. So Trump proposed giving $1.9 trillion to corporate America and taking $3.6 billion from rural America. Got it.

- **Got Milk?** No one works harder than dairy farmers. No one. My wife's family has milked cows in Wisconsin for more than a century. They're up before dawn, working till dark, risking their lives and limbs to make America healthy and strong. In 2019, it cost a Wisconsin dairy farmer $1.90 per gallon to produce milk. The corporate conglomerate, which is the only buyer for them, thanks to the corporatization of dairy, pays them just $1.35 a gallon. If there's one thing farmers know, it's math. Every farmer I know is deeply aware of the cost of production and keenly follows commodity prices. Combine the corporate squeeze with Trump's trade war (dairy sales to China dropped 43 percent in 2018, when China hit US dairy with tariffs), and you have a recipe for bankruptcy. Wisconsin lost 465 dairy farms in 2017, nearly all of them small operators—that is, family farms. They lost another 638 dairy farms in 2018 and 551 more in 2019.

- **The Rich Get Richer.** Remember that Trump welfare program for farmers—from a few pages ago? Well, I hope you're sitting down, because this is going to shock you. Most of the money goes to a few rich people. The Environmental Working Group ran the numbers and found that 68 percent of the checks that went out in the first round of Trump's welfare program went to the wealthiest 10 percent of ag operators. A thousand people who got checks don't even live on a farm—they're city dwellers who are absentee landlords. To be clear, the big boys have been squeezing family farmers for decades—even before Trump arrived—the 90 percent of farms that are small got just 27 percent of commodity payments. But Trump was supposed to be on the side of the little guy, right?

Trump's War on the Wilderness

I am a lifelong hunter and fisherman, happiest in a deer stand or a trout stream. Nothing gets my heart racing like flushing a covey of quail. Hikers, campers, sportsmen and sportswomen—all of us share a special bond. If you've ever cussed while trying to pitch a tent in the rain, or sworn when you lost a fish, or hollered when you slipped on a mud-slick trail, you know it is so worth it. But as everyone who loves the outdoors also knows, there's less of it than there used to be. Or, rather, we have less access than we used to have.

As a candidate, Donald Trump pretended to be a sportsman. He told *Petersen's Hunting* that he is "a member of Ducks Unlimited, Trout Unlimited" (more likely he's the head of Liars Unlimited). He went on to describe himself as "a lifetime member of Backcountry Hunters and Anglers," and more. He touted his undying commitment to the Second Amendment, and then hit on a key issue: access to public lands. "For me, it's all about easy access, whether it be to hunting, fishing, recreating, or owning firearms. When I watch the liberal left try to eliminate the ease of access for law-abiding Americans—it's a death by a thousand cuts mentality that I don't like." He said he would "make accessibility a priority."

Looks like he lied. Once in office, he ordered a review of all national monuments—more than two dozen of them—which have been set aside by his predecessors to be protected from development. The hook and bullet crowd loves the monuments, because they can hunt and fish and hike in pristine wilderness. Trump called protecting this wilderness an "egregious abuse of federal power." (One wonders who wrote that for him; Trump does not seem to me like a guy who says "egregious" a lot. "Egg salad," sure. But not "egregious.")

What's egregious is destroying wilderness that can never be reclaimed. What's egregious is cutting 85 percent of the land that's protected in Utah's Bears Ears National Monument. What's egregious is taking more than a million acres of Bears Ears away from sports-women and sportsmen, away from Native American tribes and middle American families. What's egregious is cutting the stunning Grand Staircase-Escalante National Monument in half.

I realize Trump is not an outdoorsman. I'm sure his idea of being in the great outdoors is driving his fat keister around one of his golf courses, and his idea of wildlife is the supermodel scene at the old Studio 54. I know he lacks an appreciation for God's creation. But it's not just a lack of appreciation at work here. Trump is gutting these precious wilderness areas for one reason:

Oil.

(Or, as we say in Texas, "ahhl.") And gas, too. Trump's removal of protections of both Bears Ears and Grand Staircase-Escalante will allow drilling and mining on that irreplaceable wilderness. This is, as the *New York Times* reports, "the largest rollback of public lands protection in United States history."

If you live in Utah, or close to Utah, or you can afford an airplane ticket to Utah, perhaps you should consider seeing these wilderness areas before it's too late. If not, use your search engine and check out photographs of these places. Their beauty is otherworldly. The colors, the geology, the history stretching back thousands of years—all of that is at risk. And for what? For oil.

This has seriously angered the anglers. Hunters, too. And hikers and campers and all kinds of folks. They spoke out, wrote letters, applied pressure; 2.8 million comments flooded the Interior Department, most of them seeking to keep the wilderness monuments safe. Keep in mind, these are not lefties. In fact, 50 percent of hunters call themselves conservative; just 10 percent say they're liberal. Chris Wood, CEO of Trout Unlimited, isn't playing around. "We will ensure the voices of sportsmen and sportswomen are heard throughout," this process. He continued, "They [the politicians] ignore us at their political peril."

Native American tribes—Navajo, Hopi, Ute, and Zuni—have

sued the Trump administration. Environmental groups, including the Sierra Club and the Wilderness Society, have also filed suit.

Here again, Democrats should reach out. Sportsmen and sportswomen are conservationists as well as conservatives. Much of the cultural resentment working-class whites feel is because they believe—often correctly—that coastal elites look down on them. Democrats could find a lot of common ground if they tried: on wilderness protection, public lands, clean air and water, even climate change. But as the great Steve Forbert once sang, "You cannot win if you do not play." Democrats need to pull on their hip boots and wade in.

How Democrats Should Run on This

First, listen. Actually listen to the white working class. You're not going to like everything you hear, but that's okay. I believe that they feel a significant amount of resentment primarily because their pain and their plight have been, in their view, ignored by elites. So listen. Don't lecture. Listen and learn. Their opinion, their views, their values matter—and we should respect them enough to hear what they have to say and understand how they feel.

The secret to a long relationship is, I believe, three little words. And, no, they're not "I love you." Sure, that's important. But over time there are three other words that are just as important: "I hear you." Democrats need to hear the pain behind the prejudice. They need to hear the desire for a return to an America that offered upward mobility to the daughter of a soldier, like my wife, or the son of a salesman, like me.

President George H. W. Bush used to say, "Ninety percent of life is just showing up." Beto O'Rourke showed up in all 254 counties in Texas in 2018. No, he didn't win, but he did better than any Democrat has in Texas in twenty-four years. Show up. Listen up.

Democrats need to stop thinking like cultural anthropologists and start thinking like neighbors. Or organizers. White working-class Americans are not some exotic, frightening species. Sure, some are prejudiced—but so are some college-educated elites. When we listen, when we show up, two things happen. First, folks open up. Second, we open up, too. We see women and men who are being screwed by the same system that's screwing communities of color in our cities. We see that there is more that unites us than divides us.

Sorry to get so preachy. Let me get back to being practical: we don't have to *win* rural America; we don't have to *win* the white working class, or high school–educated white men. We just have to stop sucking so badly. Here's a question: Do you think Joe Biden can get the same level of support from the white working class as a black guy whose middle name is Hussein? I do. Because Joe's default setting is empathy. As we saw earlier in this chapter, if Biden can simply do as well in Luzerne County, Pennsylvania, and Volusia County, Florida, as Barack Obama did, we win.

American Bridge, a progressive group I have advised, is doing just that. They have sent teams of videographers into 66 counties in Wisconsin, Michigan, Pennsylvania, and Florida—just 66 of the 3,142 counties in this country. Those 66 counties were selected because they'd swung from Obama to Trump. And boy, did they swing. Loaded with white working-class voters, they fell for Trump bigly (as he would say). If we can merely cut the margin in those counties, if we could persuade even a small percentage of Trump voters that he has betrayed them, it could be game over. Keep in mind, Wisconsin, Michigan, and Pennsylvania were all decided by less than 1 percent of the vote. The margin in all three combined was 77,744 votes. And Trump only won Florida by 1.2 percent.

American Bridge is planning on spending $50 million to reach those voters, and they're reaching them with a message much like Mike Earnest's. They have interviewed and filmed dozens of disaffected Trump voters. Their stories are heartrending: families whose health care costs are through the roof; farmers whose crop prices have collapsed; factory workers whose jobs went overseas despite all of Trump's bombastic promises.

The answer to those scourges is not, it seems to me, to promise paradise. It is both more prosaic and more practical: a job you can support a family on, a neighborhood you can raise children in, quality, affordable health care, great schools, clean air and water, a planet that's not burning, a political system that is ethical and responsive, rising opportunity, and a dignified retirement.

In other words, the American Dream.

> Democrats don't need to reinvent the wheel. In fact, a lot of voters are skeptical of grandiose promises—and if they wanted pie in the sky, they can get that from Trump. Hell, he's promising a whole floating bakery. Democrats just need meat and potatoes. (Or, if you prefer, tofu and kale.)

Abraham Lincoln (who 53 percent of today's Republicans think was not as good a president as Trump—seriously) is said to have asked, "Do I not destroy my enemies when I make them my friends?" Democrats need to emulate Lincoln and destroy a few Trump voters by making them Democratic voters.

CHAPTER 6

THE RISING AMERICAN ELECTORATE

In addition to white people switching parties based on their educational attainment, another massive shift is going on in American politics: a rising American electorate that will dominate our politics for decades. There are four elements to this new American majority: people of color, unmarried women, younger voters, and the religiously unaffiliated. Let's look at each of them.

People of Color. America is diversifying. That freaks out some older, poorly educated white people, pushing them to vote for Trump in droves. By the way, this is not new. America has been diversifying for a couple hundred years. There weren't any "Begalas" on the Mayflower.

People of color vote overwhelmingly Democratic—and more of them are registering to vote every day. When Ronald Reagan was elected in 1980, 88 percent of voters were white. By 2016, that percentage had dropped to 71 percent.

Democrats need to push the percentage of minority voters above 30 percent if they want to win in 2020. Then they need to persuade people of color to vote for the Democratic nominee. The formula is simple: Mobilization + Motivation = Victory. Any Democrat who thinks all they need to do is eat right and exercise and they will win a landslide among people of color is deluded. Let me make it clear: Democrats are not *entitled* to those votes, they have to earn them every day. No one likes being taken for granted.

An analysis published in the *Washington Post* shows African American turnout fell by 4.7 percent in 2016. The impact was, of course, especially crucial in the swing states of Wisconsin, Michigan, and Pennsylvania. African American turnout fell by a crushing 12.3 percent in Wisconsin, 12.4 percent in Michigan, and 2.1 percent in Pennsylvania.

There is a stupid, pointless debate going on in the Democratic Party, one that has raged since the 2016 election: Do we electrify our base, or search for the swing voters? It is a false choice. The Democrats have to do both. One of the reasons I believe Democratic presidents are more successful than Republicans is their party looks more like America. To succeed in the Democratic Party, you have to unite people across lines of race and religion and region; gender and generation. Democrats need to both inspire their base and expand their electorate. It's like asking if you'd like to lose your left lung or your right lung—except a person can actually live with just one lung. Democrats are doomed if they don't motivate their base—even as they reach out to bring new voters into their coalition.

> *There can't be more of them than us.*
> *There can't be more.*
>
> —Jason Isbell, "Hope the High Road"

The question is, how? And this is where the aforementioned pointless debate gets downright stupid. If you campaign on an issue that perhaps gains you votes from one community, but it loses you as many or more votes in another, you're losing ground. Politics is about addition. This is, of course, more challenging for a Democrat, as their party is richly diverse. This is also why Democrats make better presidents: bringing together a broad, diverse, multiracial, multiethnic, multireligious, multicultural party is good training for leading a broad, diverse, multiracial, multiethnic, multireligious, multicultural nation.

The key here is to actually know your voters. The *Washington Post* did a deep-dive poll of African American voters. What it found may surprise you, if you haven't been listening. Too many alleged analysts conflate "African American" and "leftist." But according to the *Post* poll, six in ten African American voters identify as moderate or conservative. The solid majority of black voters say that the most important priority in choosing their nominee is picking someone who can beat Trump. Only a third say the most important thing is choosing someone they agree with on all the issues. This stands to reason: only 7 percent of African Americans approve of the job Trump is doing. Ninety-one percent disapprove. I'm no expert on politics, but it seems to me that a 91 percent disapproval rating is, umm, bad.

African Americans are clear about their priorities—at least according to survey research. A Hart Research/Brossard Research poll asked African Americans to name their top policy priorities. Seventy-seven percent gathered around three issues: affordable health care, college affordability, and creating good jobs with good benefits. The way to appeal to African American voters is to address them. The most important reason Joe Biden is the Democratic nominee is because of the support he earned from African Americans.

The Latino community is far from monolithic; its members include Spanish Americans from Europe; Afro-Brazilians; Mexicans and Cubans; Puerto Ricans and Venezuelans. Still, the survey found some powerful areas of common ground. Like African Americans, Latinos are much less bullish about the Trump economy than Anglos. Trump won 29 percent of the Latino vote in 2016. If he wants to increase that, he is going to need more than chest-thumping on the economy. Indeed, in polling for UnidosUS, Latinos ranked the following five issues as most important to them: jobs and the economy, health care, immigration, education, and gun violence. Obviously, Democrats must stand for comprehensive immigration reform. Clearly they should support legal status for Dreamers. And absolutely, in the name of God, Democrats must stand strong against savage Trump policies of putting children in cages. But if all Democrats do is talk immigration to Latinx voters, they will be missing other key priorities. Job insecurity, wages, health care costs, gun violence—these are the issues Latinos want Democrats to address as well. Besides, voters are smart; if you only talk about immigration when you're with Latinos, people may think you're Hispandering.

Unmarried Women. There is a massive marriage gap. Even controlling for age, income, and education, unmarried women (including those who are divorced and widowed) are more progressive, period. My friend and client Page Gardner founded the Voter Participation Center and the Women's Voices Women Vote Action Fund. She coined the term "Rising American Electorate" and cringes every time someone speaks of a "gender gap." The real gap, Gardner argues, is a marriage gap.

In 2012, Barack Obama lost married women by 7 percent. He won unmarried women by 36 percent—a 43-point improvement. That's what I call a gap. More like a canyon. We saw a similar outcome in 2016, except that Hillary Clinton—who underperformed Obama in several key demographics—outpolled him significantly among married women. Hillary won married women by 2 percent and unmarried women by 29 percent.

In the midterm election of 2018, Republicans lost married women by 10 points and unmarried women by 35 percent. The marriage gap had narrowed from 43 points under Obama to 25 under Pelosi. The trouble for the Republicans is that the gap narrowed because of Democratic improvement with married women, not GOP gains among unmarried women.

But the marriage gap is still large. Why? Why are unmarried women more progressive? James Barnes, coauthor of *The Almanac of American Politics*, has hypothesized that this is programmatic: single women are more concerned about a safety net. "Government can be a lifesaver for some single people," Barnes has written. "For an elderly single person who lacks a pension or savings, Social Security and Medicare are truly vital." Others, like the scholars Christopher T. Stout and Kelsy Kretschmer of Oregon State University and Leah Ruppanner of the University of Melbourne, Australia, attribute the difference in the way married and unmarried women vote to gender-linked fate. Unmarried women, they argue, see their own fate more closely and clearly linked to the fate of other women than do married women. "Marriage alters women's perceptions of self-interest," they argue, "by institutionalizing their partnerships with men and consequently leading women to feel less connected to other women."

I don't know who's right, and as a strategist I don't really care. But this I do know: women in general, and unmarried women in particular, are a crucial part of the Democrats' hopes to defeat Trump.

Younger Voters. Young people are progressives, and likely to remain so. The idea that you're liberal when you're young and conservative when you're old is baloney. Voters who came of age under FDR remained more progressive throughout their lives, just as those who came of age under Reagan are still conservative today (yours truly being a proud exception).

How progressive are young people today? They are by far the most progressive generation in memory. In a 2018 Pew Research Center survey, 57 percent of millennials described themselves as "consistently or mostly liberal." Just 12 percent of millennials are conservative—that's a nearly five-to-one ratio in favor of progressive politics. By contrast, just 28 percent of voters over sixty-five are liberal, while 29 percent are conservative.

But labels like "conservative" and "liberal" are meaningless, right?

Well, no, actually. Look at how people vote. Barack Obama won 66 percent of the youth vote in 2008, and Democratic congressional candidates won 67 percent of it in 2018. In that same Pew survey, nearly eight in ten millennials say immigrants strengthen the country; less than half of seniors say that. No wonder Donald Trump's nativist hatemongering doesn't play with young people. Same on race. The majority of young voters say racial discrimination is the main reason many black people can't get ahead these days. Three-fourths of senior citizens disagree.

Younger voters don't remember the Cold War; they remember the Great Recession, when hundreds of thousands of jobs were lost, lives were upended, communities crushed. No wonder they have a more favorable view of socialism than do their elders, while less than half view capitalism favorably.

They have lived most of their lives under the specter of George W. Bush's forever wars in Afghanistan and Iraq. I have spoken with enlisted personnel and even some officers who have little or no memory of a time when their nation wasn't at war. And so they are not as likely as their grandparents to say that the United States stands above all other countries in the world. Nearly twice as many Americans under age thirty say other countries are better than the USA as say America is the greatest country on earth.

They are painfully aware that, while Jesus said the meek shall inherit the earth, it is the younger generation who will inherit a planet on fire, set ablaze by their parents and grandparents. And they're pissed off about it. The majority of millennials say the federal government is doing too little to reduce the effects of climate change, while less than a third of older voters feel that way. Nearly all millennials (78 percent, to be exact) want our country to prioritize renewable energy sources over fossil fuels.

They may be losing faith in capitalism and religion (which we'll get to in a moment), but young Americans really believe in democracy. Rather than following the sixties mantra "turn on, tune in, drop out," young people today are lining up and signing up to vote, volunteer, and run for office. Their numbers are significant—potentially game-changing. According to the nonpartisan group States of Change, millennials will comprise 34.2 percent of the eligible voting population in 2020. Add to that the post-millennials (those born after 2000, sometimes called Gen Z), and you gain another 3.4 percent. Their numbers could far exceed the combination of baby boomers (28.4 percent) and those older than boomers, often called the Silent Generation (9.4 percent).

But note that I said "eligible" voting population. Younger voters have always voted in smaller numbers than their elders. Less than half of eligible voters under thirty cast a ballot in the 2016 presidential contest. Those who did overwhelmingly favored Hillary Clinton, but whereas 10 percent of the voters in 2016 were age twenty-five and younger, 16 percent were sixty-five and older—and seniors solidly preferred Trump.

Democrats obviously need to put a lot of time, money, and thought into maximizing the youth vote. The good news is, where they have done so, young people have responded. Democrats picked up key congressional seats in Virginia, California, and New Jersey in 2018. Each state saw a jaw-dropping increase in youth turnout—gains of 20 percent or more. If Democrats reach out to young voters, they will respond.

The Nonreligious. The fastest-growing religious denomination is not evangelicals or Catholics or Muslims or Hindus or Jews. It is Nones: people who say they have no religious affiliation. Those who claim no particular religion were just 16 percent of the country at the end of the George W. Bush presidency. Today they account for more than one in four Americans, outnumbering my brothers and sisters in the Catholic faith, which constitutes 20 percent of adults. Sixty-eight million adults in America are Nones.

Democrats who are used to sending buses to black churches

on Election Day and Republicans who harvest votes from mega-churches are going to have to adjust to this new reality. Maybe we should be sending buses to Starbucks, hot yoga classes, and Whole Foods.

Nones tend to be more Democratic. Those who express no particular religion, according to the Pew Research Center, lean Democratic by a 23-point margin, and atheists prefer the Democrats by a 54 percent margin, making atheists more likely to vote Democratic than even the most Republican-leaning faith is to vote GOP: Mormons. And there are three times as many atheists in America as Mormons.

The rise in secular views has brought a rise in progressive political values. Whereas only one in three evangelical Protestants says homosexuality should be accepted by society, 83 percent of Nones do. Ninety-five percent of atheists believe humans evolved over time; just 30 percent of evangelicals share that view.

How Democrats Should Run on This

These groups—people of color, unmarried women, younger voters, the religiously unaffiliated—were Democratic-leaning long before Donald Trump slithered down that Trump Tower escalator, but he has accelerated and hardened their Democratic allegiance. Donald Trump's constant racist rants, his misogynistic comments, his right-wing judges, and his cozying up to white supremacists—those moves do not warm the heart of the Rising American Electorate. This is a highly nuanced observation I have come to from decades in politics: if you tell people you hate them, they don't like it. And they tend not to vote for you. Corollary: voters are not drawn to a party that calls them idiots.

Republicans drive away the Rising American Electorate at their long-term peril. But in one sense, Republicans have it easier. Instead of trying to appeal to a broad, diverse electorate, all they have to do is unite the white and the translucent; the old and the ancient; the Cro-Magnons and the Neanderthals.

Republicans have driven themselves into a box canyon. By doubling and, heck, quadrupling down on older male white working-class voters, they are missing the demographic bus. The smart ones know this and have urged the GOP to modernize and moderate. But Donald Trump has killed that effort.

Here's the cool part: wages, job insecurity, health care costs, gun violence, education, clean air and water—these are the same issues you hear about when you listen to people in the suburbs, or in the exurbs, or in the cities, or on the farm. The key for Democrats is to build coalitions, and coalitions require web issues, not a hodgepodge of separate issues for different communities. Democrats should take literally that old Baptist hymn "Blessed Be the Ties That Bind." They need to stitch together communities of color with white people; younger voters with seniors; LGBTQ+ Americans with straight allies; religious progressives with atheists. To do that they need issues with broad, diverse appeal. This is no time for boutique, artisanal, bespoke messaging.

BANANA REPUBLICANS

The Real Election Rigging

"It's Rigged!"

Trump, and many other leaders of today's Republican Party, simply do not believe in democracy. That's a harsh charge, but the facts bear it out. As he was bullying his way to the Republican nomination, Trump was undermining Americans' faith in our democracy. When an October 2016 poll showed him trailing Hillary by 11 points (which he probably was before James Comey tilted the election to Trump in the closing days), Trump whipped out his trusty Twitter machine. He banged out a few of his patented semiliterate messages:

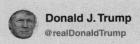 **Donald J. Trump**
@realDonaldTrump

The election is absolutely being rigged by the dishonest and distorted media pushing Crooked Hillary - but also at many polling places – SAD

 1:01 PM · Oct 16, 2016·Twitter for Android

Donald J. Trump
@realDonaldTrump

Polls close, but can you believe I lost large numbers of women voters based on made up events THAT NEVER HAPPENED. Media rigging election!

7:36 AM · Oct 16, 2016·Twitter for Android

Donald J. Trump
@realDonaldTrump

Election is being rigged by the media, in a coordinated effort with the Clinton campaign, by putting stories that never happened into news!

8:31 AM · Oct 16, 2016·Twitter for Android

President Obama, with preternatural calm, responded to a question about Trump's tweet. He was in the Rose Garden, being presidential, standing with Italian prime minister Matteo Renzi. "I have never seen in my lifetime," he said, "or in modern political history, any presidential candidate trying to discredit the elections and the election process before votes have even taken place." President Obama was incredulous. "It's unprecedented," he continued. "It happens to be based on no facts. It doesn't really show the kind of leadership and toughness that you'd want out of a president. You start whining before the game's even over?"

Perhaps President Obama (Jeez, I miss saying those two words. President. Obama. It just feels so good.) was so calm because Trump had done this before. In August he told his bestie Sean Hannity that

Republicans should be "watching closely" because he feared the election was going to be "taken away from us." He returned to the subject—and to Hannity—in October, this time with one of his patented lies: the specific statistic lie. "You have 1.8 million people who are dead, who are registered to vote," he said. "And some of them absolutely vote." He literally said that almost two million zombies would be lurching to the polls.

Trump told the *Washington Post*, "If the election is rigged, I would not be surprised. The voter ID situation has turned out to be a very unfair development. We may have people vote 10 times."

His campaign website for months was pumping the election-rigging lie. "Help Me Stop Crooked Hillary From Rigging This Election!" it blared, asking the gullible or the paranoid to volunteer to monitor polling places.

Trump's pal Roger Stone (R-Felon) was pushing the lie, of course. He formed a group called Stop the Steal. The idea was to undermine the legitimacy of a Hillary victory. But what's weird is that Trump kept up the conspiracy theory even after he was inaugurated. I've seen a lot of things in my day, but I have never seen a sore winner; never seen someone attack the system that made him president. Made him president, by the way, despite the fact that he lost the votes of the American people. More on that later.

"At Least 3 Million Votes Were Illegal!"

Even as president, Donald Jackal Trump has continued his voter-fraud fraud. Consider this tinfoil hat stuff:

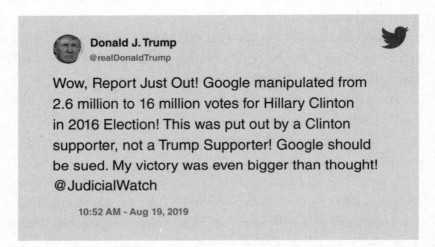

Big, if true. But, sadly, not. Trump had based his tweet on a story he'd seen on Fox News, of course. But the "report" Fox cited was described by the tech industry news site Tech Crunch as "a very bad study. Its contents do not amount to anything, let alone evidence by which to accuse a major company of election interference."

Trump has alleged that he would have won California— Cali-freakin'-fornia!—but for voter fraud. He has said that "at least 3 million votes were illegal." According to the official results of the California secretary of state, Hillary Clinton won California by 4,269,978 votes.

Who's going to tell him?

I'm guessing Trump wasn't a math major in college. Or maybe he went to Trump University.

Still, the *San Jose Mercury News* decided to commit journalism.

They put Trump's claim that 3 million illegal immigrants voted in California to the test. The first thing they found is, well, inconvenient. Turns out there are only 2.4 million undocumented people in California. And only 1.8 million of them are over age eighteen. The *Mercury News* called Trump's claim "preposterous."

Trump blamed voter fraud for his losing California by more than the total population of . . . Panama. So we shouldn't be surprised that he blamed his paper-thin loss in New Hampshire on voter fraud as well. In 2019, on his way to a rally in New Hampshire, he trotted out this theory: "New Hampshire should have been won last time."

Wait. Stop. Dude, it *was* won last time. Just not by you. Okay. Pardon the interruption. Please continue:

"Except we had a lot of people come in at the last moment, which was a rather strange situation. Thousands and thousands of people coming in from locations unknown. But I knew where their location was."

Huh?

The president did not reveal this undisclosed location, this hotbed of hordes of illegal voters who swarmed into the Granite State. Maybe they hid out in a cave in the White Mountains. Maybe they were just across the state line, in a biker bar in Lowell, Massachusetts, or maybe they were hiding out in Bernie Land—across the Connecticut River in, say, Norwich, Vermont. Probably in a quaint B&B with excellent scones and butter tea—fair-trade organic non–genetically modified po cha, harvested by superenlightened lamas in Bhutan. Wait. What am I thinking? They came over from Canada. Obviously. Quebec is on New Hampshire's northern border—a border that is unguarded. (Thanks, Obama.) Build a wall! Or, as they say in Quebec: *Construisez un mur!*

But rather than chase down these election-stealing Canadians, the people who run New Hampshire's elections did something else. They said Trump was full of it. "It's just not accurate," said New Hampshire secretary of state Bill Gardner. But what does he know?

He's just been overseeing elections in New Hampshire since Gerald Ford was president. Still, Gardner is a Democrat, so maybe he's got a partisan axe to grind. (By the way, why isn't that David Axelrod's Twitter handle: @PartisanAxe. You're welcome, David.) Former New Hampshire Republican chairman Fergus Cullen, however, threw Trump under the bus, weighing in with "logic" and "reason." (Those are air quotes, by the way.) "You've got thousands of people at polling places with phones, with cameras," he said. "And nobody has a videotape. I'm reminded how there used to be sightings of Bigfoot and aliens all the time."

Very funny, Fergus. Except: a) Bigfoot is real, duh; b) aliens are not only real, one of them represents South Carolina in the US Senate. (I'll give you a hint: it's not Tim Scott.)

The Pence-Kobach Commission

Here's the thing about moving from being a reality TV blowhard to being an Oval Office blowhard: you now have real power. So if Trump was truly concerned about voter fraud, which is a federal offense, maybe he should have ordered someone in the federal government to look into it.

That he did. In his first year in office he appointed then-Kansas secretary of state Kris Kobach and Vice President Mike Pence (who, every time he stands next to Trump, looks like he has a thought bubble over his head that says, "Take me now, Lord. Please bring the Rapture now, Lord!") to run a commission to investigate voter fraud. Kobach was one of the great proponents of the theory of massive voter fraud. An ACLU attorney called him "the nation's leading purveyor of lies about illegal voting to stir up fears and paranoia about our election system."

But that's just the ACLU. Buncha civil libertarians who believe in, you know, civil liberties. But the ACLU lawyer was not alone. A Bush-appointed federal judge in Kansas scolded Kobach for calling a couple of cases of alleged voter fraud "the tip of the iceberg." The Republican judge said, "the Court draws the more obvious conclusion that there is no iceberg; only an icicle, largely created by confusion and administrative error."

But now Kobach had all the power and resources of the federal government at his disposal. He had Pence as his wingman. And he had all fifty states to look at, not just honest, ethical, upright Kansas. But eight months after it was formed, the Pence-Kobach commission disbanded. It did not identify those millions of illegal voters in California; didn't catch any of those thousands of border crossers in New Hampshire. Didn't even write a report. Now, I've been in government. A commission without a report, well, that's just sad.

The Voter-Fraud Fraud

In the last Republican administration, there was much honking off about voter fraud, too. So President George W. Bush's Justice Department, led by John Ashcroft, set out to hunt down the fraudulent voters. (Ashcroft has the distinction of being the only senator in history to lose his Senate seat to a dead man—true story. How do you give that concession speech? "We tried our best, friends, but the other side just outworked us. My congratulations to the late Mel Carnahan.") Anyway, Attorney General Ashcroft's investigators looked into hundreds of campaigns, in which a total of 197 million votes had been cast. They convicted precisely twenty-six people of voter fraud. For those of you keeping score at home, as the writer/producer/actor/activist/podcaster Bob Cesca noted in *Salon*, "that's a voter fraud rate of 0.00000013 percent."

The Brennan Center for Justice at NYU Law School has taken the lead in spreading the truth about voter fraud. In its report, cleverly titled "The Truth About Voter Fraud," it notes that it is far more likely that an American would be "struck by lightning than that he will impersonate another voter at the polls."

The *Washington Post* reported on a study of fourteen years of elections, in which 1 billion votes were cast. It found thirty-one cases of fraud. This includes not only those that prosecutors charged and juries convicted but any that the study's authors found credible. Thirty-one in a billion.

After the 2016 election—the one that Trump claimed was rife with millions of illegal voters from sea to shining sea—Philip Bump of the *Washington Post* (no wonder Trump hates that paper so much) searched Nexis for any published report of voter fraud. He found four—out of more than 135 million votes cast. Well, Bump found a couple more cases that were under investigation but not yet proved. But my favorite case was from Iowa. A woman in Des Moines tried to vote twice but was caught. She was trying to vote twice for—oh, you just know it—Donald Trump. She was asked why she did it. "The polls are rigged," she said, echoing her hero.

Why is voter fraud so rare? Because people are smart. (Well, not the woman who tried to vote for Trump twice, but most people.) The risk-reward ratio for voter fraud is way out of whack. If you get caught, you go to federal prison, which I've never been to but I'm sure Trump campaign chairman Paul Manafort will tell us all about when he's eligible for parole. So that's a big downside risk. And the reward? Well, your favored candidate gets one more vote. Just one. You need more than 60 million votes to win the presidency, so the potential fraudster is risking prison for nothing. The gangsters in *Goodfellas* didn't risk prison in the Lufthansa heist for one measly dollar, and voters don't risk prison for one measly vote.

Voter Disenfranchisement: Bull Connor Would Be Proud

Now that we have exploded the myth of voter fraud, let's look at a very real and very serious problem: voter disenfranchisement. You would think that a man like Trump, so desperately concerned with the integrity of the franchise, would be equally concerned about actual legit American citizens being denied their right to vote. And that happens a heck of a lot more than Trump's mythical in-person voter fraud.

John Lewis had his head split open by George Wallace's thugs as he tried to cross the Edmund Pettus Bridge. He and other heroes marched from Selma to Montgomery for the right to vote. Today's tactics are less bloody, but they have the same goal: the intentional disenfranchisement of people of color, new Americans, and young people.

Georgia. Let's start with a state I love: one where I have worked and won, and the state Lewis represents in Congress: Georgia. The Peach State has kicked 1.4 million people off its voter rolls in the past eight years. According to a study by the *Atlanta Journal-Constitution*, this reduced turnout in 2018 by 1.2 to 1.8 percent. Democrat Stacey Abrams lost the governor's race by 1.4 percent.

What happened to Abrams is especially outrageous. Before she ran for governor, she had spent years registering voters through an organization she founded called the New Georgia Project. Abrams has a BA from Spelman College, a master's in Public Policy from the University of Texas at Austin (so you know she's smart), and a law degree from Yale. She is brilliant, and one of the issues on which she is a by-God expert is voting rights.

Her GOP opponent, Brian Kemp, was secretary of state, and as such, he was supposed to be registering voters. So he's a bit of an expert, too. Except his expertise is in kicking people off the voter rolls. Kemp led what the *Washington Post* described as "an aggressive effort to purge voters before the [2018] election, with nearly 700,000, or 10 percent, removed from the rolls in the year before the election." An American Public Media report said that "for 107,000 of those people, their removal from the voter rolls was triggered not because they moved or died or went to prison, but rather because they had decided not to vote in prior elections."

Voting is as fundamental a right as there is in a democracy. It cannot be a "use it or lose it" deal. Your right to vote is not like your right bicep, where if you don't exercise it, it withers. If you miss church for a few weeks—or a few years—do you lose your freedom of religion? If you haven't ever written a letter to the editor, do you lose your freedom of the press? If you have never attended a protest march in the past, do the cops bar you from attending one in the future? It is madness, and maddening, to deny a citizen her right to vote because she didn't find anyone worth voting for in previous elections.

Kemp offered this explanation: "We're following the process." Really? Following the process? That's not a rationale, it is gibberish. Yes, you're following a process. But is that process fair? Is it just? Or is it a naked attempt to disenfranchise certain voters? "I'm very proud," Kemp continued, "of my record on making sure we have secure, accessible, and fair elections." Okay. Let's look more closely at that record.

As if purging 700,000 voters wasn't enough, Kemp went further. In October 2018, in the closing weeks of an election in which he was running, he placed 53,000 voting applications on hold. The Associated Press looked into it. Turns out the list was "predominantly black." What a shock. This list, these 53,000 Georgians whose voting rights were put in limbo, was generated by a system called "exact match." Information on a citizen's voter registration must perfectly match that person's Georgia driver's license or Social Security file. Perfectly. If the applicant—or a clerk doing data entry—so much as misses, say, a hyphen, or introduces any other tiny typo, the right to vote is suspended. The AP analysis revealed that nearly 70 percent of the registrations Kemp put on hold were of African American Georgians.

Kemp also closed more than two hundred polling places. Guess where they were? Buckhead, the wealthy part of Atlanta, where massive mansions sit atop perfectly manicured grounds? Uhhh, nope. The polling places that were closed were mostly in low-income and minority neighborhoods. As the *Washington Post* reported: "Voters reported long lines, malfunctioning voting machines and other problems that delayed or thwarted voting in those areas." The *Post* went on to cite research that verifies what common sense tells us: long lines depress turnout. Folks can't afford to miss hours of work, or they just get frustrated and leave. The *Atlanta Journal-Constitution* concluded that closing precincts and requiring voters to drive farther to vote—ten miles, in some cases—prevented 54,000 to 85,000 Georgians from voting in the Abrams-Kemp election. Abrams lost by about 55,000 votes.

In 2016, Brian Kemp, when he was secretary of state, was the only state election official in America who declined federal help once the Department of Homeland Security identified the threat from Russia to our voting systems. The only one. "The question remains," he said at the time, "whether the federal government will subvert the Constitution to achieve the goal of federalizing elections under the guise of security." What a bunch of hooey. This guy wants you to believe that the government of the United States of America—you know, the people who have the Navy SEALS and those cool jets that fly over football stadiums—is a bigger threat to Georgia's elections than Putin? Really?

Yes, really. Even in 2017, after the entire US intelligence community verified that Russia was trying to hack our election, Kemp was yapping about states' rights (a bit of a dog whistle for those of us from the South). "I think it [the offer of federal help to secure voting systems] was a politically calculated move by the previous administration," he told the *Washington Post*. He went on to say, "I don't necessarily believe" that Russia was behind the effort to influence the 2016 election. Somewhere, fresh from wrestling an anesthetized tiger for the cameras, Vladimir Putin was smiling as he read the words of yet another useful idiot.

Wisconsin. The Badger State, sadly, is a leader in voter suppression. This matters. Trump won it by just 27,257 votes out of 2.8 million cast. Turnout was down in Wisconsin, the lowest since 2000—down by 91,000.

Many wags blamed Hillary Clinton, said she should have campaigned in Wisconsin. Perhaps. But there was more afoot. Turnout was not down uniformly across the state. In fact, nearly half of the decline in turnout—41,000—was in Milwaukee, the state's largest city. Milwaukee is a great city. Home of the Bucks and the remarkable Giannis Antetokounmpo, aka the Greek Freak. The Milwaukee River, which you can enjoy on the beautiful Riverwalk, runs through the city. While you're there, check out the Bronze Fonz—the statue of the coolest guy ever, played by one of the nicest guys ever, Henry Winkler. Milwaukee is so all-American that the sitcom *Happy Days* was set there, as was *Laverne & Shirley*. But for our purposes, this fact is crucial: Milwaukee County is 49 percent non-white.

The entire state (including Milwaukee) is just 19 percent minority; it is 6 percent African American. So, when turnout is way down in Milwaukee, that means minority turnout is way down in Wisconsin. Again, some of that may have been because of Hillary's campaign. But others pointed to another phenomenon: Wisconsin's controversial voter ID law. Passed in 2011, it requires voters to present a driver's license, a state ID, a federal ID like a passport or military ID, or a tribal ID. If you don't have your ID on you when you go to vote, you can cast a provisional ballot, but have only seventy-two hours to produce the proper ID.

For someone like me—white, privileged, with IDs coming out of my ears—that doesn't sound so onerous. But 300,000 Wisconsinites who are old enough to vote don't have one of those forms of photo ID. You shouldn't lose your right to vote just because you don't drive or fly on airplanes. We have already established that in-person voter fraud is less common than being hit by lightning. Indeed, when the law was challenged in court, the State of Wisconsin could not cite a single instance of someone fraudulently voting as someone else. So why would Wisconsin's political heavyweights—and at the time the law was passed, the governor was GOP darling Scott Walker—want to disenfranchise hundreds of thousands of people? Take a guess.

Because they're not Packers fans? Wrong. Everyone in that state is a cheesehead.

Well, maybe—and I hope I'm not being too cynical here—it is because most of those 300,000 people are poor, or minority, or both. One of the law's backers, Republican congressman Glenn Grothman, said the quiet part out loud. Before the election, he told a television reporter, "I think Hillary Clinton is about the weakest candidate the Democrats have ever put up. And now we have photo ID, and I think photo ID is going to make a little bit of a difference as well."

Oh, Glenn. Dear, sweet Glenn. You were being too modest. Saying the voter ID made "a little bit of a difference" in Trump winning Wisconsin is like saying Aaron Rodgers made a little bit of a difference in Green Bay winning Super Bowl XLV.

Even though we now have a Democratic governor in Wisconsin, Tony Evers, the voter suppression crowd is still pressing on. In December 2019, a state judge ordered the state to kick as many as 234,000 citizens off the voter rolls. Ozaukee County judge Paul Malloy's ruling, which came in a case in which conservatives were seeking to force the state Elections Commission to toss out voters who had not responded to a letter asking them if this was their correct address. An analysis by the *Milwaukee Journal Sentinel* found that the highest percentage of voters kicked off the rolls were in Democratic strongholds like Milwaukee, Madison, and other college towns. More than half of the letters sent went to areas where Hillary beat Trump. The Elections Commission had planned to give people until April 2021 to respond, but the judge booted them before the 2020 election. The League of Women Voters is appealing.

Texas. My beloved home state is consistently in the bottom tier of states in terms of turnout. You'd think the politicians who run the place would hate that. They wouldn't allow Texas to be ranked forty-fifth in barbecue or forty-eighth in football or forty-ninth in pickup trucks. But they seem to be just fine with Texas sucking at voting.

In fact, the Republicans keep trying to make it harder to vote in the Lone Star State. My fellow Texan Mimi Swartz, writing in the *New York Times*, described the GOP's phony "VOTER FRAUD ALERT!" of 2019. The secretary of state, David Whitley, claimed he had a list of 95,000 people who needed to be dumped from the voter rolls because, he alleged, they weren't citizens. He even hinted darkly that as many as 58,000 of them had already voted illegally.

Wow. But, Paul, you just told me in-person voter fraud only occurs 0.00000013 percent of the time.

That's right. Turns out, the Republicans in Texas were just peein' on your boots and tellin' you it's rainin'. Turns out some of the files they were citing were twenty-five years old. Harris County, the state's largest county, which includes Houston, quickly found that 60 percent of the people on the list had, in fact, become citizens. Who knows how many other errors were to be found on the list.

State Rep. Rafael Anchia of Dallas chairs the Mexican American Legislative Caucus in the statehouse. He decided to look into it. It didn't take long. He met with the secretary of state and in two questions busted the myth. According to the *Texas Tribune,* Anchia says it went down like this:

ANCHIA: Do you know for sure that any of the people on your list have actually committed the felony of voting as noncitizens?

WHITLEY: No.

ANCHIA: Isn't it the protocol that you investigate and, if you find facts, you turn it over to the Attorney General?

WHITLEY: I do not have an answer for that.

Anchia should be on one of those cop shows. Except each episode would be eight seconds. Soon, Governor Greg Abbott was treating the list like a stolen car that wound up in his driveway. "Listen," he said, "this isn't a hard and fast list. This is a list that we need to work on together to make sure that those who do not have the legal authority to vote are not going to be able to vote." Well, that's a far cry from VOTER FRAUD ALERT!

The League of United Latin American Citizens filed suit, calling the phony fraud allegations "a plan carefully calibrated to intimidate legitimate registered voters from continuing to participate in the election process." A federal judge has temporarily blocked the purge, calling the GOP's effort "ham-handed." "The evidence has shown in a hearing before this Court that there is no widespread voter fraud," Judge Fred Biery ruled. He went on to say the challenge is how best to "ferret the infinitesimal needles out of the haystack of 15 million Texas voters."

Oof. That's a gut punch to the voter fraud fearmongers in Texas, especially the state's attorney general, Ken Paxton. By the way, Paxton is under indictment for fraud. Actual fraud. Securities fraud. So there's that.

Undeterred by their epic fail on VOTER FRAUD ALERT!, Texas Republicans took aim at mobile voting. Texas has for years allowed counties to set up temporary mobile voting sites in high-volume areas. But in 2019 the GOP-controlled legislature effectively barred them. State Rep. Greg Bonnen, of course, claimed he was just trying to rein in abuses. Right, 'cause making voting easier is a real abuse. Texas Democrats filed suit. They noted that in Travis County, home of the world's greatest university, sixty-one mobile sites helped almost

30,000 Texans vote. The Texas Democratic Party filed suit, calling the law the Republicans' "latest attempt to curb the Democratic rise in the state and steal an election from the rising Texas electorate." State Democratic chair Gilberto Hinojosa accused the GOP of making it "harder for college students, seniors, the disability community, rural Texans and survivors of natural disasters to cast their ballots."

One last thing about Texas—and I say this as someone who loves, loves, loves Texas, but thinks its right-wing Republican leaders are about half a bubble off plum (Notice how my Texasisms have come roaring back? You should see me after a couple of Shiner Bocks at Scholz's beer garden in Austin)—Texas has a voter ID law, like the one we discussed in Wisconsin. But here's where the right-wing's bias is about as obvious as Trump's spray-on tan: Look at which government-issued IDs Texans can use for voting. For example, let's say you are lucky enough to be enrolled at the World's Greatest University. Or even Texas A&M. Those are state institutions. They issue photo IDs. But you can't use your state-issued photo ID to vote in Texas. What can you use? Well, your license to carry a handgun, obviously. 'Cause nothing says "I'm gonna cast a vote to change my government" like packing heat.

The Electoral College Overturns the Will of the People

If you're looking for a silver lining, here's one—there is a group of minority voters the Republicans love, a minority they fight for—the minority of voters who live in small, rural, conservative states.

For the first time in American history, one political party has won the popular vote in six out of seven presidential elections. Six out of seven. The post–Civil War Republicans didn't do that. The FDR New Deal Democrats couldn't do that. But from Bill Clinton's 1992 victory to Hillary Clinton's 2016 campaign, Democrats have been the choice of the American people every time, except for George W.

Bush's narrow reelection in 2004. If you simply look at the will of the voters, Democrats are on a roll. They won the popular vote in 1992, 1996, 2000, 2008, 2012, and 2016.

If it weren't for the archaic, antidemocratic Electoral College, Al Gore would have been president. And, of course, we would have had President Hillary Rodham Clinton.

Blame the framers, and I do. In fairness, they were dealing with a very different country. We were small in number but large in size. There was little mass media, and the framers feared that voters would only be familiar with presidential candidates from their own states. They did not want the big states to dominate the presidency, nor did they want thirteen candidates to split the vote so no one emerged as a consensus president. The Electoral College is elitist by design. The founders feared factions—political parties—would arise and appeal to the naked, ungoverned passions of the mob. So they allowed states to pick the electors, who would be an intermediating, moderating force. In most of those states, the legislature chose the electors. In some, they actually had an election—but of course voting was limited to white male property owners (a few states let non-property-owning white men vote, if they were taxpayers).

Under the original rules, each elector cast two votes. The candidate who could command a majority of electors became president; the second-place finisher was vice president. If no one had majority support, the electors would be thanked for their service and the House would make the final decision, with each state's House delegation getting one vote. That's how we got President Thomas Jefferson in 1800. Slave-owning states, whose electoral vote power was boosted by the Constitution's counting three-fifths of their enslaved people for the purposes of congressional representation, were able to block President John Adams (the only non-slaveholder of the first five presidents) from winning reelection. While Jefferson led, he lacked a majority. Because the Jeffersonians cast their votes for both Jefferson and his running mate, Aaron Burr, Jefferson and Burr were tied. Adams was out, but the House was required to choose between the top two: Jefferson and Burr.

It was a disaster. Over the course of several days, the House was deadlocked. Tempers flared—and by "flared" I mean Jefferson was threatening civil war. After thirty-six votes and five days, Jefferson was made president and Aaron Burr vice president. People realized that taking the young nation to the brink of civil war was no way to choose a president, and the whole second-place-guy-gets-to-be-veep thing virtually guaranteed division in the executive branch. They passed the Twelfth Amendment, which codified the Electoral College as we now know it. It separates the vote for president and vice president, but retains the buffer between the people and those who choose the president. Crucially, the disproportionate power of slave states was protected. So long as Electoral College power was determined by population, and slave states could count 60 percent of their enslaved people, they would have an advantage.

Thanks to Lincoln, Grant, Frederick Douglass, Harriet Tubman, and hundreds of thousands of people killed, we no longer have slavery. But the imbalance remains. California has sixty-eight times more people than Wyoming but about eighteen times the number of electoral votes. (America's first census, in 1790, counted Virginia as the most populous state, with 747,610 people. Delaware was the least populous state, with 59,094 people. Virginia was 12.6 times bigger than Delaware. A considerable difference, but nothing like the 68 times disparity we have between California and Wyoming today.)

Because twenty-first-century Democrats live mainly in packed-in cities and close-in suburbs, while Republicans dominate rural areas, the Electoral College has thwarted the popular will twice in the last five elections.

There is a clever workaround for this, one that does not require amending the Constitution. The National Popular Vote Interstate

Compact is a proposed agreement among the states wherein each state pledges its electors to vote for the winner of the national vote rather than the winner of that state's vote.

Trouble is, just sixteen states (with 196 electoral votes) have joined the compact. The good people at National Popular Vote are working in several states and hope to get the requisite 270 electoral votes committed. But they're not there yet and won't be before the 2020 election.

Until states comprising 270 commit to supporting National Popular Vote, we are stuck with the antimajoritarian Electoral College. So, we have to play on the field as it is. If you live in Michigan, Ohio, Pennsylvania, Florida, Minnesota, Arizona, North Carolina, or Georgia, expect to see a lot of rallies and a ton of ads. Voters in the other forty-two states, well, thank you for playing. Presidential elections should not be a spectator sport. National Popular Vote would put every voter back in the game.

Even though it won't be a reality in time for the 2020 election, I support direct election of the president. It is one of the issues that can help America purge the venom of Trumpism, even after Trump himself has left the stage.

The Russians Got Away with It Once. Why Wouldn't They Do It Again?

"Russia, if you're listening, I hope you're able to find the 30,000 emails that are missing. I think you will probably be rewarded mightily by our press." That's what Donald Trump said on July 27, 2016. We all remember that infamous statement. I heard it live and was shocked. A major party's nominee for the White House was asking a hostile foreign power to illegally hack his opponent. But in my shock I didn't pay close enough attention to the rest of the press conference. After he called on Russia to hack his opponent, he was asked this:

QUESTION: "I would like to know if you became president, would you recognize Crimea as Russian territory? And also if the U.S. would lift sanctions?"

TRUMP: "We'll be looking at that. Yeah, we'll be looking."

In all the excitement about Trump asking Russia to hack Hillary, I didn't even notice that he said he'd be open to recognizing the Russian seizure of Crimea and the lifting of US sanctions.

Turns out Russia was listening. According to federal indictments from special counsel Robert Mueller's office, within hours after Trump's statement, Russians started their efforts to hack Hillary Clinton's email.

Trump has not recognized Putin's annexation of Ukraine's Crimean Peninsula, though he did try to withhold aid to Ukraine, as we all know. But Trump *did* take some steps to lift sanctions on Russia. As Ken Dilanian of NBC News reported in June of 2017: "The Trump administration was gearing up to lift sanctions on Russia when the president took office, but career diplomats ginned up pressure in Congress to block the move, two senior former State Department officials told NBC News." Trump also considered handing back to Russia two diplomatic compounds in the United States that had been seized by the Obama administration, but he backed down when a bipartisan group of senators raised hell.

The Russian attack on Hillary Clinton was, in the words of the late senator John McCain, "an act of war." It is without precedent in American history, and stands as the most successful foreign intelligence attack against the United States. Russia has paid little or no price for it. Putin's attack helped install the most pro-Russian president since we bought Alaska in 1867.

They're at it as we speak. Russian bots and trolls infect our social media ecosystem, spreading lies, hate, and division. Jeanette Manfra, then-assistant secretary of cybersecurity for Homeland Security, testified before Congress in 2018 that it's likely Russia tried to hack into election systems in all fifty states.

What can we do to prevent another attack, or at least repel it when it inevitably comes? A lot of the responsibility falls on state and local governments, who administer elections. We have eight thousand different voting jurisdictions. That's both good and bad. The good is that our enemies can't easily have direct, personal influence on them. Another benefit is that our enemies can't hack all of them at once.

The bad is that many of them are underfunded. The Obama administration declared voting systems to be part of our nation's critical infrastructure—like the power grid, pipelines, and water systems. Good start. That makes it easier for federal dollars to flow to protect them. In March 2019, Congress sent $380 million to the states to help secure their voting systems. They are supposed to use it for cybersecurity, voting equipment, election auditing, and more. That money helps. They need more. The Brennan Center for Justice reports that two-thirds of the election officials they contacted say they still don't have enough funding to replace their voting machines.

But like so much of the Trump administration, the Election Assistance Commission is, in the words of one expert, "a hot mess." (I love when experts talk like human beings.) Susan Greenhalgh, of the bipartisan National Election Defense Coalition, told *Fortune* magazine, "From an election security perspective they have not adequately faced the election security threat that we've learned the severity of." Experts like Greenhalgh, and retired four-star US Marine Corps general John Allen, now head of the Brookings Institution, recommend some concrete steps, including:

- Paper, paper, paper—2020 should be the year of the Dunder Mifflin election. Every expert who has looked at this comes back to paper: paper backups, paper records. As the kids say, we want the receipts. A paper trail is essential, and in 2018, thirty-six states had one.

- Ban online voting. Too easy to hack. Thirty-two states allow some online voting. Voting and phones should not mix. (See Iowa caucus app.)

- Training. Teach local election officials about phishing, sometimes called spear phishing, whereby you receive an email from what looks like a trusted source. The email has a link. You click on the link, and BAM! Russkie malware is in your system. Phishing is reportedly how the Russians hacked the Democrats in 2016. It is maddeningly successful.

- Securing voter registration rolls. The Senate Select Committee on Intelligence report states that "at least 18 states had election systems targeted by Russian-affiliated cyber actors in some fashion . . . Almost all of the states that were targeted observed vulnerability scanning directed at their Secretary of State websites of voter registration infrastructure." In some of those states, the report went on, the Russians were capable of altering or deleting voter registration data. Although there was no evidence that vote totals were altered, the Russians may be able to delete voters from the registration rolls.

- Communicate. This may seem obvious, but simply informing the public and thousands of local election officials about a threat empowers officials to counter it. As Grandma used to say, "Forewarned is forearmed." Amazingly, as the US intelligence community was sounding alarms about Russian attempts to attack our 2016 presidential election, Mitch McConnell (R-Moscow) refused to sign on to a bipartisan condemnation of Russia and a warning to Americans. Without McConnell, Obama feared, a Democrats-only statement on election interference could have undermined the election's legitimacy, which was precisely what the Russians wanted.

  Communicating the threat can help voters and the legitimate news media identify and label misinformation. Hearing about the threat can also cause people to harden their defenses, so the thousands of election officials will, one hopes, think twice before clicking on a hyperlink in an email, or responding to a "Reset Your Password" spear phishing attempt. Voters themselves would be reminded to check their voter registration status, to make sure that they have not been wrongfully purged, either by election officials or foreign hackers.

What's Next? You Ain't Seen Nothin' Yet

In February 2020, leaders of the US intelligence community briefed members of Congress on the latest efforts by Russia. Their conclusion was at once unsurprising and unsettling: Russia is at it again. They want to divide Americans. They want to destroy our democracy. They want to reelect Trump.

Duh.

Still, for the intelligence community to come to such a conclusion, and to state it to bipartisan congressional leaders, was striking. After all they've been through, you just know the intel people were loath to state that conclusion. So you figure they really had it cold—just as they did when they looked at the 2016 Russian cyberattack on the United States and concluded then that Russia was trying to elect Trump.

Republicans on the Hill and in the White House sprang into action. They ordered immediate hardening of our election systems; they ordered countermeasures to thwart Russia's invasion; they communicated publicly with the American people about this attack.

I'm kidding. They didn't protect America. They didn't counterattack against Russia. They attacked the nonpartisan career intelligence officials. Donald Trump, in fact, fired the acting director of national intelligence, Joseph Maguire—berating him for even briefing Congress in the first place. (Note: the intelligence community is required by law to brief Congress on threats.)

To help Trump, the *New York Times* reported, Putin's cyberthugs are again using Facebook and other social media platforms. This time, the *Times* revealed, they are trying to entice Americans to repeat and amplify their disinformation. They are also using servers inside the United States this time, as well as infiltrating Iran's cyberwarfare machine, so Putin's attacks can be blamed on Ayatollah Ali Khamenei. The Russians may also use ransomware, which has already crippled cities across America—all in the service of discord, distrust, and Donald Jackknife Trump.

Trump replaced Maguire with Richard Grenell, who had been serving as ambassador to Germany. Grenell, as of this writing, was acting director of national intelligence, and not nominated for Senate confirmation by Trump—perhaps because the law requires that the DNI "shall have extensive national security expertise" and Ambassador Grenell has none. He is, however, known to be a Trump loyalist. He may not know how to protect American national security, but he seems to know how to protect Donald Trump politically.

Just after Trump removed Maguire as acting director of national intelligence and replaced him with an unqualified political ally, the *Washington Post* reported that, in addition to favoring Trump, Russia was trying to aid Bernie Sanders's 2020 campaign. As of this writing, Trump has done nothing to punish Putin for his 2020 cyberinvasions of our election. Nothing. Nada. Zip. Zilch. Or, in a language Putin would understand: Ничего.

If we are to fend off the Russians, we are going to need our best people, not our most political ones. Disinformation plays a crucial role in Russia's efforts to divide Americans and undermine our faith in democracy. Last election it was fraudulent Facebook and Twitter accounts. One especially pernicious effort was a tweet that featured a doctored photo of the actor Aziz Ansari. He is holding a sign that says, "Save time. Avoid the line. Vote from home. Tweet ClintonKaine with the hashtag #PresidentialElection on November 8th, 2016 between 8AM and 6PM to cast your vote." Of course, you can't vote via Twitter. Twitter could not tell Congress how many people may have fallen for it and thus lost their chance to actually participate in the election. Other accounts told people that they could vote by text. Wrong.

These accounts—thousands of them—spread lies, rumors, and phony "scandals." They clearly had an effect on the election. When the presidency is decided by 77,744 votes, everything has an effect. Senators Mark Warner (D-VA) and Amy Klobuchar (D-MN) have introduced the Honest Ads Act, which would require big digital platforms to disclose the content of political ads, who they are targeted at, and who paid for them. This is comparable to the disclosure that TV and radio stations must follow. Oh, and just like TV and radio ads, ads on Facebook, Google, Twitter, and other platforms will have to include clear, easy-to-read disclaimers telling the audience who paid for them.

This new law is desperately needed. Facebook and other megaplatforms simply will not police themselves. In a Senate Judiciary Committee hearing in late 2017, then-senator Al Franken was incredulous when a Facebook executive tried to claim ignorance of Russian attempts to manipulate American public opinion. "People are buying ads on your platform with rubles," Franken said, nearly coming out of his chair. "They're political ads. You put billions of data points together all the time—that's what I hear that these platforms do."

Franken, of course, was right. It strains credulity that a company that makes billions by making connections did not see the connection between a group based in Russia, which paid in rubles, and Russian interference in the election.

As of this writing, Moscow Mitch has not brought this vital, sensible legislation to the Senate floor.

Fake news, fake ads, fake Facebook posts, fake tweets—they were all part of 2018, and will be part of 2020. But if you really want to lose sleep, ponder deep fake videos. Experts are concerned that enemies of democracy, including Russia—but also perhaps China, North Korea, Iran, or other bad actors—are likely to use new technology to create fake videos. These deep-fake videos can make anyone look like they're saying anything.

The far right made a foolish first stab at this when they deliberately slowed down video to make it appear that Nancy Pelosi was drunk. They also altered a video to make it appear—falsely—that ace CNN White House reporter Jim Acosta had batted away the hand of a young woman who was reaching for his microphone. Those clumsy efforts were caught early and discredited quickly. The technology is improving at an astonishing pace.

Digitally inserting someone into a preexisting video used to be the province of the most skillful artists and technicians. Think of Tom Hanks shaking JFK's hand in *Forrest Gump*. Robert Zemeckis made that film in 1994. Today some four-hundred-pound guy sitting on his bed (as Trump might say) can do nearly as well.

There is an app for that. There always is. The app allows anyone to manipulate a video. Of course, the porno people got there first. They always do. They've made manipulated videos that seamlessly superimpose a celebrity's face onto the body of a porn star and— *voilà!*—there's your favorite actor doing nasty things, right there on your computer screen.

New York Times columnist Kevin Roose explored the technology and concluded, "It's not hard to imagine this technology's being used to smear politicians, create counterfeit revenge porn or frame people for crimes." Ya think? Roose concludes his fascinating and frightening tour with this dark conclusion: "There's probably nothing we can do except try to bat the fakes down as they happen, pressure social media companies to fight misinformation aggressively, and trust our eyes a little less every day."

I cannot accept Roose's conclusion. We have to do more to stop them. To its credit, Google is giving researchers access to its collection of fake videos, which were created to study how to develop technology to better spot deep fakes. It is, the experts say, a constant battle. As computing power increases and artificial intelligence becomes more sophisticated, deep fakes will be more difficult to detect. One expert, Subbarao Kambhampati, a professor of computer science at Arizona State, told the *New York Times*, "In the short term, detection will be reasonably effective. In the longer term, I think it will be impossible to distinguish between the real pictures and the fake pictures."

Google, as powerful as it is, is not the only heavy hitter chasing deep fakes. So is the Pentagon. The Defense Advanced Research Projects Agency, or DARPA, is on the job. In 1969, DARPA created something called ARPANET. Today, ARPANET has morphed into what we call the internet. To his credit, Senator Marco Rubio (R-FL) has taken the lead in pushing for efforts to counter deep fakes.

We do not know whether deep fakes will be a part of this election; whether Russia or some other adversary will deploy them, and whether our cybersleuths will be able to detect them. But even knowing that the technology is out there can cause us to distrust our senses—and give liars a way to deny genuine footage. Can you imagine what Donald Trump would have said if deep fakes had been around when he was caught on that infamous *Access Hollywood* tape? More than a year after apologizing for the tape, Trump was telling people, "We don't think that was my voice." Deep fakes give one more weapon to someone who's willing to lie, deny, and gaslight at every turn.

If All Else Fails, Cancel the Elections

If the voter purges, the voter suppression, the misinformation—if all of that still fails, I would not put it past Trump to try to cancel elections themselves. I know that sounds alarmist, but you should be alarmed. Trump has clearly and repeatedly stated his desire to be President for Life. He's not joking, folks. He doesn't joke. Any time you hear him use the "I was joking" defense, you can be sure of one thing: he wasn't joking.

Democrats should pull back the curtain on Trump's constant undermining of checks and balances and describe it for what it is: a naked drive to undermine democracy. Bill Maher is deadly serious—and absolutely right—when he says that if Trump is defeated in November 2020, he may not leave office.

If you start with that assumption, the rest makes more sense. Why undermine elections when you won the last one? Because you fear you will lose the next. Why claim that millions of illegal votes were cast? So you can delegitimize the legal vote that would put you out of office. Why undermine the free press when you've built your career on publicity? Because the press will call you out on your efforts to stay in power. Why deride "so-called judges" who rule against you? Because when they rule you can't stop elections, you can claim that their rulings are illegitimate and therefore not to be obeyed. Why wage an all-out war on truth, complete with Orwellian "alternative facts"? Because when the truth comes out—about a scandal you were involved in, or a crime you were complicit in, or an election you lost—you want to be able to convince millions of Americans not to believe their own eyes.

Trump has been priming his supporters for years, undermining democracy, undermining law enforcement, the press, the courts—anyone and everyone. If he were to say "The election was rigged!" after losing in 2020, he would be on well-trod ground. As far back as August 2017, just eight months into his presidency, he had so undermined his supporters' faith in elections that polls showed a shocking result:

Poll: 52 percent of Republicans would support postponing the 2020 election if Trump proposed it.

Fifty-two percent of Republicans surveyed said yes to this question: "If Donald Trump were to say that the 2020 presidential election should be postponed until the country can make sure that only eligible American citizens can vote, would you support or oppose postponing the election?" And when you add congressional Republicans to the call to postpone the election, support jumps to 56 percent.

This is no joke. The survey is legit: conducted by Dr. Ariel Malka, an associate professor of psychology at Yeshiva University, and Dr. Yphtach Lelkes, an assistant professor at the Annenberg School for Communication at the University of Pennsylvania.

Most Republicans would support canceling the next election if Trump called for it. I'm going to keep saying it: most Republicans would support canceling the next election if Trump called for it. Keep in mind that this survey was conducted in 2017. The number could potentially be even higher today, after a steady diet of conspiracy theories and attacks on every check and balance in our system. (It may be the only diet Donald Jellybelly Trump has ever been on.) There is a method, I believe, to Trump's madness. His endless undermining of democratic institutions puts him in a win-win position: if he does win the election he can say, as he did in 2016, that he won in spite of the rigged system. But if loses, he will have laid the groundwork for an all-out war against democracy itself.

Responding to Trump's War on Democracy

Here's what we can do: First, Democrats should call Trump out on this. Why is Bill Maher pretty much the only Paul Revere openly warning us that Trump will not honor the will of the people? Democratic leaders should be telling Americans who aren't mainlining Breitbart that this risk is real. That unlike Trump's phony risk of millions of illegal votes being cast, the president could call for ignoring millions of votes that were legally cast against him.

Second, ask questions of every Republican politician. Folks should go to their local representative or senator's town hall meetings and ask them this simple question: "If Trump tries to cancel or discredit the election, will you stand with democracy or with Trump?" Videotape them. Be respectful—please. Lord knows there's enough incivility. If your representative or senator is no longer having town hall meetings, write them. Email them. Call them. And keep receipts.

Third, if it comes to it, be prepared to use your First Amendment rights to free speech and freedom of assembly. I believe Al Gore made a critical mistake when he did not allow organizers to call for peaceful demonstrations while the Republicans were stealing the 2000 election from him. Gore is a true patriot. He volunteered for Vietnam when Trump was faking bone spurs. But even back in 2000, Republicans were prepared to steal an election. Twenty years later, they have only become bolder, more brazen, more contemptuous of the majority of Americans. The day after Trump took office, we saw some of the largest mass demonstrations in American history. The Women's March of 2017 may well have been just a dress rehearsal for an even bigger mass movement in 2021.

Fourth, the only cure for a war on democracy is more democracy. Stacey Abrams of Georgia, whom we met a moment ago, lost her race for governor by just 1.4 percent. After the election, Abrams decided to get better, not bitter. She has founded Fair Fight and Fair Fight 2020, organizations determined to preserve, protect, and defend the right to vote. In an interview with *USA Today*, she said that her goal "is to ensure that people know about the obstacles that are being placed in their way, but [are encouraged to] vote in even larger numbers to overwhelm the intention of the system. The best way to defeat voter suppression is by having such a high turnout that the barriers to voting have limited effect." In other words, flood the zone.

Democrats are also flooding the courts, as you learned earlier in this chapter. Marc Elias, one of the best election lawyers in America, has spent more time in court during the Trump administration than Paul Manafort. It is sometimes an uphill battle. In 2013, the Supreme Court gutted a key provision of the Voting Rights Act, eliminating "preclearance" of changes in voting procedures. Under preclearance, the Justice Department was required to sign off on any changes in the voting rules, to make sure they weren't being used to, oh, say, discriminate. So, for example, if a state like Georgia, which has a history of racial discrimination, wanted to close a bunch of polling places, the Justice Department was supposed to see if, say, the polling places it was closing were mostly in African American neighborhoods. No more. Without preclearance, voting rights attorneys like Elias are fighting with one hand tied behind their back. Elias has noted that, on December 6, 2019, the House voted to restore the Voting Rights Act. Every single Democrat in the House voted to restore voting rights. Only one Republican did.

This is a historic retreat from what had been a modern consensus in support of voting rights. As recently as 2006, Congress reauthorized the Voting Rights Act by a vote of 390–33 in the House and 98–0 in the Senate. But under Trump, the party of Lincoln has become the party that has abandoned voting rights. Elias has written powerfully about this, about the consequences elections have on voting rights, and vice versa:

> Opposing minority voting rights is not the exception in today's Republican party, it is the rule. It is a feature of what makes the Republican party attractive to its supporters, not a flaw the party wants to fix in the future. That's because Republicans know that the more they can drown out the voices of minority voters who are the backbone of the Democratic party, the more likely it is that Republicans will be elected. It is time for supporters of minority voting rights to speak in similarly loud voices. In 2020, if the country elects a Democratic president, U.S. House, and U.S. Senate, not to mention Democratic governors and majority-Democratic state legislatures, we will have new laws protecting the right to vote. If Republicans control any part of the legislative process, we won't. It is that simple.

Finally, in keeping with a central theme of this book and one of my core beliefs about politics: make it about the voters, not Trump. He's only in it for himself. How's that for a six-word message? Trump has worked tirelessly to portray himself as someone who's fighting for working-class Americans. His and his supporters' endless rants about the "deep state" are designed to provide cover for him to lay siege to any institution, any person, any force that could restrain or constrain him. Even a national election.

How Democrats Should Run on This

Hard. Strong. Aggressively. Patriotically. That's how they should run on this. Republicans have always known how to stir up nationalistic fervor. Republicans from Joe McCarthy to Richard Nixon to Ronald Reagan stoked fear of the Russians. Granted, that was the "Evil Empire," but Putin is plenty evil, and he is seeking to reconstitute the Soviet empire. Just ask the people of Georgia, which he invaded in 2008, or the people of eastern Ukraine, which he invaded in 2014. Putin is a punk—there's a bumper sticker for you. Democrats need to repeat what John McCain said about the 2016 Russian cyberattack on the United States: "When you attack a country, it's an act of war. And so we have to make sure that there is a price to pay so that we can perhaps persuade Russia to stop these kinds of attacks on our very fundamentals of democracy."

Democrats should repeat what retired four-star army general Mark Hertling has said. Gen. Hertling commanded the US Army Europe and the Seventh Army, as well as the First Armored Division in Iraq. He compared the Russian attack on our election to Pearl Harbor and 9/11. This stands in stark contrast to the media cliché: "meddling." No, it was not meddling. Meddling is what your mother-in-law does when she peeks in your medicine cabinet. What Putin carried out was an attack on our democracy as shocking and dangerous as a physical attack on our homeland. "In 2016, our country was targeted by an attack that had different operational objectives and a different overarching strategy," Gen. Hertling wrote, in an article with Molly McKew, "but its aim was every bit as much to devastate the American homeland as Pearl Harbor or 9/11. The destruction may not send pillars of smoke into the sky or come with an 11-digit price tag, and there's no body count or casualty statistics—but the damage done has ravaged our institutions and shaken our belief in our immovability."

After you have defined the attack, define the beneficiary. Take a page from the GOP: attack Trump's image of strength. Portray him as the weakling he is: a spray-tanning, cross-combing, country-clubbing, bone-spurring wussy who wets his pants every time Vladimir Putin snaps his fingers. Instead of reinforcing the image of Trump as a tough guy, shatter the myth. Trump says he's a tough guy. He says if he gets hit, he hits back ten times harder. America is under attack, and Trump is cowering under the bed—or, worse, helping the foreign punk who's attacking us. As we say in Texas, Trump is all hairspray and no cojones.

The victim in this narrative is the voter. (Again, always make it about the voter.) Trump's weakness risks robbing you of your right to vote, a right countless Americans died for. No red-blooded American wants that.

The acid test of a democracy is accepting the results when you lose. Al Gore and Hillary Clinton are the gold standard: they accepted being denied the White House even when they had won the popular vote. In Gore's case, he lost the votes of five Republican lawyers on the Supreme Court. In Hillary's, it took voter suppression plus Russia plus Jim Comey's intervention plus the Electoral College to keep her out of the White House. But here's the deal: both of them accepted the result. Does anyone think Trump will? Me neither. So we had better be prepared to stand strong for our democracy if and when Trump declares war on it.

CHAPTER 8

THIS CHAPTER WILL BEAT TRUMP. I GUARANTEE.

As a rule, I don't believe in silver bullets. I usually have contempt for people who come into the campaign headquarters yelling "Eureka!" and then tell me if we just focus on this one thing, we'll win. I was doing a campaign in Texas once and a guy told me, "I got it! If you just focus the campaign on historic preservation you'll win!" This was, mind you, a campaign for the United States Senate. Three guesses on what that guy did for a living, by the way.

You're getting good at this. He did, in fact, restore historic buildings. Who'da thunk it? With that caveat, let me say this:

Eureka!

I have found the issue that will defeat Donald Jackrabbit Trump. He wants to cut Medicare, Medicaid, and Social Security.

You're welcome.

It is his Achilles' heel, his bone spur, his fatal flaw, his soft underbelly. (I'll pause for a moment while you throw up in your mouth at the thought of Trump's soft underbelly.)

Medicare, Medicaid, and Social Security. Americans love them. Trump wants to cut them. Say it with me: Trump wants to cut Medicare, Medicaid, and Social Security. If you need a mnemonic, how about MMSS, which stands for Medicare, Medicaid, and Social Security: things that Trump wants to cut.

Trump Promised Not to Cut Medicare, Medicaid, and Social Security. He Lied.

As a candidate, Trump was adamant that he would not propose cuts to Medicare, Medicaid, and Social Security. He lied. On May 7, 2015, he tweeted:

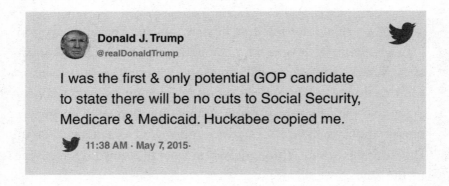

Donald J. Trump
@realDonaldTrump

I was the first & only potential GOP candidate to state there will be no cuts to Social Security, Medicare & Medicaid. Huckabee copied me.

11:38 AM · May 7, 2015·

He told the conservative site the Daily Signal in 2015: "I'm not going to cut Social Security like every other Republican and I'm not going to cut Medicare or Medicaid. Every other Republican's gonna cut."

On April 18, 2015, Trump said, "Every Republican wants to do a big number on Social Security. They want to do it on Medicare, they want to do it on Medicaid—and we can't do that. It's not fair to the people that have been paying in for years and now all of a sudden they wanna be cut."

On June 16, 2015, he said, "Save Medicare, Medicaid, and Social Security without cuts. Have to do it."

Two days before the 2016 election, Trump added a new twist to his pledge: the phony claim that Hillary Clinton was actually the candidate who would cut Social Security and Medicare. He said at a rally, "Hillary Clinton is going to destroy your Social Security and Medicare. I am going to protect and save your Social Security and your Medicare. You made a deal a long time ago." Psychologists call that "projection"—accusing someone of that which you know you yourself are guilty of. It's kind of a tell with Trump.

In his 2020 State of the Union address, he was repeating his lie: "And we will always protect your Medicare and your Social Security." He gave that speech on February 4. Six days later, he released his budget. It proved he had lied. His 2021 budget cuts Medicaid and Obamacare by $1.6 trillion dollars. That's right. Trillion, with a *t*. As in Trump. The guy who wants to cut Medicare, Medicaid, and Social Security. His 2021 budget also includes spending $451 billion less on Medicare.

John Cassidy, who covers politics and economics for *The New Yorker*, noted: "The White House is looking to achieve hundreds of billions in Medicare savings over the next decade, relative to the baseline, by changing the way doctors are paid and making other changes."

As recently as March 5, 2020, Trump admitted that he wants to cut Medicare, Medicaid, and Social Security. In a town hall meeting, he was challenged by Fox News's Martha MacCallum on his ballooning deficit. "If you don't cut something in entitlements," MacCallum said, "you will never really deal with the debt." Trump's answer was not to reject MacCallum's premise, and it certainly wasn't to call for more revenue by, say, making billionaires and corporations pay their fair share. "Oh, we'll be cutting," he said immediately. He went on to add that we will have tremendous, wonderful, earth-shattering growth. But his commitment to cut Medicare, Medicaid, and Social Security is important.

This isn't the first time Trump has tried to cut Medicare, Medicaid, and Social Security. He tried to cut them in his 2020 budget as well. As the *Washington Post* summarized that budget: "The spending plan calls for a cut of nearly $1.5 trillion in Medicaid over 10 years." The budget would have shifted Medicaid to a block grant program, which would inevitably mean cuts. On top of that, Trump wanted to eliminate funding for Medicaid expansion, the Obamacare project that has brought health insurance to more than 17 million Americans. All told, the bottom-line Trump cuts to Medicaid came to $777 billion.

What's more, Trump's 2020 budget called for reducing spending on Medicare by $845 billion over ten years, and cutting Social Security by $550 billion.

> There it is: the holy trinity of entitlements. Medicare, Medicaid, and Social Security. And have I mentioned that Trump wants to cut all three? 'Cause he does.

The people who follow these programs for a living spoke out loud and clear. Like Chip Kahn. He's the president of the Federation of American Hospitals, more than a thousand for-profit hospitals all across the country. He said that Trump's 2020 budget "imposes arbitrary and blunt Medicare cuts . . . The impact for seniors would be devastating." Kahn is an expert. He knows what these cuts would do to the hospitals he represents and the patients they treat.

Oh, no, the Trump people say, we're just going to cut "waste, fraud, and abuse." Baloney. Trump doesn't want to cut waste, fraud, and abuse; he *is* waste, fraud, and abuse. "Waste, fraud, and abuse"—the unholy trinity for people who are lying about cutting Medicare, Medicaid, and Social Security. "Waste, fraud, and abuse" my Aunt Fanny. Trump bilks the taxpayers every day. It's part of his con, his grift, his endless drive to line his own pockets at taxpayers' expense. One quick example, and then I'll get back to Trump's plans to cut Medicare, Medicaid, and Social Security: Trump charges the Secret Service rates as high as $650 a night, or $17,000 a month, to stay at his white-trash hellhole, err, country club, in Bedminster, New Jersey. Waste, fraud, and abuse indeed.

There's another euphemism I want to warn you about: "I want to *fix* Medicare, Medicaid, and Social Security." Anytime a politician says they want to "fix" something, I think of my veterinarian. He said he wanted to "fix" my dog Gus. Well, it depends on what you mean by "fix." I can tell you this: after the vet was through, that which once worked well no longer worked, and Gus was not too happy about the procedure. A "fix" is a euphemism for a cut. Just ask Gus.

Speaking of cutting: cutting Medicare, Medicaid, Social Security— it's what Republicans do. They can't help themselves. They can't stop themselves. It's in their DNA. It's a compulsion, a sickness, an addiction.

> Republicans lie awake at night, unable to sleep, worried that somebody, somewhere might be receiving quality health care or a decent, dignified retirement.

Take Mick Mulvaney, please. The now former White House chief of staff was once an active member of the House Freedom Caucus, which is basically devoted to freeing you from your Medicare, Medicaid, and Social Security. In 2017, when he was running the Office of Management and Budget, Mulvaney bragged about how he conned Trump into cutting Social Security. Mulvaney wanted to cut Social Security Disability Insurance, which is a) part of Social Security; and b) a lifeline for people who are disabled. Instead of telling

Trump that, Mulvaney simply said he wanted to cut Social Security Disability Insurance. Because "it's welfare." "OK," Trump reportedly replied, "we can fix welfare." There's that euphemism again: "fix."

Set aside what a duplicitous jerk Mulvaney was for tricking his boss into cutting Social Security, if you can. Look past the savage cruelty of cutting the subsistence payments to disabled Americans. Focus on the fact that *Mick Mulvaney bragged about it. To a reporter.* He was proud of his effort to cut Social Security payments to disabled Americans. Tell me again how Republicans believe in family values.

Almost 11 million Americans rely on Social Security Disability Insurance. *Oh, but what about waste, fraud, and abuse? I bet there's a ton of that in the SSDI program.* Ummm, no. According to the Trump administration's own analysis (dug out by the *Washington Post*'s tireless fact checker Glenn Kessler), "improper disability payment, which can result from mistakes or incorrect information" (NOTE: which are innocent mistakes, not fraud or abuse), represented a teeny, tiny percentage of disability payments. How tiny? Tinier than Donald Trump's hands. Overpayments constituted 0.99 percent of disability payments, and underpayments made up 0.22 percent. When less than 1 percent of the program is overpayments, I'd say you're running a pretty tight ship.

I'd also say Donald Trump wants to cut Medicare, Medicaid, and Social Security.

Turns out Donald Trump would say that, too. Maybe not to your face, but to the economic elite gathered in Davos, Switzerland, in January 2020. While in the Alps, Trump gave an interview to CNBC. He was asked if changes to the structure of entitlement programs might be on his plate. "At some point, they will be," he said. He went on to boast about economic growth, which he seemed to think would make it easier to cut entitlements (it also makes it easier to pay for them, if you have a sensible, progressive tax code). "At the right time, we will take a look at that," he said. "You know, that's actually the easiest of all things."

Note well not only what Trump said—that he will cut Medicare—but *where* he said it. Davos. Davos is not just a place, it's a way of life. Davos: the sun-drenched, snow-covered peaks of the Swiss Alps swaddle this picturesque village like an Hermès scarf swaddles the diamond-laden neck of an heiress. Davos: the capital of capital. Davos: where billionaires look down on millionaires. Davos: where elites listen earnestly to presentations about global warming, then jump on their private jets. Davos: where globalists stroke their chin and wonder why the bottom 99.9 percent is so angry. Davos. Sweet, sweet Davos: where the greatest beneficiaries of Trump's tax cut for the rich were delighted to hear him say that cuts to Medicare are on the table.

The fact that Donald Trump would make a statement like that in a place like that tells you all you need to know about his arrogance. He is betting that his voters don't know and don't care; that they will once again be so distracted by his call to hate the Other—Mexicans, Muslims, African Americans, LGBTQ+ Americans—that they won't notice he is planning to cut the health and retirement programs that could be the difference between dignity and destitution.

His Cuts to Medicare, Medicaid, and Social Security Are to Pay for His Tax Cut for the Rich

I bet by now you're wondering why Trump wants to cut Medicare, Medicaid, and Social Security. Motive is often difficult to discern. It could be that he is falling in line with the long-held GOP desire to gut these entitlements. Could be he's just mean. Or it could be to pay for his tax cuts for the rich. Let's take a look behind Door 3.

In 2018, when they read Trump's budget for the next fiscal year, Senators Martin Heinrich (D-NM) and Chris Van Hollen (D-MD) noted that if you add together the George W. Bush tax cuts for the rich and the Trump 2017 tax cuts for the rich, "Republicans will have sent a whopping $2 trillion to [a] small sliver of the richest Americans." The senators went on, "In their proposed budget, Republicans in Congress are now wanting to pay for those special interest tax breaks by taking that same $2 trillion out of Medicare, Medicaid, Social Security, and the Affordable Care Act."

Pairing Trump's tax cuts for the rich with his cuts to Medicare, Medicaid, and Social Security makes sense. The numbers match pretty closely, and it helps voters understand why Trump, who desperately wants to be loved, would attack such beloved programs: because he wants to help the rich even more than he wants to be loved by the middle class. Besides, he might figure, he can always con the middle class. It worked in 2016.

We will discuss Trump's tax cut for the rich in greater detail in chapter 10. You don't need to memorize all the mind-numbing detail. But you should know that the nonpartisan Congressional Budget Office says that the Trump tax cut for the rich costs $1.9 trillion over ten years. That's a lot of money. You can't come up with a way to pay for it by cutting back on donuts at the staff meeting. To find that kind of money, if you're a Republican, you have to cut Medicare, Medicaid, and Social Security. And that means hurting a lot of people.

Who Receives Medicare, Medicaid, and Social Security?

Trump voters, that's who.

To the extent that Medicare, Medicaid, and Social Security payments go to seniors (they do *to a great extent*), they are likely to disproportionately go to Trump voters. Hillary Clinton won a solid majority of voters under the age of forty; Trump won voters over forty. Trump won voters age sixty-five and older—by definition, voters who are on Medicare and Social Security—by 7 percent. Basically, the older you are, the more likely you were to have voted for Trump. And the older you are, the more likely you are to receive Social Security, Medicare, and/or Medicaid.

Obviously, everyone over sixty-five (or nearly everyone) is on Medicare and Social Security. Thus any cuts to those programs would have affected Trump voters more than Hillary voters. Hillary won Medicaid recipients. But 39 percent of Medicaid recipients voted for Trump, and in rural counties that number was even higher. The bottom line is, Trump's cuts in Medicare, Medicaid, and Social Security would harm the very people he says he cares about: many of the people who voted for him. If you are on Medicare, Medicaid, or Social Security, or know someone who is, you have a lot on the line. And if you are on Medicare, Medicaid, or Social Security and you vote for Trump, you are voting to cut your own benefits.

Medicare. Basically, Medicare is health insurance for older Americans. Every American over age sixty-five can receive it. That's 59.8 million Americans.

President Lyndon Baines Johnson signed Medicare and Medicaid into law on July 30, 1965. The first Medicare recipient was former President Harry S Truman. In fact, LBJ traveled to the Truman Presidential Library in Independence, Missouri, to sign the bill into law. He then gave Harry and Bess Truman the first two Medicare cards.

They needed it. Harry and Bess were far from wealthy. Back then, old age often meant poverty. Before Medicare, more than half of seniors (56 percent, to be exact) had no health insurance at all. Medicare is now such an integral part of the fabric of our society that it is difficult to imagine just how bitterly some opposed it. And by "some" I mean Republicans. In 1961, the new president, John F. Kennedy, was pushing for health coverage for the elderly—something every Democrat since Truman had supported. Medicare opponents, led by the American Medical Association, pulled out the big guns to shoot it down. They asked a popular movie and TV star, Ronald Reagan, to make their case. He made a record album (ask your parents), which the AMA funded. Having gotten into showbiz as a radio guy, Reagan was audio magic. His soothing, all-American delivery masked a hard-edged, right-wing line. Unless his listeners rose up to kill Medicare, he said, "one of these days we are going to spend our sunset years telling our children and our children's children what it once was like in America when men were free."

After JFK's assassination, LBJ, the master of the Senate, got Medicare and Medicaid passed. More than a half-century later, the uninsured rate for senior citizens in America has dropped from 56 percent to 0. Medicare was so successful—and so popular—that even Ronald Reagan got on board. Remember when he had that killer line against President Jimmy Carter in one of their 1980 debates, "There you go again," complete with the wry smile and the affable Gipper headshake? He said it in response to this charge—this 100 percent true charge—from Carter: "Governor Reagan, as a matter of fact, began his political career campaigning around this nation against Medicare. Now we have an opportunity to move toward national health insurance." The camera cut to Reagan, who was shaking that big, gorgeous head of his and smiling as if he'd caught his puppy chewing on his slippers again. Carter continued, outlining his plan for national health insurance, emphasizing prevention and cost containment. He concluded, "Governor Reagan again, typically, is against such a proposal." Reagan was asked to respond. "Well," said Reagan, chuckling and shaking his head, "there you go again."

That chuckling dismissal is remembered fondly. It must have driven Carter mad to realize that his wholly accurate attack was simply laughed off. Reagan won the election, but Medicare won the war. By the last year of Reagan's second term, he had given up on abolishing this "socialist" program. In fact, he signed a bipartisan bill to *expand* Medicare. It was the largest expansion of Medicare since LBJ created the program. (The law, which created catastrophic care insurance for seniors, was repealed a year later, when seniors rebelled against the surtax on middle- and upper-middle-income seniors that funded it.)

Medicaid. Signed into law the same day as Medicare, Medicaid is the health insurance program for low-income Americans. Today, more than 64.5 million Americans get their health insurance through Medicaid. Rather than automatically enrolling 100 percent of them in a federal program, which Medicare did for seniors, Medicaid was a cooperative program with the states. Each state decided whether to participate (Arizona was the last; it waited until 1982 to join).

Obamacare boosted Medicaid, setting up incentives that encouraged states to expand enrollment in the program. As of 2019, thirty-six states and the District of Columbia have expanded Medicaid; sixteen states have not. By 2015, 14.5 million people had been added to Medicaid or the Children's Health Insurance Program, which was created by President Bill Clinton. In addition, Medicaid is the number one payment source for nursing home care. Sixty-two percent of all Americans in nursing homes today have their care paid by Medicaid.

Social Security. Sixty-four million Americans receive Social Security benefits. Social Security is really three programs: retirement income, disability payments, and benefits for the survivors of workers who have died. "Without Social Security," reports the nonpartisan Center on Budget and Policy Priorities, "22.1 million more Americans would be poor." Without Social Security, the think tank found, "39.2 percent of elderly Americans would have incomes below the official poverty line."

Most elderly Americans have a household income under $50,000 a year, and one in four make do on less than $20,000 a year. For most retirees, Social Security is the majority of their income, and for many retirees—one in five, to be exact—Social Security is 90 percent of it. This is especially pronounced in states with lots of Trump supporters. Take West Virginia, for example; the state where Trump did best. He crushed Hillary Clinton in the Mountain State by a margin of 48 percent. To be clear, he didn't *get* 48 percent, he *won by* 48 percent. Eleven percent of West Virginia's seniors live in poverty. That's far better than the overall poverty rate in West Virginia, which, even before Trump's Corona-crash, was 17.8 percent. But if you took away their Social Security, the number of West Virginia seniors living in poverty would skyrocket to more than 48 percent. Social Security is truly a lifeline for nearly half of all the seniors in Almost Heaven.

You Don't Need a Poll to Know This Is Unpopular

I realize that cutting Medicare, Medicaid, and Social Security is unpopular, and that you don't need a poll to tell you that. But guess what? There have been a bunch of polls on this subject. They're not shocking, but, you know, I did look them up. In a Kaiser Family Foundation survey, a whopping 12 percent of Americans supported decreased funding for Medicaid. On the other side of the ledger, 87 percent wanted to maintain funding levels or increase them.

Medicare is even more popular. In a Pew survey, 94 percent of Democrats said they want to maintain or increase Medicare spending. Okay, but they're, ya know, Democrats. You may be interested in learning, however, that 85 percent of Republicans agreed with them.

How about Social Security, Paul? I bet people really want to cut it. Wrong. Ninety-five percent of Democrats and 86 percent of Republicans want to maintain or increase spending on Social Security. Only 10 percent of Republicans and 3 percent of Democrats say they support cutting it.

I've been in politics a long time, and I have never seen America so divided. But let's recall: in the Civil War, Lincoln saved the Union, then called on the better angels of our nature to forgive, to unify, to heal. Donald Trump has united a divided country in an entirely different way. By supporting cuts in Medicare, Medicaid, and Social Security, he has united Republicans and Democrats—86 percent of the former and 95 percent of the latter. That's not easy to do.

How Democrats Should Run on This

Is that a trick question? This one should not be difficult. Republicans have been trying to kill Medicare, Medicaid, and Social Security since Noah docked his boat. To be fair, Noah lived to be 950 (Genesis 9:29), so he would have collected Social Security benefits for 885 years.

When Republicans try to cut Medicare, Medicaid, and Social Security and Democrats call them on it, Democrats win. It's pretty simple. They cut. We protect. We win. And yet for the life of me I rarely heard the Democratic candidates for president talk about it—at least not in the early stages of the primary contest. I realize that primaries are about drawing distinctions within the party, and there is no Democrat running for president calling for cuts in Medicare, Medicaid, and Social Security the way Trump has. And I realize, therefore, that candidates don't prepare for debates by emphasizing issues they all agree on. I get all that.

Joe Biden knows how to do this. As soon as Trump promised Fox News he would be cutting Medicare, Medicaid, and Social Security—literally minutes after Trump's comments—Biden hit him with a rhetorical two-by-four, tweeting: "Here's the deal, folks: Social Security is on the ballot this year, and the choice couldn't be clearer: I'll protect and expand it. Donald Trump will cut it and take it away." Perfect. Go get 'em, Joe.

Biden needs to be especially aggressive on this, since Trump will try to turn the tables on him and accuse Biden of wanting to cut Social Security and Medicare. Bernie Sanders tried this in the primaries, and it didn't fly. Seniors voted overwhelmingly for Biden in the Democratic primaries. In his *loooong* Senate career, Biden has supported a balanced budget amendment to the Constitution, which some fear could cause cuts in entitlements. And he supported a one-year freeze in all federal spending back in the 1980s. He must not be sheepish about proposals that never passed decades ago. He needs to take the fight to Trump, as he did in that rapid-response tweet following Trump's Fox News pledge to cut Medicare, Medicaid, and Social Security.

That's how you do it, people. You just say it—early and often. Set a little buzzer on your Apple Watch that goes off every ten minutes. When it goes off, just repeat, "Trump wants to cut Medicare, Medicaid, and Social Security." Might come in handy in a debate when you find yourself down a rabbit hole, arguing the most technical details of a health care plan that will never pass. You're lost in abstruse arcana about high-risk pools when your watch goes off. You interrupt yourself and say, "And Donald Trump wants to cut Medicare, Medicaid, and Social Security." Even after the debate is over and you're driving back to your motel. (You're a Democrat. This is a low-budget campaign.) You've stopped at a red light. (You don't have Secret Service protection yet.) There's a fellow in the next lane. You roll down the window and say, "Donald Trump wants to cut Medicare, Medicaid, and Social Security." Even if you're not running for president, toss it into conversation every ten minutes. "Yep, Jim, Cleveland sure misses having Corey Kluber on the mound. And Donald Trump wants to cut Medicare, Medicaid, and Social Security." "I love Lizzo. She's so body-positive. And Trump wants to cut Medicare, Medicaid, and Social Security."

Make it a habit. When I was a kid in Missouri City, Texas, a Houston radio station, KILT, had a contest. If you answered the phone "KILT's gonna make me rich!" and KILT called you, well, you won money. My friend Steve Abbott answered the phone that way for every call, every day, for weeks. He didn't get rich, and now he lives in the Netherlands. Where he has great health care. But you don't. So if you want to defeat Donald Trump and save Medicare, Medicaid, and Social Security, repeat that sentence. No, not the one about KILT radio making you rich. Focus, people. Donald Trump will cut Medicare, Medicaid, and Social Security.

HEALTH CARE

Your Money or Your Life

Going Viral, Literally

We covered the coronavirus in chapter 2, but just to summarize a couple of the key points before we go to a larger discussion of health care.

When the global pandemic of COVID-19 first exploded in Wuhan, China, Donald Jaundice Trump leapt into action. He summoned to the Oval Office the special pandemic security team at the National Security Council that was established during the Ebola outbreak, and . . . wait. No, he didn't. Because he had fired the National Security Council's pandemic response team two years ago.

As Judd Legum of the indispensable newsletter *Popular Information* and others have reported, Trump fired the entire NSC pandemic response team in May 2018. The pandemic team, created by President Barack Obama, was led by Rear Admiral Timothy Ziemer, who, I should note, I do not know at all. But my experience in government is that there are not a lot of rear admirals who are political hacks. Trump's own homeland security adviser had called for "a comprehensive biodefense strategy against pandemics and biological attacks." He was fired, too—a month before Rear Admiral Ziemer.

The Ebola outbreak of 2014 was a big deal, or, rather, it turned out not to be as big a deal as it might have been, because the United States of America rode to the rescue. President Obama deployed resources, putting Ron Klain, an experienced government hand, in charge. Only four Americans got Ebola. Only one of them died from it.

As Kurt Bardella, a former Republican congressional staffer who has become disillusioned with his former party under Trump, has written, "In the summer and fall of 2014, Trump posted close to 100 tweets criticizing and, for lack of a better word, weaponizing, the Obama administration's response to the Ebola crisis." Trump's attacks, Bardella notes, included calling President Obama "stupid" and "incompetent."

You can imagine that President Trump would want to do better than that "incompetent," "stupid" Obama. But instead of building on Obama's robust response, he surrendered. Not only did he fire the professional national security experts who were charged with defending us from pandemics, he also cut the funding for pandemic response at the Centers for Disease Control and Prevention. He cut CDC funding for the prevention of global disease outbreak by 80 percent. He significantly reduced or even eliminated funding for epidemic prevention in thirty-nine of the forty-nine countries where the United States was operating. That funding was essential for training health care workers, improving labs, expanding emergency care—all the things you'd want to be doing to keep a virus from going viral. One of the countries where the CDC had to scale back or stop working: China.

Tom Frieden, who ran the CDC during the Ebola outbreak, spoke up when Trump gutted the funding for epidemic prevention, telling the *Washington Post*, "This is the front line against terrible organisms. Like terrorism, you can't fight it just within our borders. You've got to fight epidemic diseases where they emerge."

At the same time he was predicting zero cases soon, Trump called Democrats' concerns about the Covid-19 pandemic "a hoax." He has repeatedly suggested that we could have a vaccine for the virus in months, despite the fact that our government's experts correct him in real time, explaining that it will take a year to eighteen months to bring a vaccine to the market. He also suggested that perhaps the flu shot—"a solid flu vaccine," he called it—might do the trick. Umm, no. Then he told Fox News's Sean Hannity that the World Health Organization's estimated death rate was "a false number," based on his own "hunch."

I have a hunch that what Trump doesn't know—or doesn't tell the truth about—can hurt you.

The United States Stands Alone— and Not in a Good Way

The United States is the wealthiest country on earth. We are also the only country in the industrialized world that does not have universal health care. (By "industrialized world" I mean the thirty-six nations of the Organisation for Economic Co-operation and Development (the OECD), which includes our economic peers Japan, Germany, Great Britain, and Canada. It does not include China, which the OECD still considers "emerging.")

Some say this is because Americans are more hostile to government, more entrepreneurial, more ruggedly independent. They may have a point. But the biggest reason we don't have universal health coverage is more of an accident of history. World War II sent millions of workers, mostly men, off to war, creating a labor shortage at home. Wages had been frozen, so to compete for talent, companies began offering benefits, especially health care. After the war, Britain and many other countries converted to universal health care, but the United States maintained its employer-based system. Seventy-five years later, here we are. While the British National Health System has its problems, no British politician is campaigning to end socialized medicine in the UK. In fact, the NHS became a pawn in the Brexit fight, with Conservative Party foreign minister Boris Johnson claiming that leaving the EU could bring a windfall of 350 million pounds per week (about $455 million) to the NHS.

Canada took a slightly different path. Starting in one province in 1947, they slowly had provincial governments take over health insurance, culminating in 1984 with a national law. Today in Canada, doctors and nurses are all privately employed. But there is only one insurance company, as it were: the government. Their name for that single payer: Medicare.

Even if socialized medicine is politically unassailable in the UK and single-payer health care is beloved in Canada, the United States remains wedded to its employer-based system. And yet we want more and better health care for lower cost. As the campaign manager for Harris Wofford's upset 1991 race for US Senate in Pennsylvania, I saw up close the power of the issue. Wofford did not bury voters in a blizzard of position papers. He stated simply and powerfully: "If criminals have the right to a lawyer, I think working Americans should have the right to a doctor." In our initial poll, Wofford trailed popular two-term governor Dick Thornburgh—then serving as President George H. W. Bush's attorney general—by 47 points. On the strength of his health care message, Wofford won by 10 points.

Wofford was one of the few people I have known who I would truly call a visionary. He saw self-evident truths and spoke them clearly. When he articulated his vision of health care, he knew that less was more. If you say a hundred things, you're really saying nothing. Democrats need to state powerful truths simply.

The challenge is to translate simple truths into policy. A great many Democrats, myself included, took Wofford's victory as evidence that the country wanted universal coverage, at the least—or even single-payer Medicare for All. They didn't. Even Bill and Hillary Clinton, popular, brilliant, deeply versed in the policy details, failed to get universal coverage through a Democratic Congress in 1993. Of course, sixteen years later, Barack Obama, Nancy Pelosi, and Harry Reid got the Affordable Care Act passed. While not single-payer or even close, and while lacking even a public option, Obamacare stands as a monumental domestic accomplishment. It was also so politically toxic that Democrats lost a staggering sixty-three House seats and six Senate seats because of it—and with that, control of both chambers.

I have learned that the winning message on health care often is: "The other side is going to take away your health care." Republicans used that against Clinton, claiming that his plan would take away your right to choose your own doctor (it didn't). Democrats used that against Republicans in the Obamacare fight, claiming that the GOP status quo denied coverage for millions of people with pre-existing conditions. Rather than developing exquisitely detailed, carefully vetted position papers, Democrats should: 1) put Trump's health care record on trial; 2) pledge to protect people's health care. But don't get too deep into the weeds. You'll lose your audience, or, worse, you'll scare people. Besides, Congress is never going to enact any presidential candidate's position paper as is. Presidents set goals; Congress writes the specifics, so don't get hung up on them.

Trump Wants to Take Away Your Right to Coverage if You Have a Preexisting Condition

Donald Trump wants to give insurance companies the right to jack up rates or deny you health care coverage altogether if you have a preexisting condition. Protecting people with preexisting conditions is one of the seminal accomplishments of Obamacare. And yet Trump wants to repeal Obamacare. Badly. He is so bitter about his failure to repeal the Affordable Care Act that he continues to mock and belittle the memory of Sen. John McCain, who cast the deciding vote in the Senate against Trump's plan to repeal Obamacare.

It was late at night on July 27, 2017. The president and his GOP Senate majority leader, Mitch McConnell (R-Кентукки), were still one vote shy of the majority they would need to repeal the Affordable Care Act. John McCain, the war hero Trump had insulted ("He's not a war hero. He's a war hero because he was captured. I like people who weren't captured."), was the only senator whose position had not been made public. McCain never liked the Affordable Care Act, but he was a maverick. He disliked the closed-door process by which McConnell was ramming through repeal. Days before, he had disclosed that he had glioblastoma, a form of brain cancer that would ultimately take his life. As midnight approached and the vote neared, McCain was still publicly coy. "Wait for the show," he told reporters as he headed to the Senate floor. "Wait for the show."

And what a show it was. McCain approached Democratic leader Chuck Schumer of New York, who, according to reporters watching from the Senate Press Gallery, seemed pleased with their conversation. Then he talked with Texas Republican John Cornyn, a key McConnell deputy. Cornyn was described by observers as "dour" during the conversation. Vice President Mike Pence, in the chamber to cast the tiebreaking vote if needed, had a thirty-minute talk with McCain. Then Trump called McCain. This, in retrospect, seemed like a bad move. McCain had stood up to North Vietnamese torture. I doubt he was intimidated by Corpulent Corporal Bone Spurs.

Sure enough, when the moment of truth arrived, McCain strolled over to the clerk's table, stuck out his right arm—which had been permanently maimed by his torturers in Vietnam—and turned his thumb down. Democratic senators burst into applause before Schumer silenced them. It was over. With that dramatic gesture, McCain preserved the chief domestic accomplishment of the man who had defeated him for the presidency. He also preserved the rights of tens of millions of Americans to get health care if they have a preexisting condition.

But Trump is still at it. He won't rest until you've lost that right. He is so obsessed with repealing Obamacare and its protections for people with preexisting conditions that his Justice Department joined a lawsuit filed by a gang of GOP state attorneys general led by Texas attorney general Ken Paxton (R-Indicted for Fraud). As *Kaiser Health News* reported, it is rare, to say the least, for the federal government to go into a federal court and argue that a federal law be struck down. After all, the president swears an oath to "faithfully execute" the laws, and that doesn't mean execute as in the electric chair. The lawsuit, *Texas v. Azar*, seeks to toss out the entire Affordable Care Act. *But Paul, you say, didn't the Supreme Court already uphold the constitutionality of the Affordable Care Act in the landmark 2015 case of King v. Burwell?* Right you are. But a binding decision of the highest court in the land is nothing to these intrepid attorneys general. (I love using the plural of "attorney general" correctly. Makes me feel like I didn't waste all that money on law school tuition.) Despite the *Burwell* case, these Republicans are arguing that, since the Trump tax cut for the rich eliminated the tax penalty for those who do not carry health insurance, the individual mandate itself is unconstitutional, and that with it the whole law must go—including protection for people with preexisting conditions.

This matters. The Centers for Medicare and Medicaid Services (CMS) estimates that as many as 129 million non-elderly Americans have some sort of preexisting health condition. That's up to half of us. These range from cancer to asthma, diabetes to high blood pressure. Before Obamacare, those folks could be charged significantly higher premiums, could have had their benefits reduced, could have been forced to wait a long time before receiving coverage, and could have been denied health insurance altogether. Of course, as we age, the preexisting condition risk just increases. CMS estimated that up to 86 percent of Americans aged fifty-five to sixty-four have a preexisting condition, and that nearly a third of people who are in good health today will develop a preexisting condition before they reach sixty-five, when they can go on Medicare.

Here's how crazy the old system was. Before the ACA, according to the National Women's Law Center, "just being a woman could be considered a preexisting condition." Wait. What? Yep. As the NWLC notes, "insurance companies have denied women coverage for having a cesarean delivery or for seeking medical treatment for domestic or sexual violence." That's right. Having a C-section could be the basis of discrimination, as could being the victim of sexual assault or domestic violence.

For folks with a preexisting condition, Obamacare has been a godsend. No longer can insurance companies discriminate against you for the sin of being a woman or the crime of growing older. No longer can they cut you off, claiming you've reached your annual or lifetime limit of health care payments. ("Sorry, that's enough chemo for you, ma'am.") No longer are people locked into a job they hate, for fear of being denied coverage if they change employers. No wonder Obamacare is more popular now than ever. People have lived under it for a decade, and it is working. Approval of the ACA has jumped from a low of 33 percent in 2014 to a high of 55 percent in February 2020. When a policy as controversial as the Affordable Care Act climbs by 22 points in the polls as it is implemented, it is politically dangerous to wipe it out. Perhaps the increase in support is also because, for the Obama-haters, Obama is no longer president, so Obamacare is now just care.

More People Are Uninsured Under Trump

Before Obamacare, according to the Kaiser Family Foundation, more than 44 million Americans lacked health insurance. After the ACA, that number fell to fewer than 26.7 million—a historic low. The percentage of Americans who lacked health insurance had been stuck around 17 percent for years before the ACA. After it was fully implemented, the number dropped dramatically, to around 10 percent. Nearly 20 million Americans have health insurance today because of Obamacare. (Thanks, Obama.)

But a funny thing has happened under Trump. Not funny ha-ha, like Trump's hair. Funny strange, like his skin tone. Both the number and percentage of Americans without health insurance have gone up. As Trump has thrown sand in the gears of the ACA, some people have been hurt. The advertising budget for health care sign-up was cut a little. And by "a little" I mean 90 percent. The individual mandate, as I noted above, was eliminated in the 2017 Trump tax cut for the rich. This eliminated any penalty for those who chose not to have health insurance but instead relied on taxpayers to cover for them at the local public emergency room.

Trump also used his executive authority to allow for so-called skimpy health insurance plans—short-term plans that don't cover all of the required services under the ACA. They frequently fail to cover mental health care or maternity care or prescription drugs, for example. Some discriminate against older Americans or those with preexisting conditions. No wonder some health care advocates call them "junk insurance." Even the health insurance industry's lobbying group expressed concern about these shoddy policies, telling the *Washington Post*, "We remain concerned that consumers who rely on short-term plans for an extended time period will face high medical bills when they need care that isn't covered or exceeds their coverage limits." Harold Wimmer, of the American Lung Association, was even more blunt: "Lung disease patients need access to treatment to be able to breathe." Well, Harold, breathing is now apparently a preexisting condition.

The Trump assault on health care continues to this day. In January 2020, his administration announced new rules that would make it easier for states to turn Medicaid into block grants. This would cut Medicaid by placing a cap on how much a state spends on it, no matter the need. Currently Medicaid is an entitlement, which means that if you qualify, the program pays whatever is necessary for your treatment. God help you if you have an expensive accident or illness.

Trump's assault on your health care is having an effect. By the end of his first year in office, the number of uninsured stopped falling, as it had every year since Obamacare was fully in place. Under

Trump, the number of uninsured jumped by about a half-million people. Trump further undermined coverage through state waiver programs that made it harder for people to get Medicaid—these were programs that appeared to impose work requirements but actually just punished people for being poor and sick. By the end of Trump's second year in office, the uninsured rate had risen again, from 7.9 percent in 2017 to 8.5 percent in 2018—the first back-to-back increases in the uninsured since 2008–9, when we were in the Great Recession and the Affordable Care Act had not taken effect. And, as with everything under Trump, it is worse for people of color. While the uninsured rate is 5.4 percent for white people, it is 9.7 percent for African Americans and 17.8 percent for Hispanics. And the catastrophic job losses in the Trump/Corona crash have made the uninsured rate soar.

Rural Hospitals Are Closing Under Trump

You know that map that shows all the counties Trump carried in red, and all the Hillary counties in blue? The Trumpeteers love to show that off, often with a clever line like: "Impeach This." In point of fact, Trump did carry the overwhelming majority of counties: 2,626, to just 487 for Hillary. Of course, Hillary won more votes than counties, and in a real democracy, votes would be the sole determinant of victory. Many of my friends on the left point out that many of those counties are sparsely populated. "They have more cows than people," they sneer. And in many cases they're right. In fact, in nine states—states, mind you; not just counties—there are more cows than people: Oklahoma, Iowa, Idaho, Wyoming, Kansas, North Dakota, Montana, Nebraska, and South Dakota, in case it comes up on Trivia Night. Guess how many of those cow-states Trump won? Well, all of them, of course. He carried rural America by 61 percent to 34 percent—which almost perfectly mirrors the 60–34 drubbing he took in urban areas.

You'd think that a guy who so dominated rural America would actually enact policies that helped rural Americans. Instead, he has used them and abused them—especially when it comes to their health care.

As every rural American knows, one of the most critical local institutions is the hospital. When a buddy of mine got busted up in an accident on his ranch in West Texas, a twenty-five-bed rural hospital saved his life. He was lucky. That little hospital was only twenty-four miles from his ranch. If he had been in, say, Junction, in the Texas Hill Country, he might have had quite a wait for help to arrive. They have just one EMS worker and two ambulances to cover a 3,800-square-mile area. (Not sure why they need two ambulances if they have only one EMT, but what the heck.)

There is a crisis in rural health care. According to the National Rural Health Association, 121 rural hospitals have closed since 2010. Beyond that, 673 are vulnerable and could very well face collapse, which would mean that more than one-third of all the rural hospitals in America would be gone. The year 2019 was the worst for rural hospitals in a long time, with 19 going under. The NRHA estimates that "11.7 million patients will lose direct access to care while local economies suffer." And "seventy-seven percent of rural counties in the United States are Primary Care Health Professional Shortage Areas while nine percent have no physicians at all." The Chartis Center for Rural Health estimates that as many as one in four rural hospitals operating today has the early-warning signs that it may be at risk of closing.

You would think that a president who has the overwhelming support of rural Americans would be on this like ugly on an ape. Like white on rice. Like, umm, spray tan on a con man. You would be wrong. In his 6,400-word 2020 State of the Union address, he never mentioned the crisis of rural health care. In fact, if you listened to that speech, you wouldn't know rural America ever existed, much less the fact that 60 million people live there—and most of them voted for

Trump. The Dear Leader gave his most loyal voters a passing phrase about rural broadband—okay, we all want farmers to have access to high-quality porn. He offered another drive-by, claiming farmers and ranchers would benefit from his new US-Mexico-Canada free trade deal. That was it. Nothing more. So much for the vast majority of those 2,626 counties won by Trump.

He spent more time talking about China and Venezuela than about rural America. And not one word about the 11.7 million facing the prospect of losing their lifeline: their rural hospital.

Maybe Trump didn't talk about the crisis in rural health care because he doesn't like the solution. Chartis estimates that rural hospitals in states that expanded Medicaid as part of Obamacare have a 62 percent greater likelihood of surviving. (Thanks, Obama.) The states that have seen the greatest number of rural hospitals go under—Texas, Oklahoma, Georgia, Tennessee, Alabama, and Missouri—have this in common: none of them opted to extend Medicaid under Obamacare. Here's why extending Medicaid helps rural hospitals—and bear with me, this is technical: *poor people can't pay their hospital bills*. Medicaid pays the hospital bills for poor people. Thus rural hospitals in states that didn't take the Obamacare Medicaid deal have lots more uncompensated care, which is what the propeller-heads call poor people who can't pay their hospital bills. The National Rural Health Association is also lobbying against cuts in Medicare, which it notes hurt rural hospitals.

One more time—and this is going to be on the exam: Who supports cuts to Medicare and Medicaid? You betchum, Red Ryder: Donald Jaybird Trump.

How Democrats Should Run on Health Care

I realize that this chapter has a lot of statistics; Democrats need to animate them. They need to personalize this, since no issue is more personal than health care. They need to remember the old saying that "facts tell, but stories sell." Some Democrats talk about the millions of people who lack health care, but can't name one such person. Barack Obama and Bill Clinton would tell you the story of one, and you would know that they understood the challenges faced by every one of those millions of people. Storytelling is not a gift, it's a discipline. Democrats must develop that discipline.

Here's a story for you: Donald Trump has never had to worry about whether he could afford health care. By the time he was three years old, his father was paying little Donald $200,000 a year in today's dollars. By the time he graduated from college, his allowance was $1 million a year.

On this issue as on so many, he is out of touch with real Americans. And yet he has used his superpower—diversion—to distract us from a record on health care that should alone be enough to sink the *Trumptanic*.

Health care is the number one issue on voters' minds. Not Trump's stupid wall or his rants about the media. Eight in ten Americans in a February 2020 poll by *Politico* and Harvard's T. H. Chan School of Public Health say that "taking steps to lower the cost of health care" is extremely or very important to them. The issue cuts across parties: 89 percent of Democrats put practical concerns about the cost of health care first, and 76 percent of Republicans agree with them. Along the same lines, reducing the cost of prescription drugs is rated as important by 75 percent of voters.

Voters, however, are pragmatic, not ideological. The sweeping Medicare for All proposal ranks eleventh on the poll's list of twenty-two top issues, significantly behind the more modest public option, whereby people could keep their private health care if they want to, but have the right to buy into the Medicare system. This buy-in option, by the way, earns the support of 43 percent of Republicans. If they are skeptical of Medicare for All, voters are downright hostile to Trump's attempt to gut Obamacare, with a mere 37 percent supporting it. (Let me remind you again that 45 percent of Republicans would support Trump shooting someone on Fifth Avenue, so 37 percent overall support for his attack on ACA is pretty low.)

Knowing this, Democrats should humanize and personalize the health care issue. Too often they speak in systemic terms: cost containment, deficit reduction, enrollment levels. They need to, as we say in Texas, "put the jam on the lower shelf, where the little folks can reach it."

That's what the nonprofit Protect Our Care does. It jumps on a bus—called Care Force One, get it?—and takes its message to the people. Or, rather, it lets the people take the message to the media. Protect Our Care shines a light on people whose lives and health have been improved by decent health care through the Affordable Care Act, Medicaid, Medicare, and other vital programs. Here are just a few of the folks who have shared their stories with Protect Our Care. These are the stories Democrats should be telling:

- Laura Packard, of Denver. Laura stayed up late to watch that midnight Senate vote on the Trump effort to repeal the Affordable Care Act. When John McCain gave that thumbs-down, she danced around her home and accidentally kicked the garbage can, cutting her toe. "Bleeding around my kitchen," she wrote in an op-ed, "I didn't even care. It meant, at least for a moment, that I could breathe again." You see, Laura has cancer. Or, rather, she *had* cancer. Hodgkin's lymphoma. Stage 4. There is no stage 5. She is in remission, thank God—and, she says, thanks to the Affordable Care Act. She doesn't mince words. "If I had received my cancer diagnosis before 2014, that would have been my story. I would be bankrupt or dead." For her, that vote, that single vote—cast by a warrior fighting his own battle with cancer—saved her life.

- Erin Gabriel. Erin is the mother of three children with disabilities. She and her family live in Beaver County, Pennsylvania (home of football legend Joe Namath, whom I love, even though he didn't go to the University of Texas). Erin's kids are fourteen, eleven, and nine. Her older two have autism, and her youngest has a host of challenges.

Along with her bilateral sensory neural hearing loss, Erin's youngest child has been diagnosed with, among other challenges, a heart murmur, macrocephaly, hypothyroidism, anemia, potential bone marrow failure, epilepsy, low-functioning immune system, and encephalopathy. Erin describes the experience of seeing her little girl being diagnosed with increasingly dire conditions as "terrifying. Every cold, every common childhood germ, could send her to the hospital. And every one of these things is considered a preexisting condition—any one of these many, many conditions she has could have denied her health care." But Erin never gave up, and neither did her daughter. They have private health insurance, but it doesn't cover all of her daughter's needs. In Pennsylvania, Medicaid does. Her daughter has been outfitted with hearing aids, a wheelchair, a speech-generating device, custom-made braces for her feet and wrists, and a seizure-monitoring device. "All of them," Erin says, "paid for by a combination of private insurance and Medicaid." And all of which could be denied to her if we didn't have the protections of the ACA.

As you can imagine, this has been a handful as well as a blessing. In addition to traveling, going to the theater, and exploring the outdoors with her kids, Erin is the state chapter leader of Little Lobbyists, a parent-led organization that advocates for the health care of children with complex medical needs and disabilities. "No family," she says, "should have to decide between paying their rent and paying for their child's medicine." If the ACA is tossed out, as Trump wants, and Medicaid is cut, as Trump wants, she says, "there is simply no way we would be able to afford any of this."

Today, Erin reports that her daughter is off all pharmaceuticals. The seizures are under control. She walks in the woods and rides bikes with other children. "She has a small army of friends," Erin says as her daughter plays nearby. "She is happy and thriving, and she is a shining example of everything that can go right in the system . . . My daughter's life should not be a partisan issue. No family, no child, should ever be put in that position. Yet here we are. When Republicans talk about cutting Medicaid, they are talking about cutting the therapies that have given her life and independence. When Republicans talk about repealing the ACA, it means they are shutting the doors of the hospital in the faces of kids like my daughter."

- Jeff Jeans, of Sedona, Arizona. Jeff is self-employed, living the dream in one of the most beautiful places in America. He and his wife had insurance, or at least they thought they did. When his wife got sick, they found out they had junk insurance and wound up paying thousands of dollars out of pocket for her treatment. Jeff knew he was in trouble when he learned he had throat cancer. Jeff was a Republican. He hated Obamacare, or so he thought. But with cancer as a preexisting condition, he soon learned that the law was a lifesaver. He got insurance—good insurance this time. He got treatment for his cancer, and later confronted then–House Speaker Paul Ryan (R-WI), demanding to know why he would support repealing the ACA without a substitute that would protect people like him. Ryan yammered for a while, but Jeff interrupted him. All he wanted to do was publicly thank Barack Obama for the ACA, he said, because if it had not been for that law, he would be dead.

Democrats need to tell stories, not rattle off statistics or prattle on about their precious position papers. They ought to act like people's lives are at stake, because they are. Too often Trump has turned politics and government into a reality show, an operatic clash in which drama queens scream at each other. Politics and government are not a reality show, and they're not a s—t show. This is deadly serious. Trump doesn't want Democrats to focus on the real-life, real-world consequences of his policies. So he uses his superpower: diversion. He distracts our attention with stunts and crimes and bigoted tweets. And while people like me react to those outrages, Trump uses the smoke screen he's generated to gut health care, even for people who voted for him. Democrats cannot let him get away with it. They need to fight like hell to turn the camera away from Trump's antics and onto folks like Laura and Erin and Jeff.

CHAPTER 10

IT'S *STILL* THE ECONOMY, STUPID

Donald Jaded Trump said this in his 2020 State of the Union address: "I am thrilled to report to you tonight that our economy is the best it has ever been." Within weeks the stock market had its biggest selloff since the crash of 2008. As Rick Perry would say, "Oops."

Glenn Kessler of the *Washington Post* reports that Trump has made this claim or one like it 260 times. And each one of those 260 times, his claim was not true. For example, while low, unemployment was a lot lower (one full percentage point) in 1953, which was during the high-tax Eisenhower era. Growth has been anemic, never topping 3 percent per year—a far cry from the Clinton growth rates of 4.5 percent in 1997, 4.5 percent in 1998, and 4.7 percent in 1999.

Even as the economy is reeling from the crash brought on by social distancing, it is important to analyze Trump's economic record from before the crash. Democrats must not allow him to paint too rosy a picture of his pre-coronavirus economic policies. Trump boasted of job growth: "Since my election, we have created 7 million new jobs." Well, first, as Kessler points out, it's a bit weird to claim credit for jobs created since his *election*, since Barack Obama was still president for two months. Beyond that—and this must drive Trump crazy—job growth in Obama's last three years was stronger than job growth under Trump's first three: 227,000 per month under Obama versus 191,000 per month under Trump. Such tiny, tiny baby-like job numbers. Nothing close to the large, manly job numbers Obama put up.

"This is a blue-collar boom." Oh yeah? Then why, as Kessler notes, was manufacturing in a technical recession even before the coronavirus crash? Before anyone had heard of COVID-19, job growth had slowed or died in construction, mining, transportation, and other classic blue-collar industries.

As with one of Donald Trump's failed casinos, his economic boasts masked underlying trouble—especially for the middle class. Whereas inflation-adjusted average weekly wages for production and nonsupervisory workers—middle-class working people—have increased 2.4 percent since Trump took office, that is a far cry from the 6.4 percent they went up under President Clinton, or the 4 percent they rose under President Obama.

If the economy was booming, as Trump claims, why didn't working people—the folks he claims to fight for—see more of the gains? Because the real gains have gone to corporations. The St. Louis Fed, analyzing data over decades, wrote in 2018, "Never have corporate profits outgrown employee compensation so clearly and for so long."

Obama Saved the World for $832 Billion; Trump Spent Twice That for What?

Trump's most important legislative accomplishment is his tax cut for corporate America. They called it the Tax Cuts and Jobs Act of 2017, but it was really just a bait and switch.

I'll say this for the Trump corporate tax cut, though: it is big. Or, as Trump would say, "Yuuuuge!" It is the biggest corporate tax cut in American history—by a lot. When the bill was before Congress, White House economic adviser and former Goldman Sachs chief Gary Cohn said, "The most excited group out there are big CEOs."

I can see why. According to the nonpartisan Congressional Budget Office, the ten-year cost of the Trump tax cut is $1.9 trillion.

That's "trillion." With a *t*. To put that into perspective, the 2009 stimulus package pushed by President Obama cost $832 billion over ten years. That bill was designed to respond to the most dire, dangerous economic crisis the world had faced since the Great Depression. The Obama stimulus saved 5.3 million Americans from poverty. It created 1.6 million jobs per year for four years. It put cash directly into the pockets of working people, who in turn spent it, which in turn stimulated the economy. Our national economic output was 2 to 3 percent higher because of the Obama stimulus package. The infrastructure part of the package, expertly overseen by Joe Biden, repaired or replaced 2,700 bridges. It fixed up 42,000 miles of road, modernized water systems, paid for 12,000 buses, subway cars, vans, and other equipment for mass transit, helped our schools, invested in renewable energy, and subsidized broadband internet, especially in rural areas.

So, for $832 billion, President Obama saved the world economy. He rescued the middle class. He invested in making us healthier, smarter, cleaner, safer, and more energy-independent. It was a ton of money, but it was put to good use. If you ask me, it was worth every penny. (He also used the TARP bank bailout money to save the auto industry, which counts as a great investment.)

Congressional Republicans, of course, squealed like a pig stuck under a gate. It cost too much, the Republicans said. It explodes the deficit, they whined. It's big government, they claimed. Until Trump came along. As someone who helped President Clinton balance the budget, I think I have the credibility to say this: Republicans only care about the deficit when Democrats are investing in poor and middle-class Americans. When they get in power, they spend like it's someone else's money—because it is.

Keep that number in mind: $832 billion. That's Obama's economic rescue package. And compare it to Trump's: $1.9 trillion corporate tax cut. Trump and the Republican Congress spent nearly twice as much of your money as Obama had—and, again, Obama was facing an economic catastrophe. Trump was facing, well, a good economy in 2017. Because of Obama's skill, Trump inherited an economy that was firing on all cylinders. In the days after Trump's Electoral College victory, the bean counters at Standard & Poor's described it this way: "President-elect Trump will inherit a much stronger economy than his predecessor did. Largely forgotten in all the rhetoric and fanfare of the campaign is the fact that data show the world's largest economy continuing to expand at a reasonably good pace."

Obama inherited an economy that was hemorrhaging jobs—with as many as 700,000 lost per month. He turned that around and created 15.6 million jobs in the private sector alone. As Obama handed the keys to the Oval Office over to Trump, the Dow Jones Industrial Average had hit a record high. So had the Nasdaq and the S&P 500. Incomes were up; consumer spending was strong. "This is an economy that's pretty close to full employment," Luke Bartholomew of Aberdeen Asset Management told *Politico*.

In 2009, we had a big crisis: the Great Recession. Obama had a big answer: $832 billion in stimulus. Trump came in, things were good, no crisis. But he spent $1.9 trillion. On what? Corporate profits.

That's what the Trump tax cut was designed to boost: corporate profits. Now, I don't think that is necessarily a bad thing. I am not a socialist. America needs a thriving private sector, and many smart and sensible people were saying that we needed to modernize our corporate tax system. But when you throw $1.9 trillion at a problem, it had better be a whale of a problem.

Except there wasn't a problem with corporate profits. Far from it. As CNN reported at the end of 2017—before the Trump tax cut took effect—"Corporate America caught fire in 2017, hauling in fatter profits than ever before." John Lynch, chief investment strategist at LPL Financial, told CNN, "Profits are the story of the year." CNN went on to report that "2017's profit growth wasn't really driven by

Washington." That's right, since the Trump corporate tax cut had not yet taken effect. Some might argue that the knowledge that corporate taxes were coming down helped touch off the boom in corporate profits. Perhaps that was part of it. But earnings were strong, and China, Europe, and Latin America were all either strong or stable. The world had pulled out of the Great Recession and was finally booming again. Thanks, Obama.

Get this: with corporate profits at a record high, Trump and his fellow Republicans spent $1.9 trillion of your money to cut taxes on—wait for it—corporate profits. Perhaps "cut" is too gentle a word—like calling strip-mining "digging." Trump and his pals cut the corporate income tax rate almost in half, from 35 percent to 21 percent. Guess what—and bear with me, because this is complicated—after they cut corporate taxes, revenue from corporate taxes collapsed. I know. Who could have seen that coming? In just one quarter, the amount of revenue Washington received from corporate taxes fell from $264 billion per year to $149 billion per year. As a share of the American economy, corporate taxes fell to their lowest level in history. In the early 1950s—you know, when America was great—corporate taxes were more than 7 percent of the US economy. After the Trump tax cut, they fell a bit: to 0.77 percent.

I have seen my share of Trump rallies on TV, and I have never seen a blue-collar, MAGA-hat-wearing guy ever call for cutting taxes for corporate America by $1.9 trillion.

In his campaign, Trump pledged to raise taxes on "hedge fund guys that are making a lot of money that aren't paying anything in taxes." He later said, "The hedge fund guys are getting away with murder. They're paying nothing and it's ridiculous. I want to save the middle class . . . The hedge fund guys didn't build this country. These are guys that shift paper around and they get lucky."

A lot of voters bought it. His onetime friend, supporter, and (briefly) White House aide Anthony Scaramucci wrote a book calling him the "blue-collar president." It was all a con. The "hedge fund guys," as Trump calls them, kept their indefensible loophole, called carried interest, whereby they pay around 20 percent in taxes. If you're a firefighter and you're married to a teacher, the two of you are probably taxed at a higher rate than the hedge fund guys are.

How can that be? Well, hedge fund managers aren't actually the principal beneficiaries. Private equity managers are, as well as venture capital firms. Oh, and real estate managers.

Wait. What?

Yep, the Trump tax bill was a boon to real estate moguls. He may be a buffoon and a crook, The Donald: sure can run a con.

CEOs Got the Gold Mine, Workers Got the Shaft

Corporations took their windfall and invested it in their people. They boosted wages, improved benefits, shared profits.

Kidding. No, a great many of them took their Trump treasure and put it into dividends and stock buybacks. This makes their shareholders richer, which makes their shareholders happy. But just 10 percent of Americans own 84 percent of all stocks, so the money didn't trickle very far down. One estimate, by Just Capital, found that 6 percent of the gargantuan tax cut ever made it into the hands of working men and women, boosting their pay by $6.21 a week. That's it. One six-pack a week. Meanwhile, Amazon, the corporation run by the wealthiest man on the face of the earth, paid zero dollars in taxes on more than $11 billion in profits in 2018.

Well, that's not exactly, precisely accurate. Amazon paid zero in taxes—*and* received a $129 million tax rebate. That's right. If you bought this book, the couple of bucks you paid in sales tax is more than Amazon paid in taxes—$129 million more.

To be clear: I don't blame corporate America. It is their job to maximize profit and minimize tax. I blame Donald Trump and the Republicans for throwing $1.9 trillion down the drain when there are real crises facing the country.

Like, for example, the long, slow death of the American middle class. Most Americans do not have a college degree. If you are part of that majority, the American Dream has been slipping away for most of your life. The nonpartisan Congressional Research Service took a look at wages over the last thirty-nine years. Its findings may not shock you, but they should trouble you nonetheless.

If you're in the top 10 percent, your wages have risen. We already knew this. And, of course, the higher you are on that economic pyramid, the greater your gains. The top 1 percent far outpaces the 9 percent below them, and so it is with the top one-tenth of 1 percent, and on and on.

But if you have a high school degree or less, your wages have declined in the last thirty-nine years. A lot. If you're in the middle of the middle class—the 50th percentile of earners—you're making 12.3 percent *less* than you were making in 1979, adjusted for inflation. Think about that. You've been busting your tail for decades, and what do you have to show for it? A paycheck that in real terms is 12.3 percent lower today than when the Bee Gees were topping the charts and Jimmy Carter was in the White House.

If you are among the people, as Bill Clinton described them, "who do the work, pay the taxes, raise the kids, and play by the rules," if you are among "the hardworking Americans who make up our forgotten middle class" but you lack a college degree, the American Dream is not merely a dream deferred. It is a dream denied. And we remember what the poet told us about a dream deferred. Sometimes it explodes.

Americans with a high school education or less—18 percent of the electorate—voted for Trump by a 5-point margin. But when you disaggregate by race and gender, you see that high school–educated white women preferred Trump by 27 percent. And high school–educated white men—the very heart of the Trump vote—well, 71 percent of them voted for their blue-collar billionaire.

As we discussed in chapter 5, Trump played on their resentment like the demagogue that he is. He blamed Mexicans, trade deals, global elites. He railed against political correctness. He . . . well, let's hear from him. This is the text of his "Closing Argument"—the ad he aired the night before the election. It is perhaps the most powerful summation of the argument Trump was making to voters:

> Our movement is about replacing a failed and corrupt political establishment with a new government controlled by you, the American people. This establishment has trillions of dollars at stake in this election. For those who control the levers of power in Washington, and for the global special interests, they partner with these people that don't have your good in mind. The political establishment that is trying to stop us is the same group responsible for our disastrous trade deals, massive illegal immigration, and economic and foreign policies that have bled our country dry. The political establishment has brought about the destruction of our factories and our jobs, as they flee to Mexico, China, and other countries all around the world. There's a global power structure that is responsible for the economic decisions that have robbed our working class, stripped our country of its wealth, and put that money into the pockets of a handful of large corporations and political entities. The only thing that can stop this corrupt machine is you. The only force strong enough to save our country is us. The only people brave enough to vote out this corrupt establishment is you, the American people. I'm doing this for the people and for the movement, and we will take back this country for you, and we will make America great again.

Those words—accompanied by images of the Federal Reserve, George Soros, Goldman Sachs CEO Lloyd Blankfein, and of course Barack Obama, Hillary Clinton, and others—are a dark and dangerous stew of resentment and rage. Perhaps it struck you, as it did me back then, as borderline psychotic conspiracy claptrap; all that talk about "the political establishment" and "the global power structure." But then again, I was lucky. Unlike so many guys my age in Missouri City, Texas, in the seventies, I went to college. I went to law school. I worked in the White House. I got a prestigious post at Georgetown and a show on CNN. It worked for me. And maybe that's why I was blind to the appeal Trump was making to folks whose wages are 12 percent lower than when they were pimply-faced teenagers thirty years ago.

Trump took people's pain and weaponized it. Not, however, to make the lives of working-class Americans better. Instead, here's what he did:

- Cut taxes for corporate America by $1.9 trillion

- Opposed an increase in the minimum wage

- Is in federal court trying to allow insurance companies to cancel coverage for people with preexisting conditions

- Cut food stamps and farm subsidies

- Helped GM pay zero taxes as it closed its Lordstown, Ohio, plant and moved it to Mexico

- Put the head of Goldman Sachs in charge of the National Economic Council and another Goldman guy in charge of Treasury

- Took billions out of workers' pockets by gutting regulations that require companies to pay overtime to those who put in extra hours

- Is allowing the use of a pesticide that his own scientists say causes birth defects

- Wants to kick millions of working people off Medicaid

- Put a Harvard lawyer on the Supreme Court who ruled that a company was allowed to fire a driver who left his truck when it was stuck in a blizzard rather than freeze to death.

Democrats need to fight back. They need to go to those blue-collar voters and make the case that Trump has betrayed them, and that Democrats will fight for them.

Infrastructure Weak

In November 2015, Hillary Clinton went to Boston's historic Faneuil Hall and outlined a five-year, $275 billion infrastructure plan. "To build a strong economy for our future, we must start by building strong infrastructure today," Clinton said. "I want our cities to be in the forefront of cities anywhere in the world. I want our workers to be the most competitive and productive in the world. I want us, once again, to think big and look up, beyond the horizon of what is possible in America." Ever the policy wonk, Hillary had done her homework. Of course, her plan called for repairing roads and re-building bridges. But it also had a twenty-first-century sensibility: universal broadband and a clean energy grid. She proposed a federal infrastructure bank, which would leverage $25 billion in federal seed money to attract an additional $225 in private capital, making the entire plan a half-trillion-dollar investment. On her website was this commitment: "She'll work to pass her infrastructure plan in her first 100 days of office, as part of a comprehensive agenda to create the next generation of good-paying jobs."

The next summer, fresh from his nominating convention in Cleveland, Donald Jerkface Trump traveled to Ashburn, Virginia, and went Hillary one better. Actually, half a billion better. He saw her half-billion-dollar infrastructure plan and raised it by another half billion. Although he lacked Hillary's specifics, Trump was trying to out-progressive the progressives. The old guard Republicans clutched their pearls: a former George W. Bush economist worried about adding a trillion dollars to the deficit. The American Enterprise Institute, a conservative think tank, noted that it preferred tolls as a means of paying for roads and bridges. The progressive confusion and conservative whining combined to make it an effective issue for Trump. After all, he boasted, if he knew one thing it was how to build.

Flash-forward to his unlikely victory. During the transition I was in touch with some of the leading Democrats in the Senate. One of them told me that if Trump began his presidency with an infrastructure package like the one he talked about on the campaign trail, he'd have to be with him. It had the potential of being a political masterstroke. A large percentage of congressional Democrats—maybe even half—would have signed on to a trillion-dollar Trump infrastructure plan. The other half would have stood in solidarity with the resistance movement. The Republicans, as we have seen, would kowtow to Trump no matter what. He had the potential of creating a center-right alliance that would create jobs that pay well, repair our crumbling infrastructure, and deeply divide his opposition.

Democrats needn't have worried. Instead of building bridges, literal or figurative, Trump started his presidency with lies about his inauguration crowd size, attacks on the CIA and FBI, and an all-out assault on Obamacare. From then on, "Infrastructure Week" became a punchline, a catchall phrase for every time Trump went off the rails. Candid Trump advisers told the *New York Times*—on background, of course; I said they were candid, but they're also cowardly—that "the original Infrastructure Week was never really about what was advertised . . . It began as a public relations stunt to distract from [fired FBI director James] Comey's testimony" on Capitol Hill as part of the Russia investigation. Nancy Pelosi saw through it from the jump. She called it "little more than a Trojan horse."

The lack of investment in our nation's muscle and bones, like the collapse of bipartisanship, is one of the tragedies of the Trump presidency. The need for infrastructure work remains pressing. The

American Society of Civil Engineers gives our infrastructure a D+.
The ASCE estimates that US infrastructure needs $2 trillion in new
investment. Whereas in 1930—during the Great Depression—our
country invested 4.2 percent of its GDP in infrastructure, by 2016
that percentage had dwindled to just 2.5 percent. The cost of that
disinvestment is colossal:

- Eight hundred fifty water mains rupture every day.

- Thirty-eight percent of all the bridges in America are more than
  fifty years old and need "repair, replacement or significant reha-
  bilitation"; 9.1 percent of bridges are structurally deficient. Think
  about that next time you're driving across one.

- Forty-four percent of the major roads in this country are in poor
  or mediocre condition.

- Drivers spend $129 billion a year on car repairs that they would
  not need if the roads were worth a dang.

- Our airports are so overstressed, according to the ASCE, that "24
  of the top 30 major airports may soon experience 'Thanksgiving-peak traffic volume' at least one day every week." (Before the
  Trump/Corona crash, of course.)

- There are 90,580 dams in America. Their average age is fifty-six.
  The ASCE designates 2,170 dams as "deficient high-hazard potential." Damn.

- Most of our electrical infrastructure dates from the 1950s and
  '60s. It was built to last fifty years. Do the math.

- Let's talk about poop. Plumbing and sanitation, it seems to me,
  are the bedrock of civilization. Ever since Alexander Cumming
  invented the first flushing mechanism in 1775 (no, it wasn't
  Thomas Crapper), we have been spared the panicky run to the
  outhouse or the ignominious emptying of the chamber pot. With

56 million additional new users expected to be potty-trained over the next two decades, engineers say we need at least $271 billion invested in wastewater systems to avoid disaster.

There is so much more to do: ports that need dredging, parks that need repairing, levees that need reinforcing. Not to mention broadband; there is still a terrible digital divide. Trump's inability to make progress on infrastructure has been a massive failure. The need is great, money is still relatively cheap to borrow, and too many people need good jobs. We should have known better. Donald Trump sold himself as a builder; he can't even build his stupid wall.

"I Am the King of Debt"

"The time to fix the roof," President John F. Kennedy said, "is when the sun is shining." He said that in his 1962 State of the Union address. The budget he introduced after that speech had a deficit of $5 billion—0.7 percent of GDP. Today, under President Donald Jabberwocky Trump, the deficit in the proposed 2021 budget is well over $1 trillion—about 5 percent of GDP. And that was before the Trump/Corona crash necessitated massive deficit.

This profligate spending while the macroeconomic numbers were relatively strong will make paying back the Coronavirus deficit spending all the more difficult. Trump should have paid down the deficit while times were good. That would have left us in a stronger fiscal position when the virus closed the economy.

Not only is his annual deficit now $1 trillion plus, Trump is running up the national debt to frightening levels. Former labor secretary Robert Reich says a sensible way to look at debt is in its ratio to GDP. Trump, he notes, has increased the ratio of debt to GDP to a modern record of more than 105 percent. (By contrast, President Clinton balanced the budget, generated a large surplus, and left his successor with a debt-to-GDP ratio of just 54 percent.) Trump did this not to rescue the world economy, as Obama did, and not to re-cover from 9/11, as George W. Bush did. He did it because he does not give a ripsnort about the future.

Think I'm being hyperbolic? According to the *Daily Beast*, when Trump aides briefed him in 2017 about a looming "hockey stick"–shaped spike in the national debt, Trump noted that it would not happen until after a potential second term for him. "Yeah, but I won't be here," he said.

How Democrats Should Run on This

As populists!

This is not difficult, people. Turn all Trump's economic embel-lishment against him. Trump, like all incumbents, faces a challenge: he must defend his record, on the one hand, but also make a future-oriented appeal for a second term, on the other. Wait. I almost for-got: he's Trump. All he will do is boast and brag and bloviate.

The coronavirus crash, as we discussed in chapter 2, puts a spot-light on the two parties' priorities. Trump is for himself and his fellow swells, the Forgotten One Percent. He isn't a "blue-collar billionaire," he's a con man, a flimflam artist. When times were good, he looted the Treasury for himself and his wealthy pals. And when the crash came, his priorities were bailouts for the powerful. It was congressio-nal Democrats who fought for benefits for working men and women.

Democrats must speak to the pain and the frustration of the mid-dle class and the poor. Show folks that you get it. Take on powerful interests who align themselves with Trump because he lines their pockets. As with so many issues, personalize, humanize, localize. Don't bury us in position papers; tell stories.

One of the most powerful messages in American politics is: he's on our side. Trump was able to convince far too many working-class Americans that he was. Go right at that big lie and deflate it. By now

I shouldn't have to say this, but don't attack Trump's voters. Convert those you can, then respectfully disagree with those you can't.

Put the Trump tax cut for the rich on trial (and never call it anything other than that). Make the case that Trump is of the rich, by the rich, and for the rich. You'll be pushing on an open door. A Pew Research Center survey found that, even during the so-called boom, the overwhelming majority of Americans said "today's economy is helping people who are already wealthy." Sixty-nine percent say that—including 63 percent of Republicans.

People think the Trump economy is rigged; that the Trump deck is stacked; that the Trump game is fixed. Why? *Because it is.* Maybe you could try saying something like this:

The overriding goal for America is more prosperity, meaning cheaper consumer goods. But is that still true? Does anyone still believe that cheaper iPhones, or more Amazon deliveries of plastic garbage from China, are going to make us happy? They haven't so far. A lot of Americans are drowning in stuff. And yet drug addiction and suicide are depopulating large parts of the country. Anyone who thinks the health of a nation can be summed up in GDP is an idiot.

The goal for America is both simpler and more elusive than mere prosperity. It's happiness. There are a lot of ingredients in being happy: Dignity. Purpose. Self-control. Independence. Above all, deep relationships with other people. Those are the things that you want for your children. They're what our leaders should want for us, and would want if they cared.

But our leaders don't care. We are ruled by mercenaries who feel no long-term obligation to the people they rule. They're day traders. Substitute teachers. They're just passing through. They have no skin in this game, and it shows. They can't solve our problems. They don't even bother to understand our problems.

Under our current system, an American who works for a salary pays about twice the taxrate as someone who's living off inherited money and doesn't work at all. We tax capital at half of what we tax labor. It's a sweet deal if you work in finance, as many of our rich people do.

Our leaders rarely mention any of this. They tell us our multitiered tax code is based on the principles of the free market. Please. It's based on laws that the Congress passed, laws that companies lobbied for in order to increase their economic advantage. It worked well for those people. They did increase their economic advantage. But for everyone else, it came at a big cost. Unfairness is profoundly divisive. When you favor one child over another, your kids don't hate you. They hate each other.

That happens in countries, too. It's happening in ours, probably by design. Divided countries are easier to rule. And nothing divides us like the perception that some people are getting special treatment. In our country, some people definitely are getting special treatment. Republicans should oppose that with everything they have.

What kind of country do you want to live in? A fair country. A decent country. A cohesive country. A country whose leaders don't accelerate the forces of change purely for their own profit and amusement. A country you might recognize when you're old.

Do you know who said that? Who uttered this cri de coeur?

Elizabeth Warren? Nope.

Bernie Sanders? Uh-uh.

Andrew Yang? Sorry.

Tucker Carlson. Yes, Tucker Fox News Carlson.

My old sparring partner from *Crossfire* and I have debated well over a thousand times. He is, to my mind, wrong about pretty much everything—but he is still my friend. We share a history but not an ideology. And yet when he delivered those words in 2019, they rang true to me. I think Tucker's social and cultural views are, well, eccentric, to put it mildly. But if a guy who talks on the phone with his buddy Donald Trump can deliver such a devastating indictment of the Trump economy, then by Jove, Democrats can as well.

CHAPTER 11

CLIMATE CHANGE

Is It Hot in Here, or Is It Just Trump?

More Backward Than the Flat Earthers

The Republican Party is, my friend the journalist Ron Brownstein has noted, the only major political party in any democracy that thoroughly dismisses climate science. As Eileen Claussen of C2ES (formerly the Pew Center on Global Climate Change) told Brownstein, there is "no party-wide view like this anywhere in the world that I am aware of." The science on climate change is settled. To deny it is akin to believing the earth is flat.

Wait. Breaking News: The Flat Earth Society actually believes in the science behind climate change. I am not kidding. In 2018, the society issued a statement on the matter. It said, "Certainly, it would be nothing short of irresponsible to question something with so much overwhelming evidence behind it, and something that threatens us so directly as a species."

When the Flat Earth Society is on the cutting edge of science while you spent your life lying about graduating first in your class, the intellectual scales may not be tipped in your favor. In defense of the president, climate denial by Republicans predates the ascendance of Donald Jackhammer Trump. But Trump has taken a party that was in the Neolithic age and dragged it back to the Paleolithic age. On a November afternoon in 2012, he tapped out this beauty:

Donald J. Trump
@realDonaldTrump

The concept of global warming was created by and for the Chinese in order to make U.S. manufacturing non-competitive.

2:15 PM * 6 Nov 2012

When he was running for president and Hillary Clinton and Bernie Sanders called him on it, Trump gave a classic Trump answer:

1. Claim you were joking.
2. Repeat the charge you just disavowed.

Watch: "I often joke that this is done for the benefit of China. Obviously, I joke. But this is done for the benefit of China, because China does not do anything to help climate change. They burn everything you could burn; they couldn't care less." As the Poynter Institute's PolitiFact investigation noted, Trump frequently uses the word "hoax" regarding climate change, a charge PolitiFact rated as "Pants on Fire." For example, at a 2015 rally in South Carolina, Trump said, "Obama's talking about all of this with the global warming and . . . a lot of it's a hoax. It's a hoax. I mean, it's a money-making industry, okay? It's a hoax, a lot of it."

Again and again and again he repeats that word, knowing that repetition of simple phrases is a very effective communication strategy. You may hate it—and I do, too—but there is no denying the effect of Trump's repeating that one word over and over and linking it to climate change. Here are a few tweets that PolitiFact cited:

Donald J. Trump
@realDonaldTrump

NBC News just called it the great freeze — coldest weather in years. Is our country still spending money on the GLOBAL WARMING HOAX?

6:48 PM * 25 Jan 2014

Donald J. Trump
@realDonaldTrump

Snowing in Texas and Louisiana, record setting temperatures throughout the country and beyond. Global warming is an expensive hoax!

1:27 AM * 29 Jan 2014

Donald J. Trump
@realDonaldTrump

Give me clean, beautiful and healthy air — not the same old climate change (global warming) bullshit! I am tired of hearing this nonsense.

1:44 AM * 29 Jan 2014

Excuse the language on that last one. I have a potty mouth myself, so I don't judge Trump on that score.

The Fossilized Views of Republicans

As the science on climate change has become more certain, as experts have become nearly unanimous, opinions of Americans have moved with them. In the two decades between 1999 and 2018, according to polling by the Yale Program on Climate Change Communication and the George Mason University's Center for Climate Change Communication, belief in climate science has increased across nearly all demographic groups. As NBC News reported, "more than 60 percent of whites, Hispanics and African Americans believe more needs to be done" to combat climate change. Similarly, more than 50 percent of people in cities, suburbs, and rural areas all agree.

Same with parties. Well, almost. As NBC reported on the study: "Among Democrats, 71 percent say climate change is an urgent problem. That is a 42-point increase since 1999. For independent voters, 47 percent say they want action taken on climate change, a figure that is up 22 points since 1999."

But—and there's always a big "but" when you're dealing with Trump—the numbers among Republicans haven't moved at all. Again, according to NBC: "Only 15 percent [of Republicans] see a pressing need to deal with the issue. More noteworthy than the difference, however, is the stability of the Republican figure. That 15 percent mark is unchanged since the same question was asked in 1999."

How much of this ossified view is attributable to Trump is impossible to sort out. Republican ranks were rife with climate-change deniers long before Trump took over the GOP. Talk-radio jockeys and Koch brother flunkies and Big Oil flacks have polluted conservatives' minds for years. But Trump could have challenged that, if he'd wanted to. Just as he upended the GOP's long support for free trade, just as he overturned their long support for Bush's Iraq invasion, Trump could have challenged his party's orthodoxy on climate change. But he didn't. The only way he would care about climate change is if he could make money off it. Quick: somebody pitch him on Trump Wind Farms, Trump Solar Panels.

Indeed, in his first year in office, Trump announced that he intended to pull the United States out of the Paris climate accord. In a bizarre, grievance-filled rant, Trump described the climate agreement as a vehicle through which other countries laugh at the United States—as if reducing pollution made us look weak. "At what point does America get demeaned?" he asked. "We don't want other countries and other leaders to laugh at us anymore."

Nowadays, they're not laughing at us; they're laughing at him—as we saw Boris Johnson, Justin Trudeau, and Emmanuel Macron doing at Buckingham Palace. Bozo isn't the only orange-haired clown America is famous for.

Neither Trump nor his aides could point to a specific example of any of the 194 other signatories to the Paris climate accord laughing at the United States for signing onto the deal. Nor did Trump explain the logic behind his theory that other nations would mock the United States for signing a deal they themselves had signed. As if that weren't weird enough, Trump made the announcement in the Rose Garden, where he had a jazz band perform. No word on whether the band performed classics like "Hot House," or perhaps "Too Darn Hot."

I know it's a fool's errand to interject facts into a Trump rant, but just so it's on the record: the Paris accord is not, as Trump alleged, "very unfair, at the highest level, to the United States." First, I have no idea what he means by "at the highest level." Does he mean the deal is unfair to the president and vice president? The secretary of state? Perhaps the Speaker of the House? Second, I do know what "unfair" means. It means, in this context, requiring the United States to do what other nations are not required to do. This seems to be at the heart of Trump's criticism. But the caps on carbon pollution in the Paris accord are: a) voluntary and b) determined by each nation for itself. The agreement requires—according to its plain language—"nationally determined contributions." Which means—

and I'm going slowly here, in case Mike Pence is reading this to Trump—that the contributions are determined by each nation. This is the kind of test I'd think Trump would love: one where you get to write the questions yourself, and then grade the answers yourself.

Instead of challenging the deniers in his own party, he challenges the scientists in his own government. In 2018, the Trump administration released the Fourth National Climate Assessment. The report stated unequivocally that climate change will damage the American economy: "With continued growth in emissions at historic rates, annual losses in some economic sectors are projected to reach hundreds of billions of dollars by the end of the century—more than the current gross domestic product (GPD) of many U.S. states." It went on to warn of damage to property and infrastructure as climate-related weather events wreak havoc.

Climate Change Is Already Hurting Americans

Let's be clear: the threat is real. The damage is already happening. When my mother, who is eighty-two, was a little girl, her grandparents had a place on Lake Hopatcong in northern New Jersey. Her grandfather, Watson G. Howell, was an iceman, and Lake Hopatcong was a great source of ice. Back in the day—nearly a century ago—there was no refrigeration, so people had iceboxes: insulated crates in which they'd place a block of ice, which would keep their milk, eggs, and other food cool. Apparently old Watson made a decent living as an iceman. Uncle George still has his tongs, and regaled me when I was a kid with stories of Watson heaving a fifty-pound block on his shoulder and climbing up three flights of stairs to make a delivery.

There are no icemen anymore, of course. But that's not the point of the story. The point of the story is, there's not as much ice. In 2019 the *Washington Post* sent a team of reporters to Lake Hopatcong to see the difference climate change is making on a lake once well known for ice two feet thick. I'm talking ice thick enough to play hockey on, to race iceboats on, to drive cars and trucks onto.

According to the *Post*, no one races iceboats on Lake Hopatcong anymore. And "even the hardy souls who still try to take part in ice fishing contests here have had to cancel 11 of the past dozen competitions for fear of straying onto perilously thin ice and tumbling into the frigid water." Turns out that Lake Hopatcong has seen temperatures rise by 2 degrees Celsius in the past century. That figure is important, because that's the mark at which bad things happen, and by "bad things" I don't just mean canceled ice fishing contests. I mean coral reefs dying, gigantic ice sheets in Greenland and Antarctica retreating, sea levels rising, which causes coastal cities to flood and a cascade of catastrophic effects. The fact that Lake Hopatcong has lost its wintertime sports is the least of it. The *Post*, using data from the National Oceanic and Atmospheric Administration (NOAA), estimates that "major areas are nearing or have already crossed the 2-degree Celsius mark." These include Los Angeles, New York, and other coastal areas. In fact, 34 million Americans—more than one in ten—are living in parts of the country that are rapidly heating up: Connecticut, Maine, Massachusetts, New Jersey, and elsewhere.

But let's go back to my mother's lake. Not only did Mom vacation at Lake Hopatcong with her grandparents eighty years ago, she went to Camp Tekawitha there, too. She fondly remembers hot summer afternoons swimming in the cool lake water. I would not advise that nowadays. Without the big freeze, nasty harmful bacteria like toxic blue-green algae now blooms, just as the tourists arrive. It's not just yucky. It can give you a rash, irritate your lungs, mess up your eyes, and if the levels get high enough, the bacteria can cause liver and neurological damage. You can't eat the fish. You can't swim in the lake. Neither can your dog, because it can kill him or her.

Rhode Island is called the Ocean State for a reason. It has 420 miles of coastline, and in some areas, the ocean is advancing 3.3 feet a year. The owners of a local convenience store in Roy Carpenter's

Beach spent a ton of money to move their store farther back from the ocean. "We moved it back 100 feet," the owner, Roy Thoresen, told the *Washington Post*, "and it only bought us 10 years."

Back to the report. Remember, the Fourth National Climate Assessment I referred to a few pages back? The one from the Trump administration, written by scientists from thirteen federal agencies, from NOAA to NASA? Yeah, the one Trump said he didn't believe. That one. It says that we are on a path to increase global temperatures by 9 degrees Celsius—bear in mind that a 2-degree rise is considered catastrophic, and a 3.6-degree rise has been called "irreversible and apocalyptic." Here are some of the consequences we are already experiencing:

- Heat waves that are dangerous for your health

- Crops dying in fields from the heat

- Power outages from too much heat-related demand

- Extreme rain, causing flash floods

- Flood-driven nutrient runoff, which is causing those toxic algae blooms, harming water quality, killing dogs and fish

- Tornadoes: lots more of them, a longer tornado season, and more intense twisters

- Forest fires like we saw in Australia and California

As I mentioned earlier in the book, I love the outdoors. If you fish, you're a friend of mine. But the climate crisis is killing ice fishing in the winter and poisoning the fish in the summer. As is so often the case, the poor are at greater risk: both those in the inner city who are breathing dirtier air and often can't afford air-conditioning, and farmers, whose crops are withering, and who are being hit with increasingly devastating tornadoes and floods.

How Democrats Should Run on This

This is harder than you might think. Although it is an existential crisis for the planet, climate change barely cracks the top tier of issues on voters' minds in the 2020 elections. A Gallup survey at the beginning of the year put climate change seventh on a list of issues voters care about, with 26 percent fewer people worried about it than health care. Climate change also was seen as less important than terrorism and national security, gun policy, education, the economy, and immigration.

But Democrats have to talk about it. They need to educate people about it and earn a mandate for bold action. Here again they need to localize, humanize, personalize. Instead of talking about the planet, talk about the local lake. Talk about the young woman in Austin whose dog, Ollie, died just one hour after he went for a swim in Lady Bird Lake. Talk about the retired couple who saved all their lives to buy a cabin on the seashore, only to have it wiped out by a storm.

Don't be afraid to call out the villains, either. Sen. Sheldon Whitehouse (R-RI) has been perhaps the most fearless and powerful advocate on this issue in Washington. He has called out big business by name, dubbing the powerful US Chamber of Commerce the "Chamber of Carbon." Whitehouse says he suspects that one of the reasons the chamber does not reveal the source of its funding "is that they're taking huge amounts of secret money from the fossil fuel industry" while using less controversial businesses to front for them. He says that this "is a fissure we want to expose and exploit."

Whitehouse and other Democrats—among them Senators Brian Schatz, Martin Heinrich, and Elizabeth Warren—have kept the pressure up, and it's having an effect. Nike left the US Chamber over its retrograde climate position, as did Apple. Also Starbucks, General Mills, Costco, eBay, Hewlett-Packard, Mattel, Kraft Heinz, Mars, and others.

I love that Whitehouse and others are naming names. Villains give a story some pop, and many companies only see the light after they feel the heat. Democrats also need to praise the good companies that are stepping up. The Climate Leadership Council, for example, features among its founders such corporate titans as General Motors, IBM, and JPMorgan Chase. The group, led by former GOP secretaries of state George Shultz and James A. Baker III, has proposed a carbon fee (something President Clinton and Vice President Gore proposed back in 1993), coupled with a "carbon dividend" designed to mitigate any harm to the middle class and the poor. They estimate the fee to start at $40 a ton of carbon dioxide produced, escalating by 5 percent above inflation per year. All of the proceeds from that fee would be rebated to the American people. Baker and Shultz estimate that the first year, a family of four would receive about $2,000; the amount will increase as the carbon fee increases.

I highlight this not because I think it's the best solution but so that you know that there are still lots of Republicans out there who want to take action. Having that corporate backing can help Democrats demonstrate that they are not sacrificing the economy in their effort to save the planet.

The Climate Leadership Council wants to emphasize its "carbon dividend" over its carbon tax for a sound and sensible political reason: people like getting money more than they like paying it. (Aren't you glad you bought this book? See the kind of sophisticated political insights you're getting?) When talking about climate, Democrats need to stress the threat, obviously, but they also need to emphasize the opportunity. They must not be Calvinists, focusing on the utter depravity and sinfulness of humankind. Save that for church. Instead, they should focus on all the good that will come from rising to this challenge—especially the economic benefits.

The Green New Deal embodies that optimism in its name. It is somewhat bolder than the Climate Council's corporate-backed plan—which is like saying Shaquille O'Neal is somewhat taller than Peter Dinklage. The plan put forward by Rep. Alexandria Ocasio-Cortez

(D-NY) is far more radical on energy and environmental issues and also includes a call for free college, universal health care, a guaranteed job, and more. In the words of the great Ron Burgundy, that escalated quickly. If you're looking for a sweeping aspirational dream of what a leftist America might look like, this will do the trick. But if you're trying to focus people on climate change, I humbly suggest you keep the focus on climate change and save the health care debate and free college for another day.

I do think there is great benefit, however, in talking about new green jobs. Right now, according to the Brookings Institution, 2.7 million Americans work in the clean economy—more than work in fossil fuels. These jobs are in industries ranging from mass transit to solar, photovoltaic, and other renewable sources of energy. More than a quarter of the green jobs are in manufacturing, and the median wages for green jobs are 13 percent higher than median wages in the rest of the economy. These are good jobs, but their growth has lagged behind the growth rate of the rest of the economy. AOC and others are right that we need to jump-start this sector, and that doing so would be a win-win: people make more money, and we save the planet. (And, I gotta say, earth is one of my all-time favorite planets. Big fan of earth.) Brookings recommends a few steps:

- Put a price on carbon (which, as we have seen, even a lot of corporate leaders now support).

- Set a national clean energy standard, which would ensure a market for clean energy.

- Reform electrical markets to encourage the use of clean energy.

- Expedite permitting for green projects.

- Adopt green building standards.

- Implement "innovative financing tools to reduce the upfront costs of investing in clean technologies."

From the conservative corporate titans in the Climate Council, to the lefties pushing the Green New Deal, to the centrists at Brookings, there is a consensus among thinking people that we can save the planet and prosper economically while doing so. But I said "thinking people," so that kinda leaves out Donald Jackass Trump.

The "green" Democrats should be talking about is money. Rather than focus on how terrible the American people are for burning coal or driving cars, Democrats should focus on the jobs we will create, the wealth we will build, the cool toys we will have. Stop being scolds and nags; start being salespeople of a new prosperity. This allows you to sidestep the debate about whether climate science is real. (Why go there? It's like debating people who say that the science on gravity is not real, even after they've dropped a brick on their foot.) Try this: "Maybe you're right. But think of this: if you're wrong, and climate change makes earth uninhabitable for humans, then we all die, but first we have famines and floods and wars. But if I'm right, and we can take steps to reduce carbon pollution, those steps can build a new green economy: we get rich, build wealth, and get cool new toys."

Some of the most successful churches out there preach what is called the "prosperity gospel"—the notion that God wants you to be rich. Whatever you think of the theology behind it, you have to admire the marketing. Which preacher is going to fill a fifteen-thousand-seat arena: the one who says we're sinful and depraved and going to hell, or the one who says God wants you to drive a BMW and live in a mansion and fly on a private jet?

Preach the prosperity gospel on climate change, Democrats. "We're all gonna get rich" is a more appealing message than "We're all gonna die." In fact, both are true. I'm just advocating that we accentuate the positive.

CHAPTER 12

THE TRUMP COURTS

"Balls and Strikes" and Other BS

Congress and the presidency are, we were taught in school, the "political branches" of government. They were filled with politicians: self-centered, vain partisan hacks. But the federal courts (cue the harps and wind chimes), they aren't partisan. Blessed with life tenure, we are told, jurists take off their partisan jerseys when they put on their robes. "My job," the chief justice of the United States, John Roberts, said in his Senate confirmation hearing, is "to call balls and strikes." He claimed he had "no agenda. I have no platform."

What a crock.

Supreme Court justices don't poop marble. And they're not the most brilliant constitutional scholars in the country. They are lawyers who are politically connected to the party in power and who have sufficient credentials to pass the laugh test. They are, in the modern era, partisans through and through.

War, Clausewitz said, is politics by other means. And so is the Supreme Court. Republicans have long known this. Democrats have long pretended not to. It's time they stopped pretending.

I hope you're sitting down. The Supreme Court is thoroughly, wholly, intensively, profoundly, extremely, absolutely, completely, entirely, full-on, whole-hog, no-holds-barred, out-and-out, through-

and-through political. That's why Republicans dominate it. Republicans will hold their nose and even vote for a guy who bragged about assaulting women and mocked a POW war hero if they believe he will pick Supreme Court justices who will hew to a right-wing Republican social and economic agenda. A majority of people who said the Supreme Court was their number one issue voted for Trump in 2016. More than one in four people who voted for Trump said the Court was the most important reason why they did so. Only 18 percent of Hillary voters chose her because of who she might put on the court. As Philip Bump of the *Washington Post* noted, "Google searches for 'Supreme Court' and either of the candidates' last names consistently showed more interest in Trump than Clinton . . . For Clinton, only one of the five most searched phrases was that direct. More common was 'Hillary Clinton age.'" Spoiler alert: she's younger than Trump. And she would have put young, progressive justices on the court.

Republicans will do anything to claim and keep power. The Supreme Court has enormous power, thus calling for any level of GOP chicanery. When Associate Justice Antonin Scalia (R-12th Century) died, on February 13, 2016, there were 269 days until the next presidential election. Republicans brazenly declared their intention to block any Obama nominee. "The fact of the matter is that it's been standard practice over the last 80 years to not confirm Supreme Court nominees during a presidential election year," said Senator Charles Grassley (R-Fibber), who was at the time chairman of the all-important Senate Judiciary Committee. Grassley knew or should have known he was prevaricating. He himself voted to confirm Anthony Kennedy nine months before the 1988 presidential election. Kennedy was granted a hearing by the Democratically controlled Senate Judiciary Committee, which was chaired by then-senator Joe Biden (D-C'mon, Man!), thirty-two days after he was nominated. (Kennedy was nominated on November 12, 1987. The first day of the Judiciary Committee hearings was December 14.) He was confirmed by the Democratically controlled Senate on February 4, 1988, by a vote of 97–0.

That was, of course, a presidential election year. Despite this, and despite the fact that Biden himself was running to succeed Reagan, he moved swiftly. He treated Kennedy fairly. And he voted to confirm him. A week before that floor vote, Grassley publicly thanked Biden for "expediting this vote."

In fact, President Reagan pushed for the election-year confirmation, and said that if the Democrats tried to stall his nominee just because it was an election year, "the American people will know what's up."

Republicans in 2016 knew all that. They knew that there was precedent to confirm a justice in an election year. They didn't care. They knew that President Obama had nominated Merrick Garland, a widely respected moderate sixty-three-year-old who had served presidents of both parties.

Let's go back to the days after Justice Scalia's passing. Scalia's death was sudden, and President Obama took a little over a month to nominate Judge Garland. Obama was not naive about how blindly partisan the Republicans were, but, as Juliet Eilperin and Mike DeBonis wrote in the *Washington Post* on March 16, the day Obama announced Garland's nomination, "Obama decided that it might be more politically difficult for Republicans to deny Garland a hearing and a vote after he has been the subject of effusive bipartisan accolades for years."

How quaint.

That very day, Republican leaders in the Senate flatly stated that they would not allow a vote on Judge Garland. Some not only refused to have a floor vote but also denied Garland a public hearing. Oh, and some would not even meet with him, as if he carried a virus. This despite the fact that Garland had received strong bipartisan support when President Clinton nominated him for the US Court of Appeals for the DC Circuit in 1997, putting him on that court with a 76–23 vote. The DC Circuit is sometimes referred to as the second highest court in the land, since so many important cases come to it. Seven Republicans who had voted to confirm Garland to that powerful court were still in the Senate when Obama nominated him to the Supreme Court: Dan Coats, of Indiana; Thad Cochran, of Mississippi; Susan Collins, of Maine; Orrin Hatch, of Utah; James Inhofe, of Oklahoma; John McCain, of Arizona; and Pat Roberts, of Kansas.

None of that mattered. Not to Mitch McConnell (R-Lenin's Tomb). The Republican Senate majority leader was as solid as the Kremlin wall. "It seems clear," McConnell said, "that President Obama made this nomination, not with the intent of seeing the nominee confirmed, but in order to politicize it for the purposes of election." He said this with a straight face. Obama chose a man the public had never heard of, who was two years away from Medicare, a moderate who'd worked as a federal prosecutor in the George H. W. Bush administration. In short, Obama chose the least partisan person he could. Barack Obama is—and I don't think I'm going out on a limb here—a pretty astute politician. If he had wanted to choose someone just to fire up his party for the 2016 election, he would not have chosen the mild-mannered moderate Garland. He would have chosen, oh, I don't know, Michelle Obama. Or Meryl Streep or Oprah.

President Obama nominated Merrick Garland because he actually, honestly thought many Republicans would see him as a consensus nominee. Perhaps he thought that because Sen. Orrin Hatch had called Garland "a consensus nominee" and urged Obama to put him on the high court in 2010. Garland, Hatch said in 2010, "would be very well supported by all sides." Hatch said there would be "'no question' Merrick would be confirmed with bipartisan support."

Silly Obama, thinking a hack like Hatch wouldn't be willing to eat those words if it meant preserving a chance for the right wing to amass more power. Not only did Hatch not offer the bipartisan support he had pledged, he joined those who opposed a hearing, much less a committee vote, much less a floor vote, much less confirming

Garland, his "consensus nominee." To be fair, Hatch did meet with Garland. "Our meeting, however," he wrote in an op-ed in Salt Lake City's *Deseret News*, "does not change my conviction that the Senate should consider a Supreme Court nominee after this presidential cycle." Unfortunately for Hatch, that op-ed was written, filed, and run *before he even met with Garland*.

Democrats miscalculated. They underestimated the intransigence, the partisanship, the pigheadedness of their Republican colleagues. They also underestimated how unimportant the court is to Democrats, and how all-important it is to Republicans. The Obama White House rallied progressive groups, civil rights organizations, the usual suspects. They are passionate and brilliant and energetic, but they were unable to galvanize the nation. Not because they did anything wrong. Not because they made strategic or tactical errors, and not because they had poor messaging. Democrats just did not care about the court as much as Republicans did.

The polling was misleading. By a two-to-one margin, Americans wanted a hearing for Judge Garland. Only 32 percent thought that the Republicans were right to leave the pick to the next president; 61 percent thought that they were wrong. But for that one-third of the nation, the courts are a *voting* issue. In a razor-close race, the right's deep, emotional, passionate commitment to controlling the court might have made the difference. As we have seen, Trump carried Michigan and Wisconsin and Pennsylvania by a total of 77,744 votes, out of 14 million votes cast. As Philip Bump of the *Washington Post* concluded: if just "78,000 of the 14 million people who cast votes in those states did so to hold a majority on the court, it made the difference. There were about 6.6 million votes cast for Trump in those three states. National exit polls suggest that 1.7 million of them thought that the court was the most important reason to cast that vote."

Republicans blocked Garland: hypocritically and dishonestly, but effectively. Trump, with the help of voter suppression, Vladimir Putin, and James Comey, slipped through the cracks in the Electoral

College and became president. And while he has been disorganized, impetuous, and unfocused about nearly every other issue, when it comes to the courts, he has been disciplined, focused, and ruthlessly successful.

Unlike his predecessor, Donald Trump never taught constitutional law. He has probably violated more provisions of the Constitution than he has studied. But he knows his constituency; knows they vote based on Supreme Court appointments. And he knows this: the Constitution is not words on a page. The Constitution is what the Supreme Court *says* those words mean. And what the Supreme Court says it means depends squarely on which partisan lawyers are sitting on the court that day. Trump knows that, which is why he came to the White House with binders full of partisan, right-wing lawyers.

The List

The Federalist Society is a right-wing lawyers club. In law schools all across America, little right-wing lawyer wannabes gather together. They teach each other how to tie bow ties and how to put children in cages—you know, all the things Republican lawyers need to know. (Okay, I imagined that; I've never been to a Federalist Society meeting. I spent my free time in law school drinking beer at the Posse East in Austin.)

But the Federalist Society is more than just a bunch of right-wing law nerds. They are a bunch of right-wing law nerds who get to pick all of America's federal judges when Republicans are in power. Since federal judges have lifetime appointments, and since there are 865 of them, and since Moscow Mitch and his pals rubber-stamp pretty much all of them, yeah, I'd say the Federalist Society has a lot of power. How did they get so much power? Well, they were organized, they were mutually supportive, they were driven. They have been around since the Reagan administration and have always been influential with Republican administrations. But they also have been given an unprecedented role in selecting judges by none other than Donald Jiggery-Pokery Trump.

As a candidate, Trump flat-out promised that his judicial nominees "'would all [be] picked by the Federalist Society.'" He asked the group to give him a list of potential Supreme Court nominees. The Federalists have never had more power, thanks to Trump making them his selection committee, and thanks also to Mitch McConnell (R-Red Square) ramming through each pick.

Sen. Sheldon Whitehouse has been one of the Senate's clearest thinkers and most powerful voices on the role of the Federalist Society. A former federal prosecutor and Rhode Island attorney general, Whitehouse is a member of the Senate Judiciary Committee. He cares deeply about our legal system, having spent much of his life in it. With a prosecutor's precision, he draws a distinction between three different roles the Federalist Society plays—between three different Federalist Societies, as it were. The first Federalist Society, he says, is the debating society for law nerds that I first encountered when I was a student at the Greatest University in the World. The second is "a sort of highbrow think tank seeking to further conservative and libertarian judicial principles. It convenes fancy forums with conservative legal luminaries, from Supreme Court Justices to big-name politicians to renowned legal scholars."

Whitehouse has no major complaints with the first and second Federalist Societies. A free country is only strengthened by healthy, honest debate. He claims, however, that there is a third Federalist Society:

> This Federalist Society is the nerve center for a complicated apparatus that does not care much about conservative principles like judicial restraint, or originalism, or textualism. This Federalist Society is the vehicle for powerful interests, which seek not to simply "reorder" the judiciary, but to acquire control of the judiciary to benefit their interests. This third Federalist

Society understands the fundamental power of the federal judiciary to rig the system in favor of its donor interests—and as
the Kavanaugh confirmation so clearly illustrated, it is willing
to go to drastic lengths to secure that power.

Whitehouse claims that Leonard Leo, the Federalist Society's executive vice president, is "*the* most influential person shaping our
federal judiciary." (Emphasis in the original.) Whitehouse has followed the money, to the best of his ability, to see how Leo's organization, and those like it, are funded. Much of it is dark money, dark
as a barrel of Koch Industries oil. Whitehouse argues that giant corporations hide behind dark money to buy influence with right-wing
lawyers so they can place them in positions of power. He cites the
example of Judge Neomi Rao, whom Trump put on the DC Circuit
Court of Appeals. "Rao," Whitehouse says, "came right out of the
deep bog of special interest dark money." She is all over the Federalist
Society website, like bedbugs at a Trump Hotel. (Fact Check: True.
Bedbugs have been reported at Trump hotels. Though, in my opinion, they're less disgusting than the vermin whose name is splattered
over the hotels.)

Judge Rao had never tried a case as a lawyer, never presided over
a case as a trial judge. She was a point person for Trump and the Federalist Society in trying to kill regulations that protect health, safety,
and the environment. Questioned by Sen. Whitehouse in a hearing,
she denied under oath ever receiving Koch money for her antireg-
ulation organization. Whitehouse says he can prove otherwise. "A
Virginia open records request revealed that an anonymous donor
and the Charles Koch Foundation donated $30 million earmarked
specially for her organization. Guess whose interests she's had conveyed on to the D.C. Court of Appeals to protect?"

I'm guessing that was a rhetorical question. My solution: make
the judges wear patches showing the corporate interests that sponsor
them, like NASCAR drivers do. Then have disclaimers like they do in

political ads: *This attack on environmental laws is brought to you by Big Oil. Big Oil: when just a little bit of toxins in your water just won't do.*

Trump Is Packing the Courts

At this writing, Mitch McConnell has nearly four hundred House-passed bills sitting on his desk, on issues ranging from raising the minimum wage, to lowering the cost of prescription drugs, to cleaning up corruption in Washington. (See chapter 13 for more details.) Sen. McConnell isn't big on passing things. The guy couldn't pass gas in a men's room in a taco bar. But he is a judge-confirming machine.

Not only did he confirm two ultra-right-wing lawyers to the Supreme Court, he has allowed Trump to name more than one out of every four appeals court judges. This is enormously important, as those appeals courts often have the last word, since the Supreme Court doesn't take many cases. (They're lazy as well as political.) To put it into perspective, over the course of eight years, President Obama named fifty-five appeals court judges. In just three, Trump has named fifty. By comparison, after three years, Reagan had named only twenty-five appeals court judges. President Clinton named thirty; President George W. Bush, thirty-four. But Trump has named fifty. For life.

At the district court level, Trump has nominated 112 judges. Why has Trump been able to name so many judges? Because McConnell stalled or stopped so many Obama judges. In Obama's final two years, during which McConnell was running the Senate, just two appeals court judges were confirmed. Two. And one was for a technical court that deals with patents and other geekizoid stuff. During the last two years of George W. Bush's term, when Democrats controlled the Senate, mean old Harry Reid (D-NV) confirmed ten appeals court judges Bush sent him.

Of course, of the scores of judges Trump and McConnell have foisted on the American people, two stand out: his two Supreme

Court appointments, Neil Gorsuch and Brett Kavanaugh. Amazingly, both attended the same high school: Georgetown Prep, a renowned Jesuit school in the D.C. suburbs. One guesses Trump has spent significantly less time in church than either of these two Catholic judges, but they are his guys nonetheless.

Neil Gorsuch and the Frozen Trucker

Eleven days after he took the oath of office, Donald Trump nominated Neil Gorsuch to the Supreme Court. Gorsuch "looked the part": tall, gray, and distinguished. This, we are told, helps with Trump, who sees life through the lens of a TV producer.

The day before Trump announced his nomination of Gorsuch, he fired the acting attorney general, Sally Yates, after she refused to send Justice Department attorneys to court to defend Trump's executive order barring refugees and other people from several Muslim-dominated countries.

Looking back, those two actions, firing the acting attorney general and nominating Gorsuch, presaged Trump's drive to bend the American system of justice to his perverted will: refugees are to be feared, Muslims are to be discriminated against, and the privileged, arrogant son of a cabinet officer is to be placed on the Supreme Court.

Arrogant? Really? Oh yeah. Gorsuch oozes a smug superciliousness. He has nestled in the Federalist Society's bosom much of his career. Before he was named to the high court, he was a Federalist Society member and regularly spoke at Federalist Society events.

After he was confirmed, Gorsuch—now Justice Gorsuch—spoke at a black-tie dinner sponsored by the group. The dinner took place in the main hall of Washington's Union Station, a Beaux-Arts masterpiece. If you've never been, I highly recommend it. The arched ceiling rises 96 feet and is decorated with 22-karat gold leaf. The hall is guarded by thirty-six giant Roman legionnaires hand-carved by Louis Saint-Gaudens over a seven-year period beginning in 1906.

The notion of a sitting Supreme Court justice sucking up to a well-heeled Washington special interest group is a bit brazen, don't you think? The Federalist Society does not pretend to be neutral. It does not advocate calling balls and strikes fairly. It is a pressure group that seeks to roll back civil rights and repeal environmental protections, among other things. Its funding, as Sen. Whitehouse has noted, is carefully hidden from view behind allegedly "charitable" organizations that don't disclose their donors.

Justice Gorsuch took the occasion to suck up to the powerful and privileged. "If you're going to have a meeting of a secret organization," he said, "maybe don't have it in the middle of Union Station and then tell everybody to wear black tie. It's not a shadowy cabal in need of Joe McCarthy." The audience roared. But unless Gorsuch is a dope (which he most assuredly is not), he would know that reformers don't have a problem with the public events the Federalist Society hosts (see Sen. Whitehouse's comments above). We have a problem with the shadowy *funding* of the group. Follow the money. And we have a problem with a guy who is paid by we, the people, promoting a right-wing, oil-funded special interest pressure group. And, yes, Your Honor, it is shadowy. If it wasn't ashamed of its funding, it would disclose it.

In his speech, Gorsuch drew knowing laughter with this one: "Everyone who's not a lawyer is going to think I just hate truckers—but so be it." That was an inside joke, and a sick one at that. You see, when he was on the US Court of Appeals for the Tenth Circuit, Gorsuch wrote an opinion that said a trucking company was within its rights to fire Al Maddin for the offense of not dying on the job.

I am not kidding. Al worked for Kansas-based TransAm Trucking. One frigid January night in 2009, he was driving on I-88 in Illinois. At around 11:00, Al pulled his rig over to the side of the highway because he was low on fuel and needed to look up where the company-mandated gas station was. When he pulled back onto the highway, he realized that the brakes on the trailer had frozen and did not work. So he pulled off the highway again and called the company's Road Assist service. It told him to stay put, and that a repair person would come to him. Al agreed. But when he tried to turn on the auxiliary power unit in his cab to stay warm, he learned that it, too, was busted. So, he sat there, in frigid temperatures, and waited for help. He fell asleep. Two hours later—this is now after 1:00 a.m.— he was awakened by his phone. It was his cousin Greg. Greg says that Al was slurring his words and sounded confused. Al realized that his torso was numb. He could not feel his feet. So he called the company again. Told them that the bunk heater wasn't working. Told them he was going numb. The company told Al to "hang in there."

Al hung in there for another thirty minutes. By now he had been enduring subzero temperatures for two and a half hours. He made another call, this one to his supervisor, Larry Cluck. He told Larry about the frozen brakes and the busted bunk heater. Larry kept telling Al to turn the heater on. Al kept telling Larry that it wasn't working. Larry told Al to drag the crippled trailer—which had no brakes. Al refused.

Finally, fearing for his life, Al Maddin unhooked the cab from the trailer and drove to safety. Fifteen minutes later the repair person arrived, fixed the brakes, and all was well. No harm befell the trailer, and Al, thank God, was alive.

All's well that ends well, right? Wrong. The company fired Al for abandoning his load.

For the next seventeen years, the case was in the legal system. An administrative law judge ruled for Al. An administrative review board of the Department of Labor ruled for Al, and ordered him reinstated with back pay. The company appealed to the Tenth Circuit, and Judge Gorsuch was on the three-judge panel that heard the case. Two of the judges sided with Al, reasoning that the health and safety protections of federal law mean little if they require someone to freeze to death. Guess who the one judge was who ruled that Al should have continued to risk his life for a load of freight?

Bingo!

That's right, ladies and gentlemen, our man Neil Gorsuch. In his dissent, Gorsuch wrote that the law only empowers a driver to "refuse to operate" a truck. But that is precisely what Al did. He refused to operate the truck without the brakes, even though he was ordered to. He also refused to freeze to death. This, apparently, was his mistake, according to Gorsuch. So much for being pro-life, Neil.

This case became an issue in Gorsuch's confirmation, because Democrats, God bless 'em, still believe that Republican senators care about a truck driver's life. (Spoiler alert: they don't.) Every single Republican voted to confirm Gorsuch, a man who has probably never broken an honest sweat in his life, despite his ruling that a trucker should have been fired for refusing to freeze to death. A few months later, Gorsuch received a standing ovation when he sucked up to the Federalist Society, concluding his remarks (after that knee-slapper about making Al Maddin freeze to death) this way: "Thank you from the bottom of my heart for your support and prayers through that [confirmation] process." I have no idea if Federalists pray. But Gorsuch is right that its support, and the support of its shadowy donors, played a critical role in his elevation to the nation's highest court. One feels confident he will continue to thank them with his rulings for a long time.

Brett Kavanaugh

Most Americans know the shocking allegations of sexual assault against Brett Kavanaugh. We know that Christine Blasey Ford swore, under oath and in public, that when they were teenagers in suburban Maryland, a drunken Kavanaugh pinned her to a bed, groped her, grinding his body on hers, and covered her mouth when she tried to scream. "I thought he might inadvertently kill me," she testified. "He was trying to attack me and remove my clothing."

We know that Deborah Ramirez says that when she and Kavanaugh were freshmen at Yale, someone pushed his private parts in her face during a drinking game. She recalls seeing a drunken Kavanaugh pulling up his pants, and another student yelling, "Brett Kavanaugh just put his penis in Debbie's face."

Many people believe these women. I do. Kavanaugh's testimony in response to Dr. Ford's accusation was epic, operatic, emotional. It was unhinged. Where Ford was, to my eyes, sad, wounded, but resolute, Kavanaugh was furious, red-faced, threatening. Did he seem like a guy who would lose control and assault a vulnerable woman? Well, to me he looked like he might jump over the witness table and attack a senator.

It didn't matter. Without hard proof, without evidence other than recollection, Republicans were able to muddy the waters. Reasonable people could agree that what happened on a drunken night three decades ago was at some level unknowable.

But what is knowable is what Kavanaugh did as an adult: what he did when he had power—nearly unchecked power—as an acolyte of independent counsel Ken Starr. In 1995, Kavanaugh pushed Starr to reopen the investigation into the death of deputy White House counsel Vince Foster. Foster had known Bill Clinton all his life. Their childhood backyards abutted in Hope, Arkansas. As Bill rose in politics, Vince ascended in law. When Bill became president, he asked Vince to join him in the White House. The story ended tragically, however, as depression drove Vince to take his life in the summer of 1993.

Foster's 1993 death had already been investigated four times. Each investigation concluded that he had taken his own life. Vince (whom I knew) was being treated for depression. He was in a high-stress White House job. He was the subject of nasty editorials in the *Wall Street Journal*. Four official investigations ruled the death a suicide:

Four. Official. Investigations:

• **The Park Police:** "Mr. Foster was anxious about his work and he was distressed to the degree that he took his own life." The Department of Justice, the FBI, and the Park Police all joined in that conclusion.

- **Independent Counsel Robert Fiske**: "On the afternoon of July 20, 1993, in Fort Marcy Park, Fairfax County, Virginia, Vincent W. Foster committed suicide by firing a bullet from a .38 caliber revolver into his mouth . . . The evidence overwhelmingly supports this conclusion, and there is no evidence to the contrary."

- **House Republicans**: Rep. William Clinger Jr. (R-PA), who was at the time the ranking Republican on the House Government Operations Committee, reviewed the evidence and concluded: "All available facts lead to the undeniable conclusion that Vincent W. Foster, Jr. took his own life in Fort Marcy Park, Virginia on July 20, 1993."

- **Senate Democrats**: The Senate Banking Committee, controlled by Democrats, also looked at all the evidence. They, too, concluded that "the evidence overwhelmingly supports the conclusion of the Park Police that on July 20, 1993, Mr. Foster died in Fort Marcy Park from a self-inflicted gun shot wound to the upper palate of his mouth." The committee's Republicans concurred, saying: "We agree with the majority's conclusion that on July 20, 1993 Vincent Foster took his own life in Fort Marcy Park."

You would think that four separate investigations into an obvious case of suicide would be enough. The investigations, conducted by experts, overseen in some instances by career professionals, in other cases by Democrats, in still other cases by Republicans—well, you would think that would satisfy everyone except the loopiest wingnuts or the most hateful, spiteful partisans.

Brett Kavanaugh is definitely not a loopy wingnut. He is, however, someone willing to use power to hurt the vulnerable in pursuit of his right-wing agenda. I'd call that hateful and spiteful. Think I'm overstating? After four independent investigations, all of which came to the same incontrovertible conclusion, Kavanaugh spent three years and $2 million re-re-re-re-re-investigating Vince's suicide.

This was not merely a waste of time and money. This was cruelty. This caused incalculable pain to an innocent family. The Foster family was outraged and issued a statement to that effect. In later years, Kavanaugh has tried to distance himself from his role in this tawdry tormenting of the Foster family. Baloney. The *Washington Post* unearthed a 1995 memo, written by Kavanaugh to Starr after all those other investigations had been completed: "we have received allegations that Mr. Foster's death [was] related to President and Mrs. Clinton's involvement" with business dealings Starr was investigating. Starr's predecessor, Robert Fiske, had already resolved the Foster issue. Kavanaugh wanted to reopen it, in my opinion, to damage the Clintons, and simply did not give a damn about the pain he would inflict on a family trying to heal after a suicide.

We only learned Kavanaugh's full capacity for cruelty years later, when Princeton historian Sean Wilentz examined Kavanaugh's records from his Starr days, which are housed in the National Archives. Although Kavanaugh admitted in memos that he believed Foster had committed suicide, he kept up the investigation, which gave credence to the conspiracy theories: maybe Foster secretly worked for the National Security Agency? (No, he didn't.) Maybe the Israelis were blackmailing him over a Swiss bank account? (No, they weren't.)

Kavanaugh, Wilentz has written, "apparently took a special interest" in one particular theory: that somehow Foster had been having an affair with Hillary Clinton. In the memos uncovered by Wilentz, Kavanaugh reports that his investigators "asked numerous people about it." Kavanaugh decided to ask Clinton personally. In an especially low moment, even for a lowlife like Kavanaugh, he sent FBI agents to take hair from Vince Foster's daughter, since she, like Clinton, is blond, and blond hairs were found on Foster's body.

This conduct was more than ghoulish and creepy; more than

a waste of money and time. It was a massive abuse of power. How could Kavanaugh, who cried at his hearing when he mentioned the girls' basketball team he coached, have inflicted that kind of trauma on another man's daughter?

No, we will never know to an actual, factual, moral certainty whether Christine Blasey Ford and Deborah Ramirez are telling the truth. But we do know that, as an adult, invested with awesome power, Kavanaugh abused that power, and victimized the powerless. He now sits on the Supreme Court, a fine place to exact his vengeance, which he promised while under oath in a not-at-all veiled threat. "What comes around comes around," he said, getting the idiom wrong but conveying the threat nonetheless. "Today," he said, "I have to say that I fear for the future."

Me too, Brett. #MeToo.

How Democrats Should Run on This

By now you know my rule for this election: make it about voters' lives, not Trump's character. Donald Trump wants to use the courts to hammer the middle class.

- He is suing to take away your protections for preexisting conditions (see chapter 9). Tens of millions of Americans could lose their health care because five right-wing lawyers—who have excellent government-provided health care—could rule in Trump's favor.

- He wants the courts to take away a woman's right to choose. He was once a supporter of abortion rights, telling the great Tim Russert (whom I miss every day) in 1999 that although he hated the idea of abortion, he would not ban abortion or so-called partial birth abortions. "I am pro-choice in every respect, as far as it goes. But I just hate it."

- Today, Trump is not pro-choice in any respect. He made it clear as a candidate that this was not merely a personal view. He would seek to impose that view on the Constitution. As a candidate he pledged he would "appoint judges that are pro-life." And in an interview on Fox News, candidate Trump explicitly tied his future court nominees to his pro-life litmus test, saying, "the biggest way you can protect [life] is through the Supreme Court and putting people in the court."

  When *Roe v. Wade* is overturned—and I am convinced it's a matter of when, not if—it will likely be overturned by Trump judges. Brett Kavanaugh replaced Anthony Kennedy, who was described by one legal scholar as "the firewall for abortion rights." If Kennedy was indeed a firewall, Kavanaugh is an arsonist. He will almost certainly be joined by Justices Clarence Thomas, Sam Alito, Neil Gorsuch, and, I believe, Chief Justice Roberts. The woman who argued the case of *Roe v. Wade*, Sarah Weddington, a graduate of the Greatest Law School in the World, told *Vox* that Kennedy's retirement "would leave the *Roe v. Wade* decision very vulnerable."

- The Trump court wants to revisit civil rights laws and rulings, perhaps the proudest legacy of American jurisprudence. Chief Justice Roberts is especially hostile to voting rights protections for racial minorities. Sounding like Bull Conner if Bull had gone to Harvard, he described efforts to protect the rights of racial minorities in a Texas redistricting, "a sordid business, this divvying us up by race." Civil rights are a lot of things: essential to a democracy, a bright spot in America's long, dark history of racism, our best hope for building Dr. King's Beloved Community. But to Roberts they are "a sordid business."

  As Ari Berman has detailed in his book *Give Us the Ballot: The Modern Struggle for Voting Rights in America*, from his days as a young clerk to then-Justice William Rehnquist (who made a name for himself in Arizona right-wing politics by personally going to polling places and challenging the rights of minority voters), to his time as a lawyer in the Reagan administration, Roberts has shown a persistent and insistent hostility to voting rights. As chief justice he took the lead in tossing out one of the strongest parts of the Voting Rights Act in 2013, a ruling that set off a spate of voter suppression (as we saw in chapter 7).

- The Trump court wants to give more power to corporations, and less power to consumers, employees, and everyone else. The Trump court believes in a vast expansion of the powers of corporations. As we saw from Neil Gorsuch, Trump judges believe that your company should have the right to fire you for choosing not to freeze to death. Beyond that, corporations have free-speech rights, political rights, and the right to make unlimited campaign donations.

  Amazingly, right-wing judges have even ruled that corporations have a soul. They have religious rights. As a faithful Catholic, this is especially noxious to me. I believe that God created people and that, as Jefferson wrote, people are "endowed by their Creator with certain unalienable rights." But God did not create the Hobby Lobby corporation. People did. Corporations are not people, dadgummit. They are a legal fiction created by people. And for-profit corporations exist—stay with me here—*to make money*. For-profit corporations don't exist to receive and return the love of Almighty God, their Creator. And they damn sure don't exist to love their neighbors as themselves.

  Right-wing judges have empowered corporations to buy our democracy. They have allowed corporations—soulless, bloodless entities bereft of conscience—to decide whether their employees can have contraception. That's right. You thought you had the right to decide whether or not to use contraception. Apparently, your corporate overlords have the final word. As I write these words, the Supreme Court has a case pending in which it will decide whether for-profit corporations can opt out of providing contraception in their health care coverage, the way churches can. Pennsylvania attorney general Josh Shapiro, who is suing the Trump administration over the issue, has said that Trump's rules "would allow virtually any employer to deny women access to contraception for any reason—including the belief that women should not be in the workforce."

If corporations have religious rights (which is crazy) and they can impose those rights on their employees (which is dangerous), and your boss can deny you access to contraception, what else can your boss do? What about a boss whose religion opposes the eating of pork—or all meat? Can your boss prohibit you from eating a BLT or a burger at your desk? Or what if your boss is a Pastafarian? Can she stop you from reheating lasagna in the office microwave? On the plus side, if your boss is a Dudeist, he might run *The Big Lebowski* on the office TV all day.

- The Trump court wants to allow the air you breathe and the water you drink to become dirtier. Donald Jughead Trump has waged an all-out war against environmental protections. "All told," the *New York Times* reported in January 2020, "Mr. Trump has gone further than any president, including Ronald Reagan, in dismantling clean air and water protections," including taking aim at the landmark National Environmental Policy Act, signed into law by Richard Nixon after the Cuyahoga River in Ohio caught fire and an oil tanker spilled 3 million gallons of crude oil on the California coast at Santa Barbara.

All such outcomes would be preventable or reversible if Democrats would put as much emphasis on the courts when they vote as Republicans do. This is the only time I will ever say this, fellow Democrats, but on this issue: be more like the Republicans.

SWAMP MONSTER TRUMP

An Agenda for Reform

Welcome to Washington

After Bill Clinton was elected, I was invited, along with a few of his other close aides, to brief the Democrats on Capitol Hill. I had worked on the Hill, so I knew a lot of the members of Congress. Plus, after twelve long years in the wilderness, Democrats were psyched to have a fellow Democrat moving into the White House. As you can imagine, I got a hero's welcome. I told them Clinton wanted to move quickly on his economic plan—focused on jobs, wages, ideas to lift millions out of poverty. They cheered.

I told them he wanted to move quickly on health care, that he thought it should be a right and not a privilege. They cheered again.

I told them he wanted to pass NAFTA and welfare reform. They clapped politely.

I told them he wanted campaign reform, to curb the influence of money in politics.

Crickets.

Then one member stood up. It was a very long time ago, and I did not take notes, so I am sure my recollection is faulty. Still, this is how

I remember the harangue: *You should be ashamed of yourself*, he said. *The men and women in this room are honorable people. My colleagues are the most honest, ethical people ever to serve in Congress. Good Lord, Paul, Spiro Agnew was taking envelopes filled with cash when he was vice president. And your boss, who has never served a day in this chamber, wants to lecture us about ethics!*

Thunderous applause.

That member, by the way, resigned a few years later in an ethics scandal. It reminds me of the legend of the South Philly politician who was running for judge with the slogan "A Reasonably Honest Man," or the guy in Louisiana who promised "Pretty Good Government."

My point is that corruption infects every capital. Always has, always will. Wherever there is power, there will be money. But Donald Trump has taken it to another level. He is the Typhoid Mary of corruption.

"Drain the Swamp!"

Part of the political genius of Donald Jitterbug Trump is his constant repetition of simple slogans. Jack Shafer, *Politico*'s senior media writer, ran some of candidate Trump's rhetoric through the Flesch-Kincaid grade-level test in 2015. In a primary debate he spoke at a fourth-grade level. At a news conference Shafer analyzed, Trump clocked in at a third-grade level. Let me be clear: this is not a bad thing. Trump is appealing to a mass audience, and half of the voters in the last presidential election did not have a college education. Democrats, as they have drifted away from being the party of the factory floor and become more comfortable as the party of the faculty lounge, tend to use rhetoric rich with sesquipedalian ornamentality. Perhaps even worse, they drift off message.

Democrats need a simple message, repeated relentlessly. Here's one: Trump is a one-man crime wave. I am not going to restate the crimes he should have been charged with as a result of the Mueller investigation (obstruction of justice), nor the crimes he committed in the Ukraine scandal (bribery, obstruction of justice). Those have been covered in depth, and, frankly, revealing them did not affect Trump's political support much at all. Consider these data points: on March 17, 2017, the day Mueller was named special counsel and the Russia collusion investigation began, Trump's approval rating in the FiveThirtyEight average was 42.7 percent. His disapproval rating was 51.5 percent. On the day the Senate voted to acquit Trump, after all the Russia revelations and all the Ukraine ugliness, his approval rating was 43.9 percent, his disapproval rating 51.8 percent.

I strongly support holding Trump accountable for his crimes. Robert Mueller and his team, House chairs Adam Schiff and Jerry Nadler, all the whistleblowers and witnesses—I think that they are heroes. But none of that had much of an effect on whether Trump will be reelected. (One important caveat: at the start of impeachment, the conventional wisdom was that, due to a then strong economy and blind partisan support from his party, Trump might zoom up in the polls the way President Clinton did. Did not happen.

But when average Americans think about corruption, they don't think about Kyiv. They think about K Street, the wide Washington boulevard lined with lobbyists. If you think the system is rigged; if you think Washington is dominated by corporate interests and their lobbyists; if you think the powerful and the privileged pull the strings and working families are being screwed in Washington, I have news for you:

Under Donald Trump, it is so much worse than you think.

Democrats should take on Trump's Washington sleaze in the 2020 campaign: as with all issues, make it about the voters. How has Trump's corruption hurt an everyday working person? Let's look.

Government of the Lobbyists, by the Lobbyists, for the Lobbyists

Trump loves lobbyists. Loves them even more than he loves golf, cheeseburgers, and porn stars. He has appointed more ex-lobbyists, an Associated Press analysis found, in his first three years than his two predecessors did in eight. He has put a defense contractor's lobbyist in charge of the Pentagon. He has put an oil lobbyist in charge of the Interior Department. He has put a coal lobbyist in charge of the Environmental Protection Agency. He put a guy who lobbied against raising the minimum wage in charge of the Labor Department, albeit as an acting secretary. The permanent secretary of labor? Well, he's an ex-lobbyist, too. And the guy who preceded both of them at Labor? Well, he resigned when it came to light that, when he was a prosecutor, he had given a secret sweetheart plea deal to Jeffrey Epstein. Heck, Trump would put Walter White from *Breaking Bad* in charge of the Drug Enforcement Administration if he could.

The nonprofit ProPublica catalogued 187 lobbyists in the Trump administration, infecting policy across the government. It may shock you to know that many of those lobbyists are in jobs where they can benefit their former special interest clients. This is possible because Trump repealed President Obama's blanket ban on hiring anyone who had been a lobbyist a year before joining the government. Trump's new rule says a former lobbyist can't work on anything they specifically lobbied on for two years, but that word "specifically" is a loophole you could drive a limousine though. Trump also shortened Obama's post-employment lobbying ban from two years to one, allowing his people to cash in quicker.

Here are a few of the places where lobbyists and their former special interest clients dovetail:

- A former lobbyist for British Petroleum has a top job at the EPA.

- A former pharmaceutical lobbyist was named counsel at the FDA.

- A former lobbyist for the health insurance industry is now at the Department of Health and Human Services.

- Oh, look, there's another health insurance lobbyist at HHS.

This matters to you. To your health and your safety. That coal lobbyist over at the EPA? His name is Andrew Wheeler. He is the top person at the EPA, but before that was up to his ears in coal. Now that he's at the EPA, however, he's devoted to protecting our precious environment. Not. Wheeler has presided over a rollback of clean water rules because, you know, who really needs clean water? The Trump-Wheeler dirty water plan removes protection from wetlands and streams across the country.

Health care is also an area where Trump has turned things over to the lobbyists. The Trump administration is in court as this is being written, trying to throw out protections for people with preexisting conditions, as well as all the other provisions of the Affordable Care Act. As many as 129 million Americans under the age of sixty-five have a preexisting medical condition, ranging from cancer or heart disease to diabetes or asthma. And if you don't have a preexisting condition, wait for it. The chances of developing one are as high as 30 percent. Before President Obama, Speaker Pelosi, and Senate Majority Leader Harry Reid brought us the Affordable Care Act, insurers could charge you more, limit your coverage, or refuse to cover you altogether if you had a preexisting condition. One study found that 36 percent of people who tried to buy health insurance faced this kind of discrimination. Even being a woman was in some cases declared a preexisting condition, especially if you needed a C-section delivery or sought treatment for domestic abuse or sexual violence.

Breathing, too, is a preexisting condition. Yet the Trump EPA, led by an ex-lobbyist, is rolling back an estimated ninety-five different environmental rules. The *New York Times* examined data compiled by Harvard and Columbia Law Schools. They found sixteen air pollution rules that had been repealed, with nine more in the pipeline.

For example, it loosened a Clinton administration rule that limited the amount of toxic pollution heavy industries could pour into the air. That means more benzene in the air, more dioxin, more lead, more arsenic, more mercury. We're not just talking about the amount of hair spray Trump puts into the atmosphere every day. This stuff is serious. They cause cancer and birth defects and other nasty conditions. Trump's EPA issued a press release hailing its pro-pollution position as a policy to "reduce regulatory burden for industries and the states." Major polluters will now be able to unburden themselves of their arsenic, their benzene, and the rest of their filth—right into your lungs. Oh, and the guy who put out that press release? Bill Wehrum. He's Trump's assistant EPA administrator in the Office of Air and Radiation. Before that he worked in President George W. Bush's EPA—and, notably, in between was a lobbyist for . . . okay, guess.

No, not the Organic Baby Food Association.

Nope, not the American Cancer Society.

No, not the International Society for Kittens and Puppies.

YES! The American Petroleum Institute. Also, the American Fuel and Petrochemical Manufacturers. Oh, and the American Chemistry Council.

Trump's Interior Department is led by Secretary David Bernhardt. But before he was called Mr. Secretary, he was Mr. Big Oil, earning his law firm a reported $5 million as a lawyer and lobbyist for energy interests. As a Public Citizen exposé reported by *Mother Jones* found, Secretary Bernhardt's former clients are keenly interested in his work at Interior. They have spent a combined $29.9 million lobbying his department. "Under Trump, insiders have taken control over virtually every agency, and the Interior Department is one of the far most egregious examples," says Alan Zibel, research director of Public Citizen's Corporate Presidency Project and the report's author. "Under Bernhardt, the Interior Department appears to have priced access to our nation's resources at $30 million and counting."

*"Under Trump, insiders have taken control
over virtually every agency."*

—Alan Zibel, Public Citizen's Corporate Presidency Project

Are those energy interests getting their money's worth? Well, first, let's stipulate that they wouldn't be spending that kind of dough if they didn't think they were getting a return on their investment. Their mamas didn't raise no fools. One particular regulatory rollback hit me especially hard: Trump's Interior Department gutted safety rules for offshore drilling that were put in place after the *Deepwater Horizon* debacle of 2010.

I'm sure you recall the disaster: nearly five million barrels of oil gushing into the Gulf of Mexico. You may remember all those wonderful volunteers cleaning off those oil-soaked birds. Most of all, I hope you remember the lives lost: eleven hardworking family men whose lives were briefly profiled in *USA Today*.

- Jason Anderson, who called coworkers his "rig brothers."

- Aaron Dale Burkeen, a crane operator from Philadelphia, Mississippi, who once told his sister, "Anything ever happens to me on that rig, I will make it. I'll float to an island somewhere. Y'all don't give up on me, 'cuz I will make it."

- Donald "Duck" Clark, who loved to fish and hated to leave home; he and his wife had four children.

- Stephen Ray Curtis, who served in the US Marine Corps, then as a police officer in Grant Parish, Louisiana, and as a volunteer firefighter.

- Gordon Jones, who finished his last phone conversation with his wife, Michelle, ten minutes before the rig blew up. Michelle gave birth two months after Gordon's funeral.

- Roy Wyatt Kemp, whose Christian faith was so deep he listened to sermons while out on the rig. He'd told his wife that there were safety problems. He was so concerned he had even planned his funeral, and asked to be buried with photos of his daughters.

- Karl Kleppinger Jr., who served in the army during Desert Storm. He and his wife and son shared their home with numerous animals they'd adopted from the Natchez, Mississippi, Humane Society. The family asked that, in his memory, donations be made to help more animals there.

- Keith Blair Manuel: the other guys on the rig called him Papa Bear; his Louisiana hunting buddies called him Gros Bebe (Big Baby). But his fiancé was never able to call him her husband.

- Dewey Revette: he left behind his wife of twenty-six years and two daughters. Since his passing, two grandsons have been born. Both were named for him.

- Shane Roshto was just twenty-two. He had a strand of steel cable—the kind they used on the rig—embedded in his wedding ring. Under the brim of his hat he'd written the date of his anniversary and his son's birth—the reasons he was doing such dangerous work.

- Adam Weise: Every three weeks he drove ten hours from his home in Yorktown, Texas, for another shift on the rig. His roots were deep in that small town, where he'd been a standout high school football player.

Real people pay the price when safety regulations are rolled back. I grew up with guys like them in southeast Texas. One summer my brother worked on one of those offshore rigs. What happened to those men could have happened to him. I worked onshore at a warehouse, loading pipe and other equipment into shipping containers to be hauled out to the rigs. We called ourselves "oil field trash," but as college boys, my brother and I were just making money for the next year's tuition. Those other men were the real deal. They did not deserve to die. We owed them more than that. No, Democrats, these men were not "deplorable." But they damn sure weren't expendable, either, Mr. Trump. And for Donald Trump to put lobbyists and corporate interests ahead of the safety of working people on rigs, well, it is nothing less than a sin.

H.R. 1

The Democrats who stormed the House in 2018 understand this, as does their leader, House Speaker Nancy Pelosi. (I just love using that phrase: "House Speaker Nancy Pelosi." Her place in history is secure; people will be naming their daughters "Nancy" in her honor.) Upon taking back the gavel in 2019, Speaker Pelosi designated as her number one priority a sweeping reform bill written by Rep. John Sarbanes (D-MD): the For the People Act, H.R. 1.

The For the People Act may be the most consequential bill you've never heard of. We all know that Mitch McConnell is burying it in the Senate. It's also true that not enough Democrats have repeated its simple three-word description: For. The. People.

Here's what this massive, sweeping anticorruption bill does:

Ethics in Government

- Requires the president and vice president, as well as candidates for president and vice president, to publicly disclose ten years of tax returns.

- Requires an actual code of ethics for the Supreme Court, which right now has fewer rules than a Nevada bordello.

- Bans the practice of members of Congress using taxpayers funds to settle sexual harassment claims.

- Prohibits members of Congress from serving on the boards of for-profit corporations.

- Tightens lobbyist disclosure and registration requirements, and includes a requirement that there be more oversight for foreign agents.

Voting Rights

- Makes Election Day a federal holiday.

- Institutes automatic voter registration.

- Implements same-day registration for federal elections.

- Puts online voter registration in place.

- Makes colleges and universities voter registration agencies (the way the Department of Motor Vehicles is now).

- Restores voting rights to felons who have completed their prison sentences.

- Prohibits voter roll purging—this would include banning the use of non-forwardable mail to remove people from the voter rolls.

- Requires fifteen days of early voting.

Election Security

- Requires states to have paper ballots.

- Sets cybersecurity standards for voting machines.

- Requires the director of national intelligence to assess threats six months before an election.

- Requires the president to develop a national strategy to protect democratic institutions, and creates a National Commission to Protect Democratic Institutions.

Campaign Finance

- Establishes a system of public financing for elections: a six-to-one match for donations under $200, which would encourage low-donor fund-raising.

- Requires super PACs and "dark money" groups to make all their donors public.

- Forces Facebook and other online giants to disclose the source of funding for political ads, just as TV and radio stations must, and requires them to disclose how much money was spent.

- Discloses political spending by government contractors.

- Makes it more difficult for foreign money to infect our campaigns by targeting shell corporations.

- Restructures the moribund Federal Election Commission, giving it five commissioners instead of the current six, which often leads to stalemate.

End *Citizens United*

Going into the 2008 election, Hillary Rodham Clinton was the Democratic front-runner. This freaked out the Hillary-haters on the right. Not sure why, but there has always been a cadre of mouth-breathing knuckle-draggers on the kook right who just hate Hillary. Maybe their mamas didn't breastfeed them, but for whatever reason, they hate her. So a right-wing group called Citizens United decided to make a ninety-minute attack ad—or documentary film, depending on your perspective. I must say, I haven't seen it, but I don't think I'm going to give it a positive review on Rotten Tomatoes.

Citizens United had already achieved some measure of notoriety; its founder, Floyd Brown, had helped create the "Willie Horton" ad against former Massachusetts governor Mike Dukakis in 1988. The ad lives in infamy as a racial dog whistle. Democrats, no doubt, didn't want to see the same thing happen to Hillary, this time under the guise of a ninety-minute "documentary." The group wanted to run their film on video-on-demand services, where it would air free of charge. The issue of whether Citizens United, which was a corporation, could run their political film the same way, say, Michael Moore aired his liberal documentaries, eventually made it to the Supreme Court. I can actually see the argument for letting the ninety-minute hatchet job air as a film rather than banning it as an ad. I love the First Amendment, so if it were up to me I would allow the group to run their film as they'd hoped to. But the court didn't just give the right-wing organization the ruling it sought; the Supreme Court went beyond what Citizens United even asked for. Way beyond.

In a sweeping ruling, the court threw out the century-old ban on corporate spending in elections. Bear in mind that Citizens United did not go to court asking for the ban on corporate spending in campaigns (which went back to 1907) to be overturned. But the Supreme Court ruled that spending is speech and thus protected—that corporations are people and thus have the same First Amendment rights to political speech. Again, spending had not even originally been at issue in the case. The right-wing majority on the Court became aggressive judicial activists, rewriting a century of settled law when they weren't even asked to do so.

The ruling blew up what little regulation there was of money in campaigns. Wealthy Americans and giant corporations now had the green light to buy elections. A week after the ruling, President Obama, a former constitutional law professor, declared in his State of the Union address that the decision would "open the floodgates for special interests." Sitting in the House chamber, Justice Samuel Alito, snug in his judicial robes, shook his head vigorously and mouthed the words "Not true."

A decade later, it is clear that Obama was right and Alito was wrong. Billions and billions of dollars have flowed into super PACs (like the one I used to advise). As Tiffany Muller, who runs a terrific group called End Citizens United, has written, the ruling has made super PACs more important players in many campaigns than the candidates themselves. "For example," Miller notes, "in Pennsylvania's 2016 US Senate race, outside spending topped $123 million, while the candidates combined for less than $50 million."

Muller and End Citizens United are advocating for a Twenty-Eighth Amendment to the Constitution to overturn *Citizens United*. Democrats are wise to support it. The current Supreme Court, dominated by Republicans appointed by George W. Bush (who lost the popular vote in 2000), and Donald Trump (who lost the popular vote in 2016), are not too keen on the rights of human beings to participate in elections, especially if those human beings are racial minorities or young people. They gutted the Voting Rights Act, which was written with the blood of civil rights martyrs. But they get positively *verklempt* about the rights of giant corporations and billionaires.

How Democrats Should Run on This

As my fellow Texan Jim Hightower reminds us, "the water won't clear up till you get the hogs out of the creek." If you want to know why we can't get prescription drug prices down, it's because Big Pharma has big money, which buys them big influence in Washington. If you want to know why we can't get health care for every American, it's because big insurance companies have big money, which buys them big influence. If you want to know why our air is dirty, our water polluted, and our planet on fire, it's because Big Oil has big money, which buys big influence. If you want to know why we can't get common-sense gun safety laws, it's because the NRA has big money, which buys big influence.

Name me an issue.

Go ahead.

The chances are that what's standing in the way of America moving forward on that issue is not a lack of good ideas. It's not a lack of public support. It's not a lack caring or compassion. It is the over-whelming power of money in politics. Scripture says, "For the love of money is the root of all evil." That timeless wisdom has never been more applicable than in Donald Trump's Washington. Donald Trump is for the lobbyists. Donald Trump is for the special interests. Donald Trump is for the big corporations. That's why they are for Donald Trump.

Democrats under Nancy Pelosi have made themselves the party of reform, of ethics, the party that is, as she says "for the people." They should run hard on this. They should take the no-corporate PAC pledge pushed by End Citizens United. They should explain to every voter that their health care, their schools, their air and water, every aspect of their lives is affected by the institutionalized corrup-tion that is the Trump administration.

For the People. End *Citizens United*. Two simple three-word phrases. Use them, Democrats.

CHAPTER 14

AMERICA LAST

Trump's Foreign Policy

The sun never sets on Donald Trump's sellouts of the United States. The man whose sworn, solemn obligation to protect America has instead put his own interests ahead of our nation's. Because he has sold out American national security, our nation is weaker, more vulnerable, less respected. Donald Trump is the first president in a century who cannot accurately be called the leader of the free world.

When he took office, Donald Juggernaut Trump had business interests in 144 companies in at least twenty-five countries. He had business relationships in South America, Asia, Europe, Africa, and North America. He had golf courses in the United Arab Emirates, condos in Mumbai, and a residential tower that has licensed the use of his name in Uruguay.

His conflicts of interest are varied and vast. But if you look at it another way, there is really no conflict of interest. With Donald Trump, his only interest is Donald Trump. See? No conflict.

The nonprofit group Citizens for Responsibility and Ethics in Washington (CREW) has kept count of all of Trump's conflicts of interest. As of late 2019, the number was 2,905. In the previous chapter, we examined Trump's swampy behavior here at home. For now, let's look at how the commander in chief has acted like the con man in chief when it comes to American foreign policy.

His financial conflicts are legion—and we will cover some of them in this chapter. But his first, most important sellout of America is even more unpardonable than mere greed. Trump's fawning, sycophantic, lickspittle obsequiousness toward Vladimir Putin is his greatest foreign policy disgrace. It is, I believe, a profound betrayal of American security interests, a betrayal of our intelligence services, a betrayal of our allies. Indeed, it is a betrayal of our fundamental mission as a democracy, as Trump has repeatedly sided with Putin in his efforts to undermine our system of free, fair, and honest elections.

All Roads Lead to Putin

Russia, John McCain accurately said, "is a gas station masquerading as a country." Take a minute. Look around your home, your office, your garage. Where were the things you see manufactured? Your coffee maker may be German, your car may be from Japan, your shirt may be from Bangladesh, your New Balance running shoes were probably made in the good ol' USA, your Canada Goose jacket came from . . . you know. The toothpaste you used this morning might have been put in the tube in Mexico. The medicine you take each day may have been manufactured in India, the Dell server in your office probably came from Austin, your Samsung TV came from South Korea, and your iPhone was made in China. You have a veritable United Nations right here in your home. But I bet you a hundred rubles you don't have anything stamped: Сделано в россии (MADE IN RUSSIA). Stoli vodka, maybe, although Tito's Handmade from—you guessed it—Austin is much better.

Russia is simply not an economic superpower. Their gross domestic product, which according to the World Bank was a puny $2.3 trillion in 2013, was down to $1.65 trillion in 2018. To put it into perspective, the State of New York has a larger economy. So does Texas.

And, of course, California. But, keep heart, Russkies, your economy is bigger than Florida's—although you have 141.7 million people, compared with Florida's 21 million.

But for its enormous nuclear arsenal, Russia would not be a major military power. The Russians spend an estimated $46.4 billion a year on defense. That's a lot of money, to be sure, but it is less than Japan or France or the Brits or the Saudis spend. To put it into perspective, the proposed 2020 US defense budget is $718.3 billion—but that doesn't come close to counting everything the United States spends on national security. One estimate puts total American spending for national security at $989 billion. Per year. Again, Russia spends $46 billion; we spend close to a trillion. And yet Putin is pushing America around? It makes no sense.

Russia has one aircraft carrier, the *Admiral Kuznetsov*. It took nine years to build and was commissioned in 1990. A few days later, the Soviet Union ceased to exist. Oopski. It made just six patrols over the next fourteen years. If you can call them patrols. The carrier, which runs on diesel, is so unreliable it travels with a tugboat to tow it. Indeed, at one point it had to be towed back from the French coast by tugboat. Last I checked—in December 2019—it was in drydock. In Russia. On fire. The United States Navy, by contrast, has eleven aircraft carriers, all of them nuclear-powered. As of this writing, none of them was on fire.

Why would a self-styled tough guy like Donald Trump be so intimidated by the punk leader of a failed economy and a dilapidated military?

House Speaker Nancy Pelosi said it best when she stood up in the Cabinet Room, stared daggers at Donald Trump, and said, "All roads with you lead to Putin." She is, of course, right. Trump has always had a thing for Putin. It is inexplicable, and dangerous.

It seems to have started when Trump brought his Miss Universe pageant to Moscow in 2013. He really wanted Putin to attend. "Do you think Putin will be going to The Miss Universe Pageant in November in Moscow," he tweeted, getting all fanboy about the Russian dictator—"if so, will he become my new best friend?"

When Russia "annexed" Crimea and invaded eastern Ukraine in 2014, Trump called Putin's aggression "so smart." "Well, he [Putin] has done an amazing job of taking the mantle," Trump told Fox News in April 2014. "And he's taken it away from the president [Obama], and you look at what he's doing. And so smart. When you see the riots in a country because they're hurting Russians, okay, 'We'll go and take it over.' And he really goes step by step, and you have to give him a lot of credit." Trump went on to claim that when he was in Moscow for the Miss Universe pageant, Putin "could not have been nicer. He was so nice and so everything. But you have to give him credit that what he's doing for that country in terms of their world prestige is very strong."

Trump went on to sort of make Putin his imaginary friend, like the sad, lonely boy in *Jojo Rabbit* does with Adolf Hitler. In July 2015 Trump told CNN's Anderson Cooper, "I think I get along fine with him." At that point there was no evidence Trump had ever met Putin. No evidence he had ever spoken with Putin by phone. No evidence Trump had ever even texted a desperate, cringey, insecure emoji to Vladimir. That didn't stop Trump from telling the National Press Club in 2014 that when he was in Moscow (presumably for the 2013 Miss Universe pageant), he spoke "directly and indirectly with President Putin, who could not have been nicer."

And at a 2016 GOP primary debate he claimed to be buddies with Vlad, telling his fellow Republicans, "I got to know him very well because we were both on *60 Minutes*, we were stablemates, and we did very well that night." In fact, Trump was interviewed in the United States, and Putin was interviewed in Russia. They were not even on the same continent.

In 2016, when our allies in Britain publicly accused Putin of complicity in the poisoning of former Russian spy Alexander Litvinenko, Trump defended his imaginary friend, telling Maria Bartiromo of

Fox Business, "Have they found him guilty? I don't think they found him guilty. If he did it, fine," Trump went on. "But I don't know that he did it. You know, people are saying they think it was him, it might have been him, it could have been him. But Maria, in all fairness to Putin—I don't know." The word salad went on like that but never included a word of criticism of the former KGB hack, even though our closest ally was accusing him of using chemical weapons in Britain.

Later in the campaign, when Russia hacked the Democratic National Committee, he called on Russia to hack Hillary. (For more, see chapter 7.) His team changed the GOP platform within days of that request, softening its previous tough-on-Russia language.

In a July 2016 appearance on ABC's *This Week*, Trump was all over the map. First, he said he would "look at" whether the United States would recognize Russia's seizure of Crimea as legitimate. Then he defended the theft of a sovereign country's territory, echoing Putin's talking points: "You know, the people of Crimea, from what I've heard, would rather be with Russia than where they were." Then he claimed that if he became president, Putin would cease his incursions into Ukraine: "He's not going into Ukraine, okay, just so you understand," he told George Stephanopoulos. "You can mark it down. You can put it down." And *then* he said Russia was indeed already in Ukraine, "in a certain way." Yes, in a certain way. In the certain way of tanks and troops and killing thousands of Ukrainians. Yeah, in that way. But with the fertilizer hitting the ventilator over Putin, Trump denied knowing him, telling Stephanopoulos, "I don't have a relationship with him. I didn't meet him. I haven't spent time with him. I didn't have dinner with him. I didn't—go hiking with him . . ." (Huh? Has Trump ever gone hiking with anyone? I mean, Trump is the kind of guy you'd expect to ride a golf cart through the all-you-can-eat buffet. And where did that weirdly specific denial come from? Why not "We didn't play Parcheesi"?) He continued, "I wouldn't know him from Adam except I see his picture, and I would know what he looks like."

Trump's clumsy crush on Putin was a sideshow during the campaign. It became a security risk once he entered the White House. President Obama had slapped sanctions on Russia as punishment for their cyberattack on our election. Some may say this was too weak a response. Indeed, one hothead called for bombing the headquarters of Russian intelligence. (Umm, that hothead was me.) Apparently Trump didn't see things my way. I only hope my tough talk didn't make his bone spurs flare up.

Even before he took office, Trump's national security adviser Mike Flynn spoke with Russian ambassador Sergey Kislyak about the sanctions. Flynn reportedly asked Kislyak not to escalate in response to the US sanctions. Kislyak reportedly told Flynn that Russia would, in fact, moderate its response as a result of his request. (Flynn later pleaded guilty to lying to the FBI about whether he had discussed the sanctions, but to the astonishment of career prosecutors, Trump's Attorney General, William Barr, ordered the charges dropped. He dropped charges that Flynn had already pleaded guilty to; charges Flynn swore under oath he was guilty of.)

In May 2017, Trump hosted Kislyak and Russian foreign minister Sergey Lavrov in the Oval Office. This meeting was wrong in so many ways. First, protocol generally reserves Oval Office visits for the head of government or the head of state, not a minister and an ambassador. Second you don't give an Oval Office audience to a man like Kislyak, who has been described by current and former American intelligence officials as "a top spy and recruiter of spies." Third, Trump allowed a Russian photographer into the Oval Office, despite the fact that he or she could have used the photography equipment as cover to smuggle in espionage devices. Fourth, although a Russian photographer was given access, no American media were allowed to attend any part of the meeting. Fifth, Trump reportedly told the Russians that firing FBI director James Comey, which he had done the day before, would make his life easier. "He was crazy, a real nut job. I faced great pressure because of Russia. That's taken off," he said.

Each of those five things was eye-popping. But here was the worst thing: in the meeting with the Russian spy/ambassador, Trump gave our Russian adversaries highly classified information about Syria. This disclosure, the *Washington Post* reported, "jeopardized a critical source of intelligence on the Islamic State." Let me decode that for you: sources and methods are the holy grail of intelligence. Not mere information, but the sources and methods used to attain it. Sources and methods must be protected at all costs—because to compromise them could cut off all future information from those sources and methods. People could die. And yet Trump blithely blabbed to his Russian pals about information that threatened the sources and methods of critical intelligence on ISIS.

Here's how the *Post* described the intel Trump leaked: "This is code-word information," said a U.S. former official familiar with the matter, using terminology that refers to one of the highest classification levels used by American spy agencies. Trump 'revealed more information to the Russian ambassador than we have shared with our own allies.'"

If I had done that when I was a White House aide, I would not be writing this book today. I would at best be furtively scratching notes to my kids on smuggled scraps of toilet paper from my cell in Gitmo.

Two months later, Trump had his first face-to-face meeting with Putin, at the G20 summit in Hamburg. And, without telling anyone, he had his second meeting with Putin there as well. The first meeting, on July 7, 2017, had the obligatory handshakes and flags. "It's an honor to be with you," Trump said to Putin. "I'm delighted to be able to meet you personally, Mr. President," Putin replied. "And I hope as you have said, our meeting will yield concrete results." The meeting, Trump aides said, was scheduled to last forty-five minutes, but it went so well that the two presidents wound up talking for two hours and fifteen minutes. That's a hell of a first date. Trump was so excited when he saw Putin I imagine he kept trying to swipe right.

American officials later leaked that Trump asked Putin about the

2016 cyberattack. Putin, as per usual, denied involvement. Trump replied, "I believe you." Love at first sight.

But there was a second, initially undisclosed meeting that same day—because two hours and fifteen minutes just isn't long enough for this bromance. In the second meeting, the only translator was Putin's. Curious. No other US staff was present. Admiral John Kirby, who had served as chief spokesman for both the Pentagon and the State Department, told CNN that the lack of US staff and translator was problematic, since the American side would not have a careful translation of the conversation, nor even a record of what was discussed. "In this case," Kirby said, "we have none of these things. And the Russians will have a transcript. Not good."

For a guy who wears his psyche on his Twitter fingers, Trump is remarkably closed-mouthed about his dealings with Russia. It turns out that after that first meeting with Putin in Hamburg, Trump went so far as to confiscate the notes from the US translator, according to the *Washington Post*. He also ordered the translator not to discuss the meeting with other administration officials. That is, other *Trump* administration officials. Diplomacy often involves discretion, of course. But why would Trump not want his own team to know what he had discussed with Putin?

Trump's secrecy regarding Putin is so important to him that there is little or no record—even a classified record—of at least five personal meetings he had with Putin. As the *Washington Post* put it, "Such a gap would be unusual in any presidency, let alone one that Russia sought to install through what US intelligence agencies have described as an unprecedented campaign of election interference." Former deputy secretary of state Strobe Talbott is a Russia expert. As a student at Oxford, he translated Nikita Khrushchev's smuggled memoirs into English. (Quick historical note: in the Clinton days I often translated James Carville's remarks into English.) As a journalist, Talbott wrote several books about Russia. As a diplomat, he participated in more than a dozen meetings between Russian president Boris Yeltsin and President Bill Clinton. He told the *Post* that Trump's secrecy "is not only unusual by historical standards, it is outrageous. It handicaps the US government—the experts and advisers and Cabinet officers who are there to serve [the president]—and it certainly gives Putin much more scope to manipulate Trump."

But all of that was just a windup for Trump's meeting with Putin in Helsinki. That meeting, on July 16, 2018, will live in infamy as the most ignominious presidential surrender in history. Even Neville Chamberlain would be thinking, "For goodness sake, show some backbone, man!" Standing next to Putin, and in front of the world's press, Trump rebuked US intelligence agencies and sided with a hostile foreign power against his own country. The Russian cyberattack of 2016 was, again, center stage. Trump was asked about it. Then Trump grabbed a knife, a giant knife, and plunged it squarely into the back of American intelligence operatives who devote their working lives—many risk their lives—to bring policymakers the truth. He wasn't finished. Then he threw them under the bus—a Russian bus. "My people came to me," he said with Putin beside him. "Dan Coats came to me, and some others. They said they think it's Russia. I have President Putin. He just said it's not Russia. I will say this: I don't see any reason why it would be."

Wait. What?

I can think of one reason Russia would have tried to manipulate the 2016 election:

*TO HELP MAKE THEIR PREFERRED
CANDIDATE PRESIDENT!*

"I have great confidence in my intelligence people," Trump said, "but I will tell you that President Putin was extremely strong and powerful in his denial today." This debacle, this surrender, came after a two-hour private meeting. And by "private" I mean, once again, Trump did not let any US aides in the room (except this time he did allow an American translator in).

The outrage from Americans was universal. "Donald Trump's press conference performance in Helsinki rises to & exceeds the threshold of 'high crimes & misdemeanors,'" tweeted former CIA director John Brennan. "It was nothing short of treasonous. Not only were Trump's comments imbecilic, he is wholly in the pocket of Putin. Republican Patriots: Where are you???"

Dan Coats, the former Indiana GOP senator who was Trump's choice to serve as director of national intelligence, publicly and courageously broke with his boss. "We have been clear in our assessments of Russian meddling in the 2016 election," he said, "and their ongoing, pervasive efforts to undermine our democracy, and we will continue to provide unvarnished intelligence in support of our national security."

Sen. Bob Corker (R-TN), then-chairman of the Senate Foreign Relations Committee, put it more succinctly. Trump, he said, "made us look like a pushover." Former director of national intelligence James Clapper called Trump's comments "truly unbelievable." He went on to say, "On the world stage, in front of the entire globe, the President of the United States essentially capitulated and seems intimidated by Vladimir Putin. So it was amazing and very, very disturbing." Former defense secretary and Republican senator Chuck Hagel was also gobsmacked. "A sad day for America," the Vietnam veteran said. "A sad day for the world." Another former Pentagon chief, Ash Carter, likened watching Trump tear down US intelligence to "watching the destruction of a cathedral. In almost four decades with national defense, starting in the Pentagon under Ronald Reagan, I never saw or imagined so uneven a handover of American security interests and principles with nothing in return at a meeting."

House Republican leader Kevin McCarthy (R-CA) once put forth a theory of why Trump is so pliant with Putin. "There's two people I think Putin pays," McCarthy told a group of his colleagues on June 15, 2016. "Rohrabacher and Trump." (Dana Rohrabacher was at the time a GOP congressman from McCarthy's home state of California.)

Some of the Republicans laughed. McCarthy added, "Swear to God." When the *Washington Post* asked McCarthy about the comment, in May 2017, he denied it forcefully. After the *Post* told him they'd read a transcript and heard an audiotape, McCarthy said he was only joking. Whether serious or humorous, the comment came after McCarthy, then-Speaker Paul Ryan, and others had met with the prime minister of Ukraine. After the Ukrainian leader had left the meeting, at which he had detailed Russian efforts to influence Ukrainian politics, the conversation among the GOP House members turned to the hack of the Democratic National Committee, which had occurred the previous day. McCarthy had a theory about that, too. "I'll guarantee you what it is . . . ," he said. "The Russians hacked the DNC and got the opp [opposition research] that they had on Trump."

I have no idea why Trump sucks up to Putin. I have no idea if McCarthy—joking or not—is right. Since Trump won't release his tax returns, we have no idea whether Putin in fact pays him, as McCarthy suggested. But I do know this: Trump's passion for Putin has consequences. It has made America weaker, more vulnerable. It has made our allies distrust us. It has made the world more dangerous.

Cui bono? The ancient Romans knew how to ask the right questions. When you see some action that you don't understand, ask who benefits. Let's ask, shall we?

- Who benefits from Trump withholding military aid to Ukraine? Putin.

- Who benefits from Trump denying the Ukrainian president an Oval Office meeting? Putin.

- Who benefits from Trump denigrating NATO? Putin.

- Who benefits from Trump attacking the European Union—even calling the EU "a foe"? Putin.

- Who benefits when Trump says Crimea is part of Russia? Putin.

- Who benefits from Trump calling for Russia's reinstatement in the G7 gathering of the world's leading democracies (which would then go back to being called the "G8")? Putin.

- Who benefits from Trump reversing the Republican Party's decades-old tough-on-Russia stance? Putin.

- Who benefits when Trump draws a moral equivalence between the Russian thugocracy, which murders journalists, and the United States—which, for all our faults, enshrines press freedom in our First Amendment? Putin.

- Who benefits when Trump, in a White House interview aired before the Super Bowl, declares he "respects" Putin? And when Bill O'Reilly challenged him, saying "Putin is a killer," who benefits when Trump runs down America, saying, "We have a lot of killers. Well, you think our country is so innocent?" Putin.

- Who benefits when Trump undermines faith in American elections, repeatedly and falsely claiming they're rigged and riddled with voter fraud? Putin.

- Who benefits when Trump repeatedly delayed implementing sanctions on Russia for its chemical weapons attack on Russian dissident Sergei Skripal and his daughter in England? Putin.

- Who benefits when Trump lifts sanctions on companies connected to a pro-Putin oligarch—sanctions imposed to punish Russia for the 2016 cyberattack? Putin.

- Who benefits when Trump ignores his own national security team's memo—"DO NOT CONGRATULATE" Putin after his rigged 2018 election, the memo said—and congratulates him anyway, thus legitimizing the fraudulent Putin victory? Putin.

- Who benefits when Trump gives code-word classified intel to an alleged Russian spy in the Oval Office? Putin.

- Who benefits when Trump insults seventeen US intelligence agencies by saying that he believes Putin's denial of responsibility for the 2016 cyberattack over their conclusion that Putin was behind it? Putin.

- Who benefits when Trump follows Putin's suggestion that the United States cancel military exercises with South Korea? Putin.

- Who benefits when Trump repeats Kremlin talking points that the Soviet invasion of Afghanistan was in response to terrorism? Putin.

- Who benefits when a US withdrawal from Syria increases Russian influence in the region? Putin.

- One more: Who benefits from a Russian cyberattack that helps to install Trump as president? You got it.

Putin's Pet

Trump acts like a lovesick fanboy whenever Putin's name comes up. Campaigning for president, he said that Putin was more of a leader than President Obama: "The man has very strong control over a country. Now, it's a very different system and I don't happen to like the system, but certainly in that system, he's been a leader. Far more than our president has been a leader."

Putin's human rights violations are numerous—so vast and varied it's hard to know where to begin. But let's begin with the killings. On the night of February 27, 2015, opposition leader Boris Nemtsov was walking across the Bolshoy Moskvoretsky Bridge, next to the Kremlin. A former deputy prime minister under Boris Yeltsin, he was a charismatic figure whose political career had been derailed by Putin. As he crossed the bridge that night, he was shot four times from behind. His girlfriend watched in horror. Five Chechens were convicted of the assassination, but observers have their doubts. As David Satter, who has written four books about Russia, wrote in the conservative

National Review, "The evidence . . . indicates that the defendants were not guilty and the murder was organized by the regime."

According to the Committee to Protect Journalists, twenty-six journalists have been murdered in Russia under Putin. Many of them were investigative journalists. Yet Trump joked about "getting rid" of reporters in a meeting with Putin at the 2019 G20 summit in Osaka, Japan. Gesturing to the swarm of journalists and photographers covering their meeting, Trump said, "Get rid of them. Fake news is a great term, isn't it? You don't have this problem in Russia, but we do." Putin responded, "We also have. It's the same." I bet Trump wishes it were the same.

When candidate Trump praised Putin on MSNBC's *Morning Joe,* host Joe Scarborough reminded him, "Well, also, this is a person that kills journalists, political opponents." Trump replied, "He's running his country and at least he's a leader, unlike what we have in this country." Scarborough tried a second time. "But again," he said, "he kills journalists that don't agree with him." Trump deflected, making the astonishing claim that the United States was just as vicious: "Well, I think our country does plenty of killing also, Joe."

Trump's foreign policy is Putin, Putin, Putin. In regions where Putin does not play a critical role, however, Trump has another touchstone. No, not freedom, like Reagan. Not peace or stability or the advancement of American values. Trump's north star is Trump. That's "Trump"—spelled "M-O-N-E-Y." If you live by the advice Deep Throat gives Bob Woodward in the movie *All the President's Men,* "Follow the money," you get a pretty clear picture of Trump's foreign policy.

"I Have a Little Conflict of Interest"

In several countries, Trump has or has had business interests that could be a conflict of interest. Let's look at a few:

Turkey. In September 2017, Recep Tayyip Erdogan was in the midst of a crackdown on political dissent. Within the space of a week, his government jailed numerous journalists, with Erdogan himself declaring that most of them "aren't journalists whatsoever. Most of them are terrorists. Many have been involved in bombing incidents or burglary." (Did not know that burglary was a major terrorist activity.) He closed more than a hundred media organizations and transferred the assets of many publications to the Turkish government. When one columnist referred to Erdogan as a "would-be dictator," Erdogan threw him in jail.

That same week, Erdogan came to New York for the annual United Nations General Assembly. Trump met with him—which was wise. Turkey is a NATO ally and hosts key US military bases, including the Incirlik Air Base and Izmir Air Station. Still, one hoped that the American president might mention human rights and freedom of the press to a leader who, that very week, was jailing journalists. Not only did Trump not stand up for imprisoned journalists and impounded newspapers, he praised Erdogan lavishly. He said that Erdogan was "getting very high marks," and that it was "a great honor and privilege" to introduce him—"because he's become a friend of mine." Trump went on to explicitly endorse Erdogan's antidemocratic crackdown, saying, "He's running a very difficult part of the world. He's involved very, very strongly and, frankly, he's getting very high marks."

Think of that. First off, Erdogan should not be "running" any part of the world. He is a political leader and should be accountable to his people and to civilized, democratic norms. Trump's praise of Erdogan was especially disconcerting, because the previous time the Turkish leader had been on US soil, his thugs beat protesters outside the Turkish embassy in Washington. Then-secretary of state Rex Tillerson condemned the attack, calling it "simply unacceptable." Not a peep from Trump or the White House.

Why would Trump suck up to Erdogan? As we have seen, sucking up to autocrats is his go-to move. But beyond that, he has a little conflict of interest. Wait, I should have put that in quotes. In 2015, Trump gave an interview to Breitbart radio's Steve Bannon. "I have a little conflict of interest, 'cause I have a major, major building in Istanbul, Turkey. It's a tremendously successful job. It's called Trump Towers—two towers, instead of one, not the usual one, it's two." We get it, Donald. It's two towers. But it is one towering conflict of interest. So towering that even the morally blind Trump can see it. In fact, Trump does not own the buildings in Istanbul. As is common in Trump Land, he licenses his brand to the real owner, in this case Turkish businessman Aydin Dogan, who is reported to be a close ally of—wait for it—Recep Tayyip Erdogan. Trump has collected up to $17 million in royalties from Trump Towers Istanbul since 2012, when the towers opened—with Erdogan in attendance.

This licensing deal means that Erdogan, through his friend, has enormous leverage over Trump. In fact, in 2016, when Trump announced his proposed Muslim ban, Erdogan and Dogan threatened to remove Trump's name from the buildings. "Trump has no tolerance for Muslims living in the US. And on top of that they used a brand [in Istanbul] with his name. The ones who put that brand on their building should immediately remove it."

Erdogan must be an enormously persuasive person, because time after time he has moved Trump to support the Turkish line. Most notoriously, in December 2018, Trump abruptly ordered the withdrawal of all two thousand US troops from Syria. This decision went against his senior military and diplomatic advisers and reportedly stunned our close allies in places like Israel and the United Kingdom. Opposing the move were James Mattis, the defense secretary; Gen. Joseph Votel, US Central Command leader; and Brett McGurk, the America envoy to the coalition fighting ISIS. They said that the withdrawal would abandon our Kurdish allies, who bore the brunt of the fighting against ISIS, while surrendering US influence in the region to Putin's Russia and to Syrian leader Bashar al-Assad. Mattis was so outraged he resigned.

But you know who loved the US withdrawal so hated by our generals? Recep Tayyip Erdogan. In fact, Erdogan was reportedly the first to learn of Trump's decision—before even our own military. In a call with Erdogan on December 14, 2018, Trump agreed to withdraw US troops. He did it, the Associated Press reported, "hastily, without consulting his national security team or allies, and over strong objections from virtually everyone involved in the fight against the Islamic State group." According to the AP, the national security team gave Trump talking points for the call with the Turkish leader. Far from agreeing to withdraw troops, the talking points reportedly called for Trump to pressure Erdogan to back off from attacking the United States' Kurdish allies. The talking points agenda was seemingly ignored as Erdogan bullied Trump. "Why are you still there?" he reportedly asked him, arguing that ISIS had lost 99 percent of its territory. This fact was confirmed by US security officials, including then-national security adviser John Bolton, who was listening to the call. Bolton hastily argued that the victory over ISIS could be reversed if the United States pulled out.

But Trump had heard enough. Suddenly he told Erdogan that the United States would withdraw all its troops. Bolton, according to the AP, was shocked. Apparently so was Erdogan. Perhaps he did not expect Trump to fold like a Trump casino. Even Erdogan, who had sought the withdrawal, urged Trump not to go too fast. Trump is said to have restated his decision to withdraw and hung up without offering any more specifics.

The bromance continues. At a NATO meeting in Brussels in July 2018, Trump was spotted fist-bumping Erdogan.

The Philippines. In 2017, Philippine leader Rodrigo Duterte was in the second year of his bloody "drug war." More than twelve thousand Filipino drug suspects, some of them children, have been killed in

Duterte's war. His critics have been arrested, including Senator Leila de Lima, who had been leading an inquiry into the killings. Duterte has urged attacks on human rights groups, telling police to shoot them "if they are obstructing justice." Human Rights Watch reports that "the killing of journalists remains a concern in the Philippines as well as reports of attacks on schools by government forces."

An American president, of course, has a special duty to call out such savagery. At a summit of the Association of Southeast Asian Nations (ASEAN) in 2016, that is exactly what Barack Obama did. He publicly decried the extrajudicial killings in the Philippines, calling on Duterte to respect human rights and follow the rule of law. "We're not going to back off," he said, "on our position that if we're working with a country, whether it's on anti-terrorism, whether it's going after drug traffickers, as despicable as these networks may be, as much damage as they do, it is important from our perspective to make sure that we do it the right way."

Duterte flipped. He called Obama "a son of a whore," and the United States in turn canceled a planned one-on-one meeting. Displaying his preternatural cool, Obama shrugged off the insult. "I don't take these kinds of things personally," he said. "I think it's just a habit, a way of speaking for him." Lord, I miss Barack Obama. Both his strong moral compass and his unflappable manner are sorely needed today.

While Rodrigo Duterte has never besmirched the memory of Donald Trump's mother, he did snub Trump when Trump invited him to Las Vegas for the 2020 ASEAN summit. Worse, Duterte has terminated the Visiting Forces Agreement with the United States. The VFA is a pact negotiated in the 1990s that ensures that US troops in the Philippines are under the jurisdiction of US, not Filipino, law. This is an important protection for US military personnel, especially in a place like the Philippines, where Duterte has made a mockery of the rule of law. To add insult to injury, when he canceled the VFA, Duterte not only slammed the door on a new deal, he nailed it shut.

Saying through a spokesman, "The president will not entertain any initiative coming from the US government to salvage the VFA, neither will he accept any official invitation to visit the United States." The American embassy in Manila decried the move, calling it "a serious step with significant implications."

Donald Trump, who never fails to overreact to a slight, said nothing. I must say, this was one time Trump's penchant for insults would come in handy. I was looking forward to the demeaning nickname he would give Duterte, to the string of exclamation points and misspelled taunts. Nothing.

One would hope that Trump would stand up for our troops, if not for the rule of law generally. But one worries that Trump has different priorities. At least one different priority, and it's 822 feet tall. You guessed it. There's a Trump Tower Manila, a $150 million luxury condo tower. As in Turkey, Trump is licensing his name and receiving royalties.

This conflict of interest is why we have an emoluments clause in the Constitution. It bars any federal official from accepting a gift or profit from a foreign ruler or government. Members of Congress and senators filed suit—215 altogether—alleging Trump is violating the emoluments clause. In February 2020, the Court of Appeals for the DC Circuit tossed out their lawsuit, saying that they did not have the standing to bring the challenge because they didn't constitute a majority of either chamber of Congress.

China. As we saw in chapter 5, American farmers are the biggest losers in Trump's trade war with China. Their incomes collapsed, their markets dried up, their communities were hammered. But someone has prospered from deals with China, even as our farmers have suffered. You have one guess.

That's right. Industrial and Commercial Bank of China, China's largest bank—which is owned by the Communist Chinese government—is a major tenant of Trump Tower in New York. According to *Forbes*, the Chinese bank pays the Trump Organization $2 million a year in rent. The lease, *Forbes* reported, expired in October 2019, according to a debt prospectus *Forbes* obtained.

In January 2019, it was reported that ICBC would retain some space in Trump Tower but would move the bulk of its operation to a different Manhattan building—one not owned by Trump. This was a big deal. With three floors to house its one hundred employees, it planned to reduce its Trump Tower presence to just one floor.

To this day, neither Trump nor his sons, who run the Trump Organization, have disclosed the content or results of whatever negotiations they may have had with the Chinese over the lease.

China, of course, has been notorious for its lack of protection of intellectual property. The Office of the United States Trade Representative has estimated that $225 to $600 billion is lost each year to Chinese theft of American intellectual property. China has rightly been dubbed "the world's principal IP infringer." So it is striking when China takes steps to protect the intellectual property of an American company. Guess whose company?

Yep. Ivanka Trump's. She won preliminary approval of five trademarks from the Chinese government in 2019, even as the Trump administration, in which she serves, was negotiating a trade deal with Beijing. According to the Associated Press, the trademarks were for "child care centers, sunglasses and wedding dresses" and "brokerage, charitable fundraising and art valuation services."

Beyond these, the AP says that thirty-four trademarks were granted to the Trump family by the Chinese, including sixteen to Ivanka Trump Marks LLC. They cover everything from handbags and shoes to jewelry and sunglasses. And, of course, voting machines.

Huh? Voting machines? Are there really going to be Ivanka Trump Voting Machines? Or did she do this just to show us she has a lively sense of humor?

Ivanka Trump shuttered her brand in July 2018 but kept pursuing new trademarks, leading the watchdogs at CREW to speculate that she may intend to revive her businesses when she leaves the White House, as several of the trademarks will remain viable until 2028.

The US-China relationship is one of the world's most important, especially now. China sees itself as ascendant, and it is increasingly assertive. It is moving aggressively, both economically and militarily, and those moves do not benefit America. Wouldn't it be nice if we had a president who could focus on the challenge of China without numerous financial conflicts of interest?

North Korea. There is no evidence that Trump has any business dealings with North Korea—so that's good. And early in his presidency, when Kim was rattling sabers, Trump lashed out, threatening to hit North Korea with "fire and fury like the world has never seen."

Nowadays, of course, Trump is lovey-dovey with the North Korean dictator. Trump has said Kim "wrote me beautiful letters—and they're great letters. And we fell in love." He has called his relationship with the murderous Kim a "special relationship"—a designation without formal consequence, but which traditionally has been reserved for the United States' long alliance with Great Britain.

Even before the love letters, Trump saw something to admire in Kim: his brutality. By 2018, Trump was gushing about Kim and looking forward to meeting him. "Kim Jong Un was—he really has been very open," Trump said about the most secretive leader on earth. "I think very honorable, from everything we're seeing."

Cindy and Fred Warmbier disagree. Their son Otto was a twenty-two-year-old University of Virginia student who visited North Korea. He saw a propaganda poster on the wall of his hotel and thought it would make a cool souvenir. Otto was arrested, imprisoned, and tortured. His teeth were twisted and mangled. After a year of relentless torture, he was flown back to the United States. When Cindy and Fred boarded the plane, they found their boy lying on a stretcher. There was a feeding tube in his nose. His head was shaved. He was blind and deaf. He was semiconscious and jerking involuntarily. His poor, mangled body was emitting what his dad called "this howling, involuntary, inhuman sound." Days later, Otto was dead.

"Kim and his evil regime are responsible for the death of our son Otto," they said in a statement after Trump praised the North Korean dictator. "Kim and his evil regime are responsible for unimaginable cruelty and inhumanity. No excuse or lavish praise can change that."

Trump ♥s Autocrats

In places where there is no obvious reported financial conflict, Trump seems to have a preference for strongmen over democratic leaders. Even more than *Playboy* models and porn stars, Trump loves dictators. "Trump has dictator envy," the Rice University presidential historian Douglas Brinkley told the *Washington Post*. "You just destroy your enemies' lives with a phone call. That's attractive to Trump." Indeed, Trump heaps praise on some of the most ruthless autocrats in the world. This list is illustrative, not comprehensive, but consider his affection for:

- **Mussolini.** I wish I were kidding. When he was running for president, Trump sent out one of his patented 6:00 a.m. tweets. Someone calling themselves "@ilduce2016" had tweeted this quote, attributing it to Trump: "It is better to live one day as a lion than 100 years as a sheep." Trump jumped on it and retweeted it to his millions of followers. Trouble is, the account was a bot, created by journalist Ashley Feinberg. Feinberg, then with Gawker, wanted to see if she could bait Trump into claiming credit for a Mussolini quote. She could. Mussolini, of course, was the founder of fascism.

- **Mohammed bin Salman.** The Saudi crown prince, who some believe was complicit in the murder and dismemberment of US resident and journalist Jamal Khashoggi, is a Trump fave. And when I say "some believe," I mean a bunch of people—including

United States senators. Bob Corker, the Tennessee Republican who in 2018 was chair of the Senate Foreign Relations Committee, emerged from a CIA briefing on the Khashoggi murder and told reporters that if MBS were on trial, "he'd be convicted in 30 minutes."

Donald Trump disagreed. Even as reports of MBS's complicity were coming in, Trump praised him, telling the *Washington Post* that he "is a person who can keep things under check." Trump called him "a very strong person" with "very good control."

Just weeks after Khashoggi's brutal murder—and presumably after receiving the same intelligence briefing that produced Corker's response—he issued a bizarre, rambling statement. The statement was on official White House letterhead—it was not just a tweet. Trump parroted the Saudi line that perhaps Khashoggi was "an enemy of the state and a member of the Muslim Brotherhood." He noted that both MBS and his father, King Salman, denied being behind the murder, which occurred in a Saudi consulate in Turkey. Then this: "Our intelligence agencies continue to assess all information, but it could very well be that the Crown Prince had knowledge of this tragic event—maybe he did and maybe he didn't!"

- **Abdel Fattah el-Sisi.** While campaigning for president, Trump met with the Egyptian strongman. After the meeting, Trump called the dictator "a fantastic guy" with whom he has "great chemistry." He went out of his way to praise the bloody coup by which Sisi seized power in 2013: "He took control of Egypt," Trump said. "And really took control of it." Took control? Well, that's one way to describe the massacre of 817 protestors. Or the incarceration of sixty thousand political prisoners. Or excluding your political rivals from running against you. So we should not be too surprised that, when he was waiting to meet with Sisi on the sidelines of the 2019 G7 summit in France, Trump called out, "Where's my favorite dictator?"

In each of these instances, Trump didn't merely voice support for a leader whose cooperation America might need, in spite of that leader's poor record on human rights. The United States needs to deal with dictators, I get that. Some of them have oil, like MBS. Others have a strategic location, like Erdogan. Still others, like Putin and Kim Jong Un, have nuclear weapons. It is a fact of life that the United States needs to have relationships with dictators. But Trump's view is different from all his predecessors of either party. He admires the dictators not despite their human rights violations but *because* of them.

Ronald Reagan negotiated with the Soviet Union, but he didn't praise the gulags.

Trump Is a Global Joke. Literally.

The video has to be Donald Trump's worst nightmare. World leaders of some of America's closest allies—Britain's Boris Johnson, France's Emmanuel Macron, Dutch prime minister Marc Rutte, and Canada's Justin Trudeau—were caught on tape ridiculing Trump. At a 2019 NATO reception at Buckingham Palace, the leaders were taped mocking and guffawing at Trump's asshattery. Johnson asks Trudeau, ". . . is that why you were late?" Trudeau responds, "He was late because he takes a forty-minute press conference off the top." Macron then says something, which is inaudible on the tape, but to which Rutte responds, "Fake news media?" mocking Trump's press-bashing. Later, Princess Anne, the daughter of Queen Elizabeth, joins the group. We can't make out what she says, but then, with exaggerated gestures, Trudeau responds, "You just watched his team's jaws drop to the floor." The snickering continues as Johnson makes a comment. Trudeau responds, referring to a Trump golf property, "Yes, no, no, I think that's Doral. Doral, yes, in Miami." Trump had floated the idea of hosting the G7 summit at his Doral resort, which the *Washington Post* described as "struggling financially," but reversed course when people thought it was a bad idea for the president to give himself a big fat government contract.

Donald Trump is a joke. He is an object of scorn and ridicule and contempt all around the world. In his 2020 State of the Union address, he began his speech by crowing that "our country is thriving and highly respected again! . . . The days of our country being used, taken advantage of, and even scorned by other nations are long behind us."

Really? That's not what the world says. The Pew Research Center studies global attitudes, and has done so for years. Simply put, America under Trump is a laughingstock. While 64 percent of the world expressed confidence in President Obama, just 22 percent has confidence in Trump. Favorable views of the United State have collapsed: from 64 percent at the end of the Obama presidency to 49 percent in Trump's first year in office.

The world sees Trump pretty much the same way Johnson and Trudeau and Macron and Princess Anne do: 75 percent say he's arrogant; 65 percent say he is intolerant; 62 percent say he is dangerous. At first I thought that was a poll of his original cabinet.

But there is one place where Trump gets significantly higher marks than either President Obama or President George W. Bush. Guess where? (No peeking.)

No, not Norway.

Nope, not Ireland.

Not Australia.

Russia. After he spoke out against Russia's invasion of Ukraine in 2014, Obama's support among Russians dropped to just 11 percent. But Trump's pro-Putin policies have him sitting pretty in Russia, with 53 percent approval—a level of support he has never had among Americans. But then again, his policies have been a lot more pro-Russia than pro-America.

Angela Merkel, the German chancellor, gets much higher marks around the world than Trump. Whereas just 22 percent have confidence in Trump's leadership, 42 percent trust Merkel. Even more troubling in terms of US national prestige, the world has more confidence in the autocratic leaders of China (28 percent) and Russia (27 percent). This matters. Leadership matters. Trust matters. Prestige is a force multiplier. When America is respected, allies are more willing to stand beside us, militarily, diplomatically, economically.

At the end of Trump's first year in office, a year in which Trump belittled NATO, the European Union, and pretty much all of America's democratic allies while sidling up to Putin, the Germans had had enough. Foreign minister Sigmar Gabriel gave an important speech in which he said that US leadership was beginning to "crumble." He said that the US retreat from world leadership was deeper than any one president, and would not likely be reversed after the next election. Gabriel noted Trump's withdrawal from the Iran nuclear deal and said this would increase the risk of war. He criticized Trump's unilateral decision to move the American embassy in Israel from Tel Aviv to Jerusalem. Whether you agree with Gabriel or not, the people of Germany do. According to a survey conducted by the Körber Foundation, Germans view Trump, in the words of a Reuters report, "as a bigger challenge for German foreign policy than authoritarian leaders in North Korea, Russia, or Turkey." This is infuriating to me, as well as tragic.

France, too, is pulling away from America. Without France, there might not have ever been a United States of America. As Britain's chief rival, France was happy to see the upstart colonists punch King George III in the nose. France sent us weapons, supplies, uniforms, and troops to reinforce General Washington's ragtag patriots. Names like Lafayette and Rochambeau should forever be close to the hearts of Americans. But let's face it: the relationship has had its ups and downs in the centuries since. Right now, we seem to be at a low point.

Trump pulling out of the Paris climate accord and the Iran nuclear deal, both strongly supported by the French, didn't help. Nor was it wise for Trump to give a speech in which he claimed his friend

"Jim" had stopped going to France due to its immigration policies, which Trump implied led to terrorism. Speaking at the 2017 Conservative Political Action Conference, Trump said: "I have a friend, he's a very, very substantial guy. He loves the City of Lights, he loves Paris. For years, every year during the summer, he would go to Paris, was automatic with his wife and his family. Hadn't seen him in a while. And I said, 'Jim, let me ask you a question: How's Paris doing?' 'Paris? I don't go there anymore. Paris is no longer Paris.' That was four years—four or five years hasn't gone there."

If you're interested in fact-checking: had "Jim" stopped going to Paris "four or five years" ago, that would mean he'd stopped going in 2012 or 2013. The terrorist attack against the magazine *Charlie Hebdo* occurred in 2015. So did the attack against Paris's Bataclan concert hall. The terrorist attack in Nice was in 2016. So "Jim" is not only "a very substantial guy," he is clairvoyant.

Trump's ignorant broadside brought an elegant rebuke from France's president at the time, François Hollande. "I think it's never a good idea," Hollande said, "to show the least disapproval with respect to an ally. I wouldn't do that to an ally and I would ask that the American president not do that with regard to France."

Hollande's successor, Emmanuel Macron, has been more assertive. At first he tried to befriend Trump, giving him macho handshakes and inviting him to military parades. But in time Macron sensed a vacuum. In April 2018 he came to the United States and threw down the gauntlet. Speaking to a joint session of Congress, Macron defended multilateralism and rejected "isolationism, withdrawal, and nationalism." In other words, Trumpism. He said he understood the urge to retreat, "but closing the door to the world will not stop the evolution of the world. It will not douse but inflame the fears of our citizens." He reminded his American hosts that the United States "invented" the postwar multilateral system that has kept the peace for decades. "You are the one now who has to help preserve it and reinvent it." Then, as if those comments were too subtle for Trump, he said the new multilateralism he envisioned would "make our planet great again" by saving us from climate change.

Macron took dead aim at Trump's trade protectionism and international isolationism: "I believe facing these challenges requires the opposite of massive deregulation and extreme nationalism. Commercial war is not the proper answer to these evolutions. We need free and fair trade, for sure. A commercial war opposing allies is not consistent with our mission, with our history, with our current commitments to global security. At the end of the day, it would destroy jobs, increase prices, and the middle class will have to pay for it."

It was as thorough and thoughtful a repudiation of Trump's worldview as one could imagine. Two months later, as he headed to the 2018 G7 summit in Canada, Macron dismissed Trump as transitory. "You say the US president doesn't care at all [about being isolated]," he told reporters. "Maybe, but nobody is forever. The six countries of the G7 without the United States, are a bigger market taken together than the American market."

What's the French word for "SNAP!"?

Macron went on, brashly assuming the mantle of leader of the free world: "Maybe the American president doesn't care about being isolated, but we [the G7] don't mind being six, if needs be. Because these six represent values, represent an economic market, and more than anything, represent a real force at the international level today."

If Trump is reelected, American withdrawal from world leadership will accelerate. Not only will Trump continue to pull back, but other leaders of free, wealthy democracies like Macron will pull away. The American Century will truly be over.

How Democrats Should Run on Foreign Policy

Rather than dissect every facet of foreign policy, Democrats should stick to the basics: Trump is in it for himself, not for you. He has sold out American soldiers, American farmers, American companies.

He has allowed Russia—a country with a dirty, corrupt leader—to humiliate the most powerful nation on earth. He has diminished America and degraded our strength. He has emboldened our adversaries and alienated our allies.

Don't ever let Trump get away with saying "America First." He is America Last—and Donald Trump first. Democrats should say:

Donald Trump is America Last, Trump First. He has sold out your very freedom, your democracy, your vote, to a bunch of Russian hackers who want to rig the election for him. He sold out your farm, your income, your family's ability to retire for his stupid, selfish trade war, while getting special favors for his own business from the Chinese. He sold out your sons and daughters, your brothers and sisters in uniform, betraying those who gave their lives to defeat ISIS. He sold out the family of an American college kid who was brutally tortured and murdered by the North Korean dictator who sends him love letters. He sold out our allies in the free world and sucked up to dictators. Perhaps worst of all, he has sold out the spirit of America, the idea that JFK and Ronald Reagan and every president and every one of you believes: that America is a unique and special place; that God shed his grace on us. Trump sold out the freedom that has inspired souls around the world since 1776—and for what? To line his own pockets, to rig his own elections. Well, Donald Trump may think America is no better than the corrupt thugs of Putin's Russia, but we know better. And on Election Day we're gonna show him.

CHAPTER 15

YA GOTTA SERVE SOMEBODY

In the novel *The Kite Runner*, the father, Baba, tells his son Amir, "there is only one sin, only one. And that is theft. Every other sin is a variation of theft . . . When you kill a man, you steal a life . . . You steal his wife's right to a husband, rob his children of a father. When you tell a lie, you steal someone's right to the truth. When you cheat, you steal the right to fairness. Do you see?"

No, actually, Baba, I don't see that at all. To my mind, there is only one sin, and it is selfishness. When you kill someone, you're putting your life ahead of theirs. When you rob someone, you put your own greed ahead of their need. When you cheat, you put your ambition ahead of theirs. Sorry to get so philosophical, but I have long believed that selfishness is the root of all wrongdoing, and empathy is the path to goodness. Martin Luther King Jr. taught us, "I believe that what self-centered men have torn down, other-centered men can build up."

Donald J. Trump is the Mt. Everest of selfishness. But I am backsliding into the very character obsession I warned about in the beginning of the book. So instead, I am going to propose a solution, if not to Trump's selfishness, then to our culture's. I want to see Democrats run on and enact a program through which other-centered people can build up our country again, build up their own prospects, build up their skills and their education, and build up the fraying bonds that should unite us across income levels and ideology, gender and generation, religion and region: universal national service.

The Challenges

It seems to me that two of the major challenges we face are a skills/education gap and deepening division in our society. A bold program of voluntary national service can address both. People who choose to serve can earn benefits for their education, and while serving they will work side by side with people who are radically different from them, and serve people who may be just as radically different from them. And from that experience can come radical empathy.

I am not the only one who views national service as a way to mend the ties that used to bind. A generation ago, President George H. W. Bush began his Points of Light program, celebrating voluntary service. "Any definition of a successful life," he said, "must include service to others." Toward the end of his long, remarkable life, he was asked to name his proudest accomplishments in his seven decades of public service. He had been a congressman, ambassador to the United Nations, envoy to China, chair of the Republican National Committee, director of the CIA, vice president and president. But here's how he responded: "I guess it would be that the Points of Light Institute is still going strong, helping spread the word about volunteerism in cities all over the country." In fact, in his final moments in the White House, as he was handing over the nuclear codes to the man who defeated him, my boss Bill Clinton, President Bush had just one request of him: save the Points of Light. President-elect Clinton was more than happy to accommodate him. Can you imagine Trump's final request of his successor on January 20, 2021? Pardon me.

Clinton, in fact, put Bush's Points of Light on steroids. He had campaigned in support of national service, and from the other side of the political aisle shared Bush's commitment to giving back. When he accepted his party's nomination as president, in what was at that time the most important speech of his life, he insisted on a call to service. "Just think of it," he told the crowd at Madison Square Garden and on TV, "Think of it. Millions of energetic young men and women serving their country by policing the streets or teaching the children or caring for the sick. Or working with the elderly and people with disabilities. Or helping young people to stay off drugs and out of gangs, giving us all a sense of new hope and limitless possibilities."

As president, Clinton kept his word, both to his predecessor and to the nation. On September 21, 1993, he signed legislation creating the Corporation for National and Community Service, through which AmeriCorps operates. President Barack Obama picked up the torch and in 2009 signed the Edward M. Kennedy Serve America Act. President George W. Bush carried on the tradition, creating USA Freedom Corps to help foster an ethic of service and to match those who wanted to serve with organizations that needed the help. Between 2002 and through the Obama administration, more than a million people gave more than a billion hours in service. That service has made America a better country and made those service volunteers better Americans.

In 2014, I wrote a piece for CNN about AmeriCorps. CNN was kind enough to grant permission to reprint part of it here. This is the sort of positive agenda I think could heal America:

Chad Clanton was in the first class of AmeriCorps volunteers. An idealistic kid from Waco, Texas, Clanton had just graduated from the University of Texas, the Greatest University in the World. He joined VISTA (Volunteers in Service to America) and was soon building houses for—and with—the poor in San Antonio.

"It really was one of the greatest experiences I've ever had," he said. "I just met the most wonderful people. And all kinds of people: hippies, yuppies, cowboys, church people, corporate executives, plumbers, electricians, rich, poor, you name it. Everyone was out there because they wanted to do something—swing a hammer, hang some Sheetrock, paint a fence—to chip away at the problem of poverty housing." Clanton went on to become a successful international political consultant, advising politicians across the country and around the world, but he says sweating in the South Texas sun was the best job he ever had.

Ely Flores did not come to AmeriCorps wanting to save the world. He was sent there by a criminal justice system that was trying to save him. "At 17 years old, I was at a crossroads," he said of his youth in Hollywood and South Central Los Angeles.

"I had a choice. Either I was going to continue the lifestyle that had forced me into community service or choose an AmeriCorps program called YouthBuild. My year in AmeriCorps with YouthBuild not only helped put my education back on track, put money in my pocket and ultimately helped me shape the foundation of social justice I stand on, but it completely transformed my view of service."

Ely helps young people affected by the incarceration of family members. He has rebuilt homes and schools and lives. When asked his occupation, he proudly says, "community builder." He has earned his undergraduate degree, is looking to get a master's and is organizing LEAD: Leadership through Empowerment, Action, and Dialogue, which seeks to breathe new life into Lincoln Heights, Los Angeles' oldest—but far from wealthiest—neighborhood.

Just as the members of the Greatest Generation were bound together by their common service in the second World War and just as Vietnam vets have a kinship that crosses partisan lines, so too should today's young people.

Be Like Alan

Alan Khazei is one of my favorite people. His dad is a surgeon who emigrated to America from Iran. His mom is a nurse whose family came from Italy. This Italian Iranian represents the best of the American experience. With the zeal of one who was raised by parents who did not take the American Dream for granted, Alan got himself accepted into Harvard College, which, I am told, is a pretty good school up in Massachusetts, and well suited to those who cannot get into the University of Texas at Austin. (Although Harvard does have a reputation as a football factory—touch football.) Lacking creativity, perhaps, he also went to Harvard for law school. So, yeah, he's kind of a dope.

After Harvard—and Harvard—Alan went to Silicon Valley and made billions with an app that secretly spies on people and sells their most intimate secrets to the highest bidder. Wait. No, he didn't. Instead, he and his law school buddy, Michael Brown, founded City Year, a nonprofit that matches young people who want to serve with disadvantaged kids in underfunded schools. The City Year volunteers mentor, tutor, and inspire. At first, City Year was in one city: Boston. But under Alan and Michael's leadership, it expanded to twenty-nine cities.

I first heard of Alan when I was working for Bill Clinton. President Clinton was a great advocate of service, and a sponge for new ideas. Alan is a classic social entrepreneur, brimming with practical idealism that can change the world. His combination of idealism and pragmatism won Clinton's respect. When President Clinton was working to make his dream of AmeriCorps a reality, he based it on City Year. To this day, President Clinton proudly rocks the City Year jacket Alan gave him.

Word of City Year's remarkable success spread. In 2001, former South African president Nelson Mandela phoned his old friend, former U.S. President Bill Clinton. "*My President*," Mandela began.

Clinton knew that greeting. "It meant Mandela was going to ask me for something," Clinton reminisced years later. "Mandela and a man named Roelf Meyer, an Afrikaaner, who had played a key role in the transition from President F.W. de Klerk to Mandela, were organizing a conference on civil society and asked me if I would participate. Of course, I said yes, but I said I would do more than that. I brought Eli Segal, the first head of AmeriCorps, and Alan Khazei, the cofounder of City Year, with me to South Africa. Their groups are a model of how to bring people together across racial and economic divides." Clinton says City Year South Africa is still going strong. "Every time I go back to South Africa," he says, "I visit City Year South Africa. I've seen them doing physical work, teaching kids, all kinds of things." Barack Obama spoke to the group's Chicago Ripples of Hope dinner back then. Like Alan and Michael, Obama was a social entrepreneur who could have cashed in after Harvard Law but decided to serve instead. "Who's the next generation that is going to lead us and inspire us and build an America we can all be proud of?" he asked the group. Then, answering his own question, he said, "When I look at all of the City Year corps members in this audience who have been giving so much of themselves, I think I have an answer to that question." When your group is an inspiration to Bill Clinton, Nelson Mandela, and Barack Obama, you're probably on to something.

Ten months. That's what City Year asks. Ten months of service: teaching and tutoring children who may not have been blessed with the opportunities that Alan or Michael or Presidents Clinton and Obama had. City Year reaches at-risk kids early, knowing that if we can get them to tenth grade on track and on time, they have a 75 percent chance of graduating. City Year changes lives—both of the students that receive tutoring and the young people who serve. Turns out being exposed to a world that's different from the one you knew gives you a deeper appreciation of others, even a sense of empathy. Which, at least to me, is the soul of morality.

But can empathy be a winning political message? Can a call to service win you votes? Well, it did for Bill Clinton and Barack Obama. And despite not reaching the White House, John McCain had a thirty-six-year career in elected office with this motto: "Nothing in life is more liberating than to fight for a cause larger than yourself, something that encompasses you, but is not defined by your existence alone." Alan Khazei would be the first to tell you he's no McCain, no Obama, no Clinton. But at this writing he is running for Congress in Massachusetts. The seat is held by Joseph Kennedy III, who is running for Senate. I have no idea if Khazei will win the crowded Democratic primary, but if he does, he will bring to Congress a commitment to service I think all Democrats can rally around.

The Causes of Earthquakes

The political earthquakes we are experiencing come from somewhere. In geology, earthquakes happen when pressure builds over time and then is suddenly released. (Okay, also if there's a volcanic eruption or an explosion, but bear with me: the metaphor works.) There are several kinds of pressure that can cause earthquakes: compressional pressure and tensional pressure are two I want to focus on. Compressional pressure is when rock gets squeezed. Think of a sumo wrestler sitting on your chest. That compressional pressure, it seems to me, is what is happening in our economy: the middle class, working families, poor people—they are getting squeezed. The three wealthiest people in America—Jeff Bezos, Bill Gates, and Warren Buffett—have a combined wealth that exceeds the wealth of the bottom half of the country's population. Think about it: those three men would probably fit comfortably in your car. And if you wanted to equal the combined wealth of those three guys, you'd have to have a car that held more than 160 million people.

It wasn't always this way. After World War II, economic blessings rose for all Americans pretty much equally. This was the era in which JFK could accurately say that "a rising tide lifts all boats."

That equality petered out in the 1970s. By 1989, according to the Federal Reserve, the top 1 percent controlled 23 percent of all America's wealth. That seemed unfair and unequal, but it was nothing compared to today. Now the top 1 percent controls 32 percent of all wealth. The middle class: those between the 50th and 90th percentiles, controls just 29 percent of wealth. And the bottom half of the country? Those 160 million people you couldn't fit in your car? They have seen no gains over the past thirty years. In fact, their share of national wealth has collapsed, from a meager 4 percent in 1989 to just 1 percent today.

This kind of wealth gap exerts enormous pressure—kind of like the compressional pressure on rock that can cause an earthquake. That's bad. What's worse is we also have another kind of pressure: tensional pressure. Geologists tell us tensional pressure is pressure that stretches rock, pulls it apart. With enough tensional pressure, the rock splits and the earth quakes. I liken that kind of tensional pressure to the way our society, our culture, and our means of communication are pulling us apart. I bet you see it in your daily life: progressives, young people, people of color, women, LGBTQ+ Americans, are growing in numbers and growing tired of being shut out of the corridors of power. When they are shut out or shouted down, the pressure rises. On the other side, conservatives feel aggrieved. Fed by right-wing media, they believe their culture is being undermined. Some fear their heritage is being erased as Confederate monuments topple and Confederate flags come down. Others worry that gun safety measures are an attack on their culture, that political correctness has run amok and they get reported to HR for using the wrong pronoun. They feel like the guy in the Bellamy Brothers song "Old Hippie": "He ain't tryin' to change nobody / He's just tryin' real hard to adjust."

All of this is hard enough when you're trying to sit around the table at Thanksgiving and Uncle Fred is honking off about something. It's worse, though, if you never talk to anyone who has the opposite worldview. And for an astonishing number of us, we never do. Pauline Kael, the brilliant, sophisticated, urbane film critic of *The New Yorker* for two decades, is said to have been stunned in 1972 when Richard Nixon won in a landslide forty-nine-state reelection. She supposedly said, "I don't know how Richard Nixon could have won. I don't know anybody who voted for him." That's the legend. In truth, she was more self-aware, more empathetic, more insightful. Kael's actual comment, according to James Wolcott of *Vanity Fair*, was: "I live in a rather special world. I only know one person who voted for Nixon. Where they are, I don't know. They're outside my ken. But sometimes when I'm in a theater I can feel them." The fundamental point Kael was making is that we are divided, and we don't really know each other. Things are far worse today in that regard.

The journalist Bill Bishop has written an important book on this problem called *The Big Sort*. More than ever, he says, we are sorting ourselves out: our neighborhoods are more homogenous, our workplaces as well. Our media preferences differ greatly depending on our political views. And Lord knows our churches are segregated—racially, culturally, and of course theologically. Our "pockets of like-minded citizens," Bishop wrote, ". . . have become so ideologically inbred that we don't know, can't understand, and can barely conceive of 'those people' who live just a few miles away."

Repairing the Breach

I don't want to be a reductionist. I realize that there is not a magic answer to rising inequality and increasing social alienation. But if I could do one thing to address both, it would be national service. Americans need more education and better skills to get better-paying jobs. Some on the left want to address that issue through offering free college. I have two problems with free college: it's free and it's college. I think earned educational benefits—which could include community college, technical school, all sorts of skills training, as well as a university education—are far better. No one ever called the

GI Bill "free college." The men and women of our armed forces earn those educational benefits. I realize not everyone is cut out for the military—I never finished the Boy Scouts. But if you're not the right person to serve in the Marine Corps, maybe the Peace Corps is right for you. Or maybe AmeriCorps.

And by serving with people who are different from you, we can repair the breach. I know this can have wonder-working power. My brother-in-law, Yves Istel, is one of the more remarkable people I know. His family were immigrant refugees who came to America in 1940, fleeing the Nazis, and Yves loves the United States with a passion only an immigrant can feel for their country of choice. Although a well-off young man from New York, he joined the Army ROTC at Princeton and underwent artillery training during the Korean War. He was sent to Fort Sill, Oklahoma, and graduated first in his class at Basic Officer Leader Course. "The usual army stuff," he says in his understated way. "Marksmanship, digging slit trenches, setting up camps, handling hot metal in one-hundred-plus-degree heat." He has had a stunningly successful business career, but if you're lucky, after a glass of French wine, he'll tell you about cussing the Oklahoma heat in Fort Sill with guys who had never even heard of Princeton. But those guys had his back. They forged a bond. After the army, Yves went back to New York. But he never fell victim to Pauline Kael syndrome. Serving with people from different backgrounds made him appreciate the richness, breadth, and diversity of America.

How Democrats Should Run on This

A moment ago, I boasted about the 1 million people who have served in AmeriCorps. But that's over the span of a quarter century. The number of people currently serving in AmeriCorps is 75,000. The Peace Corps currently has about 7,400 volunteers. And 1.29 million Americans are currently serving on active duty in our military.

But there are more than 45 million Americans between the ages of twenty and thirty.

Democrats should throw open the doors of service to any American who wants to take it on. Benefits might include forgiveness of one's existing college debt, stipends for future education and training, or maybe even a stake with which someone could start a small business or buy their first home. Think of the contributions they would make to our country: the children who could be tutored, the homes that could be refurbished, the buildings made energy-efficient, the national parks that could be fixed up, the community centers that could be staffed, the senior citizens who could be comforted, the special-needs adults who could be helped.

The social transformation would be as vast. When a kid from the prosperous suburbs has to hang Sheetrock with someone from the inner city; when a farm kid has to work side by side with a young person from a reservation, they get insights they carry with them for a lifetime. It is simply more difficult to hate someone whom you have come to know, someone you have worked with, someone you have served alongside, someone you have struggled with. Think about all those World War II movies, the composition of the platoon. Yes, there was racial segregation, which was evil. But within those strictures, the filmmakers showed some real diversity: there was usually a group of guys with names like Tex and Geno and Harold and Sarge and Jose. Lots of tension at first, but over time they came to know and respect one another, pulled together and formed a cohesive band of brothers. That's what this country could be: service could bring us together across all the lines that divide us.

Democrats must not be the party of something for nothing. In fact, a bold program of national service would allow them to define the Republicans as the party of something for nothing. Democrats should say that Trump wants a world in which a wealthy heir (like him) can win the genetic lottery and inherit millions tax-free. He wants a world of entitlement for the few; we want a nation of opportunity for all. Let him be the defender of the idle rich, the moneyed elite, the American oligarchs. Democrats should be the party of every person whose drive and dreams are being stymied by an economy that holds them down and a society that pulls us apart. If you don't stand for something. the saying goes, you'll fall for anything. Millions of Americans fell for Trump's line of bull in 2016. It is my fervent hope that does not happen again. If Democrats stand strong, and stand for the people—for unity and community; for the ideas I put forth in these pages and others; better ideas I am too dull to come up with—we will not only win, we will deserve to win.

ACKNOWLEDGMENTS

This book, like all books, was a leap of faith. My pal Jon Macks was the first person to read the manuscript. He encouraged me to jump and made sure I landed safely. His wit, which is legendary, is marbled through it. So is his political genius. He has my deepest appreciation.

As he has for a quarter century, my attorney, counselor, and friend Bob Barnett guided and encouraged me throughout.

The faith shown in me by Simon & Schuster is humbling. Jonathan Karp believed in me and in this book. His faith is deeply appreciated. Priscilla Painton was wonderfully encouraging at the beginning, and appropriately exacting through the editing process. She is a rare talent, and I am a grateful author to be working with her. Andrew Heyward, who has the good fortune to be married to Priscilla, came up with the title, which is perfect. Hana Park was always helpful and patient and kind. Jonathan Evans and Janet Byrne are careful, thoughtful copyeditors for whom I am grateful.

James Carville, my friend and partner since 1983, is an endless source of wisdom. Rahm Emanuel challenges my assumptions ("Paulie, what if we're *wrong*?!") and makes me a better analyst and a sharper combatant. I have spoken with James and Rahm every day since the 1980s, often more than once a day. I am blessed by their friendship. I call Bill Burton every day, too, but have done so "only" for the last eight years or so. Rookie. But he is way smart and deeply principled, and I benefit from his perspective each day. There is a group of "Georgia Boys" whose brains I pick all the time. Jim Butler, Steve Wrigley, and Keith Mason are the kind of guys you want holding the rope if you're hanging off a cliff. We cuss and argue politics and shoot quail. Their perspective is invaluable to me. Steve Diminuco, Jim Smith, Scott Gale, and Dane Strother form another cohort of old guys who have been together for decades. We came of age as Democrats in the Age of Reagan. We sustain each other in the Era of Trump.

As you will see in the hundreds of endnotes, this book relies heavily on the remarkable work of scores of journalists who have covered the Trump presidency hour by shocking hour. Even as the free press has been under relentless assault by the most powerful person on earth, America's journalists have risen to the occasion. I am indebted to them, as are we all. My colleagues at CNN are a godsend. They challenge me, humble me, inform me, support me, and keep me honest.

As in everything, my family is at the center. Diane, who runs our consulting firm, has allowed me to draw insights from her remarkable brain and inspiration from her beautiful heart since we were nineteen years old. Our sons, John, Billy, Charlie, and Patrick, made me laugh and made me think when I would have otherwise been too cranky to do the former and too weary to do the latter. Patrick, especially, leapt in to help with research and endnotes when I needed him most. Madhu Chugh, who has since 1996 been the daughter Diane and I always wanted, lent me her brilliance, her advice, and her support. My mom, Peggy Howard, is a marvel. She regaled me with stories of her childhood summers at Lake Hopatcong and lifted my spirits. My big brother David is cited herein more than once for his wisdom. My brother-in-law, Yves Istel, shared his stories of being an immigrant serving in the army, and how service made him a better American—and there is no better American than Monsieur Istel. Yves is married to my favorite sister, Kathleen, who has been in my corner since the day I was born. My brothers, Chris and Mike, are sources of support and encouragement. I am blessed to be their brother.

Hillary was right: it does take a village. But any errors, omissions, or mistakes are entirely my own. As I wrote this, I thought of all the people who have come up to me these last three years, worried about the country they love. I have seen their heartache harden into resolve; their pain channeled into purpose. From the Women's March the day after Mr. Trump took office, to the high school kids (including my own son) who walked out of school to call for gun safety after Parkland, to the tens of thousands of volunteers who knocked on millions of doors—your love for America inspires me. If there is a silver lining in the deep darkness that is the Trump presidency, it is this: America is the greatest country in human history not because of our leaders—or in this case, misleaders—but because of our people, the folks who live out "E pluribus unum" and still strive to form a more perfect union.

NOTES

CHAPTER 1: MEA CULPA

2 *GOP strategist Frank Luntz called it the most effective ad of 2012*: Scott Conroy, "Ad with Former Obama Backers Deemed Most Effective," CBS News, August 27, 2012, https://www.cbsnews.com/news/ad-with-former-obama-backers -deemed-most-effective/.

3 *"And you can tell them to go [BLEEP] themselves!"*: Amy Chozick and Nick Corasaniti, "Hillary Clinton 'Super PAC' to Air First Attack Ad Aimed at Donald Trump," *New York Times*, May 17, 2016, https://www.nytimes.com /2016/05/18/us/politics/ad-super-pac-clinton-trump.html.

3 *"And I didn't like what I saw"*: Sarah McCammon, "Why Would the Pro-Clinton SuperPAC Target Conservative Christians?" NPR, June 9, 2016, https://www.npr.org/2016/06/09/481376839/why-would-the-pro-clinton -superpac-target-conservative-christians.

3 *George W. Bush, who is an actual, honest-to-goodness born-again Christian*: Sarah Pulliam Bailey, "White Evangelicals Voted Overwhelmingly for Donald Trump, Exit Polls Show," *Washington Post*, November 9, 2016, https://www .washingtonpost.com/news/acts-of-faith/wp/2016/11/09/exit-polls-show -white-evangelicals-voted-overwhelmingly-for-donald-trump/.

3 *paying zero dollars in federal taxes*: "Priorities USA: '$0 in Taxes' Campaign 2016," *Washington Post*, September 28, 2016, https://www.washingtonpost .com/video/politics/priorities-usa-0-in-taxes—campaign-2016/2016/09/28 /1c8f8168-858e-11e6-b57d-dd49277af02f_video.html.

3 *He also did better with voters making less than $50,000 than Romney*: "Exit Polls 2012: How the Vote Has Shifted," *Washington Post*, https://www.wash ingtonpost.com/wp-srv/special/politics/2012-exit-polls/table.html; "Exit Polls," CNN, November 23, 2016, https://www.cnn.com/election/2016/results /exit-polls.

3–4 *"We're going to have a deportation force"*: "Priorities USA: 'The Choice Is Ours' Campaign 2016," *Washington Post*, June 10, 2016, https://www

.washingtonpost.com/video/politics/priorities-usa-the-choice-is-ours—
campaign-2016/2016/06/10/d87f2ce8-2f44-11e6-b9d5-3c3063f8332c_video
.html.

4 *Trump got 1 percent more of the Latino vote than Mitt Romney had in 2012*:
"Exit Polls," CNN; Michael Suh, "Pew Research Center's Exit Poll Analysis
on the 2012 Election," Pew Research Center, November 7, 2016, https://www
.pewresearch.org/2012/11/07/pew-research-centers-exit-poll-analysis-on-the
-2012-election/.

4 *"I moved on her like a b—h"*: Priorities USA ad, October 9, 2016, https://www
.youtube.com/watch?v=vB5OGsDqjzw.

4 *Trump won just 3 percent fewer female voters than Romney*: For Romney data:
"Exit Polls 2012: How the Vote Has Shifted," *Washington Post*; for Trump data:
"Exit Polls," CNN.

4 *"your schools are no good, you have no jobs"*: Darren Sands, "New Pro-Clinton
Super PAC Ad Attacks Trump on 'Least Racist' Claim," *BuzzFeed News*,
October 20, 2016, https://www.buzzfeednews.com/article/darrensands/new
-pro-clinton-super-pac-ad-attacks-trump-on-least-racist-c.

4 *albeit by a measly 2 percent*: "Exit Polls 2012: How the Vote Has Shifted,"
Washington Post; "Exit Polls," CNN.

4 *"He's unfit to be president"*: Maureen Groppe, "In New Ad, Former Gov. Joe
Kernan Calls Donald Trump Unfit to Be President," *Indianapolis Star*, August
3, 2016, https://www.indystar.com/story/news/politics/behind-closed-doors
/2016/08/03/new-ad-former-gov-joe-kernan-calls-donald-trump-unfit-presi
dent/87999654/.

4 *defeated Hillary by 27 percent among veterans*: "Exit Polls of the 2016 Presidential Elections in the United States on November 9, 2016, Percentage of
Votes by Military Service," *Statista*, November 9, 2016, https://www.statista
.com/statistics/631991/voter-turnout-of-the-exit-polls-of-the-2016-elections
-by-military-service/.

4 *surpassing Romney's 20-point margin from 2012*: Scott Clement, "Veterans
Are Voting Republican. And That's Not Likely to Change," *Washington Post*,
November 11, 2014, https://www.washingtonpost.com/news/the-fix/wp/2014
/11/11/veterans-are-voting-republican-and-that's-not-likely-to-change/.

CHAPTER 2: CORONAVIRUS

10 *first reported case of the coronavirus, or COVID-19, in the United States*: Ken
Alltucker, "First Case of Coronavirus in US: Patient Got Pneumonia, but Now
Only Has Cough, Study Says," *USA Today*, January 31, 2020, https://www

.usatoday.com/story/news/health/2020/01/31/china-coronavirus-us-antiviral
-meds-used-treat-first-patient/4622612002/.

10 *Austin, Texas, where he addressed the American Farm Bureau Federation*:
R. Mitchell, "President Donald Trump's Schedule for Sunday, January 19,
2020, *Conservative Daily News*, January 19, 2020, https://www.conservativeda
ilynews.com/2020/01/president-donald-trumps-schedule-for-sunday-january
-19-2020/.

10 *"and we're taking care of you"*: Remarks by President Trump at the American
Farm Bureau Federation Annual Convention and Trade Show, The White
House, January 19, 2020, https://www.whitehouse.gov/briefings-statements
/remarks-president-trump-american-farm-bureau-federation-annual
-convention-trade-show/.

10 *Tom Bossert, his White House adviser for homeland security*: Vivian Salama,
Ken Dilanian, and Dartunorro Clark, NBC News, April 10, 2018, https://
www.nbcnews.com/politics/politics-news/tom-bossert-trump-s-homeland
-security-adviser-resign-n864321.

11 *"reckless disregard for the dangers we face"*: Lauren Weber, "Sudden Departure
of White House Global Health Security Head Has Experts Worried," *Huffington Post*, May 10, 2018, https://www.huffpost.com/entry/tim-ziemer-global
-health-security-leaves_n_5af37dfbe4b0859d11d02290.

11 *"a situation that should be immediately rectified"*: Ibid.

11 *He cut the pandemic prevention budget of the Centers for Disease Control and
Prevention by 80 percent in 2018*: Lena H. Sun, "CDC to Cut by 80 Percent
Efforts to Prevent Global Disease Outbreak," *Washington Post*, February 1,
2018, https://www.washingtonpost.com/news/to-your-health/wp/2018/02/01
/cdc-to-cut-by-80-percent-efforts-to-prevent-global-disease-outbreak/.

11 *One of the countries where we dramatically scaled back our efforts was China.*
Ibid.

12 *Trump said that in a few days the US number of cases would be zero*: Suzanne
Nossel, "Truth Has Become a Coronavirus Casualty," *Foreign Policy*, March 9,
2020, https://foreignpolicy.com/2020/03/09/truth-coronavirus-china-trump
-pence/.

12 *"Came out of nowhere"*: Aaron Blake, "Trump Keeps Saying 'Nobody' Could
Have Foreseen Coronavirus. We Keep Finding Out About New Warning
Signs," *Washington Post*, March 19, 2020, https://www.washingtonpost.com
/politics/2020/03/19/trump-keeps-saying-nobody-could-have-foreseen
-coronavirus-we-keep-finding-out-about-new-warning-signs/.

13 *7.7 million were hospitalized; 586,000 were dead*: David E. Sanger, Eric Lipton,
Eileen Sullivan, and Michael Crowley, "Before Virus Outbreak, a Cascade of

Warnings Went Unheeded," *New York Times*, March 19, 2020, https://www
.nytimes.com/2020/03/19/us/politics/trump-coronavirus-outbreak.html.

14   *"had been fired or moved on"*: Ibid.

14   *"Nobody knew there would be a pandemic or epidemic of this proportion"*:
Blake, "Trump Keeps Saying 'Nobody' Could Have Foreseen Coronavirus. We
Keep Finding Out About New Warning Signs."

14   *"Anybody who wants a test gets a test"*: Laureen Hirsch, "Trump Says
'Anybody Who Wants a Test Gets a Test' After Pence Says US Can't Meet
Coronavirus Testing Demand," CNBC, March 6, 2020, https://www.cnbc.com
/2020/03/06/trump-anybody-who-wants-a-test-gets-a-test-amid-shortage
-for-coronavirus.html.

15   *as the contagion was spreading rapidly in the United States*: Chris Lu, "The
Coronavirus Is Bad. Trump Could Make It Worse," *Washington Monthly*,
February 26, 2020, https://washingtonmonthly.com/2020/02/26/the-corona
virus-is-bad-trump-could-make-it-worse/.

15   *twelve to eighteen months away, at best*: Bill McCarthy, "Fact-Checking
President Donald Trump on the Coronavirus," PolitiFact, February 28, 2020,
https://www.politifact.com/article/2020/feb/28/fact-checking-president
-donald-trump-coronavirus/.

15   *appears the mortality rate for coronavirus is significantly higher*: Lisa Lockerd
Maragakis, MD, MPH, "Coronavirus Disease 2019 vs. the Flu," Johns Hopkins
Health, accessed March 20, 2020, https://www.hopkinsmedicine.org/health
/conditions-and-diseases/coronavirus/coronavirus-disease-2019-vs-the-flu.

15   *"this is their new hoax"*: Aaron Rupar, "Trump's Friday Night Effort to Weap-
onize Coronavirus Against His Enemies Has Already Aged Poorly," *Vox*,
February 29, 2020, https://www.vox.com/2020/2/29/21159294/trump-corona
virus-hoax-south-carolina-first-death.

16   *"We're going very substantially down, not up"*: Lauren Egan and Mansee
Khurana, "Trump's Response to U.S. Coronavirus Outbreak Under Scrutiny,"
NBC News, March 8, 2020, https://www.nbcnews.com/politics/donald-trump
/just-my-hunch-trump-contradicts-health-experts-coronavirus-n1151006.

16   *"this is just my hunch"*: Ibid.

16   *"Avoid using public transportation, ride-sharing, or taxis"*: Ibid.

16   *"historically, that has been able to kill the virus"*: Ibid.

16   *where it was considerably warmer than in the United States or China*: "Coronavirus (COVID-19), Case Comparison, WHO Regions, Overview and
Explorer," World Health Organization, accessed April 13, 2020, https://who
.sprinklr.com/.

16   *"it's like a miracle, it will disappear"*: Jon Heilemann, "Trump's Coronavirus

Calendar," The Recount, March 17, 2020, https://therecount.com/watch/trump
-coronavirus-calendar/2645515793.

17 *"Therapies is sort of another word for cure"*: Ibid.

17 *would not be available by prescription*: Andrew Dunn, "Trump and Top US
Health Officials Are Expanding Access to Potential Coronavirus Treatments,"
Business Insider, March 19, 2020, https://www.businessinsider.com/trump
-fda-coronavirus-remdesivir-chloroquine-clinical-testing-compassionate-use
-2020-3.

17 *"I've been right a lot"*: David Knowles, "Fauci Tempers Trump's Optimism
on Chloroquine for Coronavirus," Yahoo.com, March 20, 2020, https://news
.yahoo.com/fauci-tempers-trumps-optimism-on-chloroquine-use-for-corona
virus-181035811.html.

18 *about how seriously to take the virus*: Daniel Dale and Tara Subramaniam,
"Trump Made 33 False Claims About the Coronavirus Crisis in the First Two
Weeks of March," CNN, March 22, 2020, https://www.cnn.com/2020/03/22
/politics/fact-check-trump-coronavirus-false-claims-march/index.html.

18 *That was not accurate*: Ibid.

18 *He claimed he had not shaken hands with anyone on his recent trip to India*:
Ibid.

18 *"We aren't sure what rule is being referenced"*: Ibid.

19 *the number of deaths went up 100 percent*: Ibid.

19 *Delta, American, United—had already halted service from China to the United
States*: Aaron Blake, "Trump Claims China Travel Restrictions Prove He Took
Coronavirus 'Very Seriously.' There Are Two Major Problems with That,"
Washington Post, March 18, 2020, http://www.washingtonpost.com
/politics/2020/03/02/trumps-airing-grievances-coronavirus-is-overcooked/.

19 *"I was right: He is incompetent!"*: Ibid.

20 *Trump fell for a falsehood that had been posted on conservative websites*: Ibid.

20 *"I think the virus is going to be—it's going to be fine"*: Shane Harris, Greg Miller,
and Ellen Nakashima, "U.S. Intelligence Reports from January and February
Warned About a Likely Pandemic," *Washington Post,* March 20, 2020,
https://www.washingtonpost.com/national-security/us-intelligence-reports
-from-january-and-february-warned-about-a-likely-pandemic/2020/03/20
/299d8cda-6ad5-11ea-b5f1-a5a804158597_story.html.

20 *Trump was downplaying the threat*: Ibid.

21 *"Trump continued publicly and privately to play down the threat the virus posed
to Americans"*: Ibid.

21 *could not get through to Trump for days or weeks*: Ibid.

21 *"he did not believe the virus had spread widely throughout the United States"*: Ibid.

21   *"The Coronavirus is very much under control in the USA"*: Ibid.

21   *Trump did vouch for the Chinese government and President Xi Jinping, tweeting on January 24*: Ibid.

22   *$1.9 trillion of projected federal revenues into the pockets of corporate America*: John McLelland and Jeffrey Werling, "How the 2017 Tax Act Affects CBO's Projections," *Congressional Budget Office*, April 20, 2018, https://www.cbo.gov /publication/53787.

22   *Trump's federal budget had a $1 trillion deficit*: "The Budget and Economic Outlook: 2020 to 2030," Congressional Budget Office, January 28, 2020, https://www.cbo.gov/publication/56020.

23   *no one ever lost an election for spending too much*: James Hohmann, "The Budget Deal Shows How Unserious the GOP Is About Deficits in the Trump Era," *Washington Post*, July 23, 2019, https://www.washingtonpost .com/news/powerpost/paloma/daily-202/2019/07/23/daily-202-the-budget -deal-shows-how-unserious-the-gop-is-about-deficits-in-the-trump-era /5d3676781ad2e5592fc35aa8/.

23   *"we're working also with the hotel industry"*: Jonathan Chait, "Trump Wants Coronavirus Bailout for Oil and Hotel Industries," *New York Magazine*, March 10, 2020, https://nymag.com/intelligencer/2020/03/trump-coronavirus -bailout-oil-hotel-industry-stimulus-recession.html.

23   *Trump, other senior administration officials, and their families from benefiting from the bailout*: Ryan Lucas, "Coronavirus Package Would Bar Trump and Lawmakers from Funds, Top Democrat Says," NPR, March 25, 2020, https:// www.npr.org/2020/03/25/821431823/coronavirus-package-would-bar-trump -and-lawmakers-from-funds-top-democrat-says.

24   *anticorruption (aka, anti-Trump) provision was put back in*: Anita Kumar, "Democrats Delayed Stimulus Bill to Tighten Ban on Trump Family Profiting," *Politico*, March 26, 2020, https://www.politico.com/news/2020/03/26 /democrats-delayed-stimulus-bill-ban-on-trump-family-profiting-150282.

24   *"a Trump supporter and an adviser to the president on energy issues"*: Jeff Stein, Will Englund, Steven Mufson, and Robert Costa, "White House Likely to Pursue Federal Aid for Shale Companies Hit by Oil Shock, Coronavirus Downturn," *Washington Post*, March 10, 2020, https://www.washingtonpost .com/business/2020/03/10/trump-oil-bailout/.

24   *a 52.6 percent jump from the previous year, before the Trump tax cut*: Anne Marie Knott, "Why the Tax Cut and Jobs Act (TCJA) Led to Buybacks Rather Than Investment," *Forbes*, February 21, 2019, https://www.forbes.com/sites /annemarieknott/2019/02/21/why-the-tax-cuts-and-jobs-act-tcja-led-to -buybacks-rather-than-investment/#7d24fe6a37fb.

25 *"record number of Americans losing their jobs"*: Press Release, "Pelosi Statement on President Trump Signing Third Coronavirus Bill," Office of the
Speaker of the House, March 27, 2020, https://www.speaker.gov/newsroom
/32720-0.

26 *issued a statement proclaiming that he would not obey some of the provisions*:
Kyle Cheney, "Trump Chips Away at Congress' Role in Coronavirus Relief
Oversight," *Politico*, March 27, 2020, https://www.politico.com/news/2020/03
/27/trump-congress-coronavirus-relief-oversight-152560.

26 *"impermissible forms of congressional aggrandizement with respect to the execu-
tion of the laws"*: Ibid.

27 *January 15, when the first reports of COVID-19 in Wuhan came to light*: Dan
Solomon and Paula Forbes, "Inside the Story of How H-E-B Planned for the
Pandemic," *Texas Monthly*, March 26, 2020, https://www.texasmonthly.com
/food/heb-prepared-coronavirus-pandemic/.

27 *didn't even bother to attend*: "Remarks by President Trump at Signing of the
U.S.–China Phase One Trade Agreement," The White House, January 15,
2020, https://www.whitehouse.gov/briefings-statements/remarks-president
-trump-signing-u-s-china-phase-one-trade-agreement-2/.

27 *"so we basically mirrored what that might look like [in Texas]"*: Solomon and
Forbes, "Inside the Story of How H-E-B Planned for the Pandemic."

28 *"a great sense of pride"*: Ibid.

CHAPTER 3: BUT TRUMP *IS* DIFFERENT

32 *"the bride at every wedding, and the baby at every christening"*: William
O'Connor, "Eleanor Roosevelt's Vicious Family Feud," *Daily Beast*, April
14, 2017, https://www.thedailybeast.com/eleanor-roosevelts-vicious-family
-feud.

32 *both men lost to Wilson in an Electoral College landslide*: Don Linky, "Gov.
Woodrow Wilson and the Election of 1912," Center on the American
Governor, Rutgers University, http://governors.rutgers.edu/on-governors/us
-governors/gov-woodrow-wilson-and-the-election-of-1912/#linky.

34 *59 percent of McCain voters said the same about their candidate*: A. W. Geiger,
"For Many Voters, It's Not Which Presidential Candidate They're For, but
Which They're Against," Pew Research Center Fact Tank, September 2, 2016,
https://www.pewresearch.org/fact-tank/2016/09/02/for-many-voters-its-not
-which-presidential-candidate-theyre-for-but-which-theyre-against/.

34 *he and his allied super PAC had spent a whopping $130 million*: Nicholas
Confessore and Sarah Cohen, "How Jeb Bush Spent $130 Million Running for

President with Nothing to Show for It," *New York Times*, February 22, 2016, https://www.nytimes.com/2016/02/23/us/politics/jeb-bush-campaign.html.

35 *(Hillary was a very distant second, with $746 million)*: Dylan Byers, "Donald Trump Has Earned $2 Billion in Free Media Coverage, Study Shows," CNN, March 15, 2016, https://money.cnn.com/2016/03/15/media/trump-free -media-coverage/index.html.

35 *By November, Trump was the beneficiary of $4.96 billion in earned media*: Tim Marcin, "Donald Trump Attacks Mainstream Media While Downplaying Russian Election Ads on Facebook," *Newsweek*, October 21, 2017, https:// www.newsweek.com/donald-trump-attacks-mainstream-media-networks -downplays-russian-ads-facebook-690240.

35 *the two least-liked presidential candidates in history—and it wasn't even close*: Matthew Yglesias, "What Really Happened in 2016, in 7 Charts," *Vox*, September 18, 2017, https://www.vox.com/policy-and-politics/2017/9/18 /16305486/what-really-happened-in-2016.

35 *Trump won those voters by a crushing 17-point margin (47–30)*: "Exit Polls," CNN, November 23, 2016, https://www.cnn.com/election/2016/results/exit -polls.

36 *"what was he doing with Lee Harvey Oswald shortly before the death? Before the shooting? It's horrible"*: Nolan D. McCaskill, "Trump Accuses Cruz's Father of Helping JFK's Assassin," *Politico*, May 3, 2016, https://www.politico.com /blogs/2016-gop-primary-live-updates-and-results/2016/05/trump-ted-cruz -father-222730.

37 *(Just 29 percent would disapprove)*: Tim Marcin, "Trump Voters, Republicans Overall Actually Don't Care If the President Shoots Someone on Fifth Avenue: Poll," *Newsweek*, July 18, 2017, https://www.yahoo.com/news/trump-voters -republicans-overall-actually-200200054.html.

37 *"'I need to check with the President if it's true'"*: Frances Langum, "Cult 45: Trump Voter Would Ask Trump to Verify What Jesus Said," Crooks and Liars, November 20, 2017, https://crooksandliars.com/2017/11/cult-45-trump-voter -would-ask-trump-verify.

40 *"they are in federal court trying to take your healthcare away"*: Sen. Brian Schatz (@brianschatz), Twitter, December 22, 2019, 11:23 a.m., https://twitter .com/brianschatz/status/1208785246621093889.

41 *"competent and truthful and idealistic as are the American people"*: Robert A. Strong, "Jimmy Carter: Campaigns and Elections," UVA Miller Center, https://www.politico.com/blogs/ben-smith/2008/09/obama-media-critic-cites -ailes-011800.

CHAPTER 4: THE LESSONS OF 2018 AND 2019

43 *turnout dropped dramatically and Democrats lost, bigly*: Ella Nilsen, "The 2018 Midterms Had the Highest Turnout Since Before World War I," *Vox*, December 10, 2018, https://www.vox.com/policy-and-politics/2018/12/10 /18130492/2018-voter-turnout-political-engagement-trump.

44 *remarkable and unprecedented*: John Haltiwanger, "Democrats Did Something Virtually Unprecedented in the 2018 Midterms, and it Says a Lot About Trump's Unpopularity," *Business Insider*, November 19, 2018, https://www .businessinsider.com/democrats-did-something-virtually-unprecedented-in -the-2018-midterms-2018-11?op=1.

45 *the DCCC raised a record-shattering $296,422,428 for the 2018 elections*: "Democratic Congressional Campaign Cmte, Fundraising Overview, 2018 Cycle," OpenSecrets.org, Center for Responsive Politics, https://www.open secrets.org/parties/totals.php?cmte=DCCC&cycle=2018.

45 *the DCCC outraised the NRCC by more than $90 million*: "National Republican Congressional Cmte Fundraising Overview, 2018 Cycle," OpenSecrets .org, Center for Responsive Politics, https://www.opensecrets.org/parties /totals.php?cmte=NRCC&cycle=2018.

45 *Democrats nominated more women and people of color than they did white men*: "A Rising Tide? The Changing Demographics on Our Ballots," *Reflective Democracy Campaign*, October, 2018, https://wholeads.us/2018-report/.

47 *Finkenauer is fighting for rural broadband, biodiesel, and farm programs*: Christal Hayes, "She Made History with AOC, but Congress' Second-Youngest Woman, Abby Finkenauer, Is Her Own Democrat," *USA Today*, August 26, 2019, https://www.usatoday.com/story/news/politics/2019/08/26 /abby-finkenauer-alexandria-ocasio-cortez-democrat-split/1837766001/.

47 *clearing it just eleven days after Finkenauer was sworn in*: Press Release, Office of Rep. Finkenauer, "Finkenauer Small Business Bill Passes House, Is First Legislation Passed by New Member of Congress," January 14, 2019, https:// finkenauer.house.gov/media/press-releases/finkenauer-small-businesses-bill -passes-house-first-legislation-passed-new.

47 *"It's far more important to her to get things done than to get on the national news," her Republican colleague Curtis told* USA Today: Hayes, "She Made History with AOC, but Congress' Second-Youngest Woman, Abby Finkenauer, Is Her Own Democrat."

47 *immigration lagged far behind*: Melissa Herrmann and David R. Jones. "How Democrats Won the House," CBS News, November 7, 2018, https://www

.cbsnews.com/news/how-democrats-won-the-house-2018-midterm-elections
-today-2018-11-06/.

48 *the DNC reached a staggering 50 million voters*: Daniel Marans, "Top Liberal
Groups Plan Get-Out-the-Vote Blitz on Weekend Before Midterm Elections,"
Huffington Post, July 17, 2018, https://www.huffpost.com/entry/liberal-groups
-get-out-the-vote-blitz-last-weekend_n_5b4d511ce4b0b15aba87a2a7.

48 *beat the GOP among women by a 20-point margin*: Ibid.

49 *crushing Republicans in the crucial independent vote by a 14-point margin*:
Ibid.

49 *among white evangelical Christians by 6 points*: For 2016 data, see "Exit Polls,"
CNN, November 23, 2016, https://www.cnn.com/election/2016/results/exit
-polls. For 2018 data, see: "Exit Polls," CNN, https://www.cnn.com/election
/2018/exit-polls.

50 *Orange (County) is the new blue*: Jorge L. Ortiz, "Orange Is the New Blue:
California Democrats Sweep 7 House Seats in Former GOP Stronghold," *USA
Today*, November 18, 2018, https://www.usatoday.com/story/news/politics
/elections/2018/11/18/california-democrats-sweep-house-seats-orange
-county/2048696002/.

50 *The Union had prevailed*: "Missionary Ridge," *Sharing Horizons*, November 20,
2015, https://sharinghorizons.com/missionary-ridge/.

52 *United States-Mexico-Canada Agreement (USMCA)—one of Trump's top
priorities*: Josh Israel, "House Democrats Passed Almost 600 Bills in 2019,"
National Memo, December 26, 2019, https://www.nationalmemo.com/house
-democrats-passed-almost-600-bills-in-2019/?cn-reloaded=1.

52 *sent President Clinton's approval rating soaring up to 73 percent*: CNN, Poll:
Clinton's Approval Rating Up in Wake of Impeachment," December 20, 1998,
https://www.cnn.com/ALLPOLITICS/stories/1998/12/20/impeachment.poll/.

52 *A majority of Americans supported not only impeaching Trump, but convicting
him and removing him from office*: Jennifer Agiesta, "CNN Poll: 51% Say Senate
Should Remove Trump From Office," CNN, January 20, 2020, https://www.cnn
.com/2020/01/20/politics/cnn-poll-trump-impeachment/index.html.

53 (*"we're gonna impeach this m——f——"*): Aaron Rupar, "New Congress
Member Creates Stir by Saying of Trump: 'We're Going to Impeach this
motherfucker!' *Vox*, January 4, 2019, https://www.vox.com/policy-and-poli
tics/2019/1/4/18168157/rashida-tlaib-trump-impeachment-motherfucker.

53 *"we shouldn't avoid impeachment for political reasons"*: Veronica Strazqualursi,
"New House Democrat Rashida Tlaib: 'We're Gonna Impeach the
Mother****r,'" CNN, January 4, 2019, https://www.cnn.com/2019/01/04
/politics/rashida-tlaib-trump-impeachment-comments/index.html.

53 *"liberal Andy Beshear sides with illegal immigrants"*: Tim Craig, "In Kentucky, a Governor's Trumpian Personality Is on the Ballot," *Washington Post*, October 19, 2019, https://www.washingtonpost.com/national/in-kentucky-a -governors-trumpian-personality-is-put-on-the-ballot/2019/10/18/ba2b8460 -f11c-11e9-89eb-ec56cd414732_story.html.

54 *"helps our local businesses flourish and workers get ahead"*: Andy Beshear, "Why I'm Running," Beshear/Coleman 2019, https://andybeshear.com/why -im-running/.

54 *"you can't let that happen to me!"*: Aaron Rupar, "'You Can't Let That Happen to Me!' Trump's Plea to His Supporters in Kentucky Aged Extremely Poorly," *Vox*, November 6, 2019, https://www.vox.com/2019/11/6/20951250/trump -kentucky-bevin-rally-bad-message.

54 *showed Bevin leading by five points, Beshear won*: "Kentucky Statewide Governor Survey," The Trafalgar Group, October–November, 2019, https:// drive.google.com/file/d/1v7FI6EDsEFMyrauwT3oGBMIcENE93KyY/view.

55 *"'Continue telling the story that we've been telling all along'"*: Melinda Deslatte, "Campaign Strategists Unpack Edwards' Victory in Louisiana," Associated Press, November 20, 2019, https://apnews.com/4bad6c908d2745a8a51ca223 da3ff2b7.

55 *"'Louisiana issues, not Washington, D.C. issues'"*: Sam Karlin, "John Bel Edwards, Warding Off Trump Rally, Says 'Partisan' Event Won't Work for Republican Eddie Rispone," *The Advocate*, November 6, 2019, https://www .theadvocate.com/baton_rouge/news/politics/elections/article_8918cc1a-00c7 -11ea-94af-3343ea5f16b1.html.

55 *highlighted his criminal justice reform*: Edwards for Governor, "My Priorities." https://johnbelforlouisiana.com/issues/.

55 *"Nancy Pelosi hates the United States of America"*: Vandana Rambaran, "Trump Blasts 'Bull—Impeachment' at Louisiana Rally, Says Nancy Pelosi 'Hates the United States'" Fox News, October 12, 2019, https://www.foxnews .com/politics/trump-rally-lake-charles-louisiana-nancy-pelosi-eddie-rispone -ralph-abraham-john-bel-edwards.

55 *"You gotta give me a big win, please. Please!"*: John Fritze and David Jackson, "Trump Rallies for Louisiana Governor Race, Mocks Diplomats in Impeach-ment Hearings," *USA Today*, November 19, 2019, https://www.usatoday .com/story/news/politics/elections/2019/11/14/trump-rally-louisiana-eddie -rispone-amid-impeachment-hearings/2514599001/.

56 *free community college to low-income Virginians*: Editorial Board, "How Ralph Northam Came Back from the Political Dead," *Washington Post*, December 27, 2019, https://www.washingtonpost.com/opinions/how-ralph-northam

-came-back-from-the-political-dead/2019/12/27/941e4a46-282b-11ea-b2ca
-2e72667c1741_story.html.

56 *He was armed with two .45-caliber pistols, high-capacity ammunition magazines, and a sound suppressor*: Whit Johnson and Bill Hutchinson, "Suspected
Virginia Beach Shooter Used Legally-Bought Gun Suppressor," ABC News,
June 4, 2019, https://abcnews.go.com/US/suspected-virginia-beach-gunman
-resigned-personal-reasons-massacre/story?id=63449625.

57 *surrender firearms if he is a threat to himself or others*: WRC Newsroom and
Associated Press, "'Votes and Laws, Not Thoughts and Prayers': Northam
Calls for Special Session on Gun Control," WRC-TV, June 4, 2019, https://
www.wric.com/news/virginia-news/votes-and-laws-not-thoughts-and
-prayers-northam-calls-for-special-session-on-gun-control/.

57 *They didn't consider a single one of the governor's bills*: Gregory S. Schneider,
Laura Vozzella, and Anotnio Olivo, "Gun Debate Ends Abruptly in Virginia
as GOP-Controlled Legislature Adjourns After 90 Minutes," *Washington Post*,
July 9, 2019, https://www.washingtonpost.com/local/virginia-politics/gun
-debate-hits-full-throttle-in-richmond-as-legislature-convenes/2019/07/09
/caf20590-a1d4-11e9-bd56-eac6bb02d01d_story.html.

58 *photoshopping a picture of her into a picture of MS-13 gang members*: Gregory
S. Schneider and Laura Vozzella, "Days Before Nov. 5 Election, Virginia
Republicans Take Hard Right Turn," *Washington Post*, October 30, 2019,
https://www.washingtonpost.com/local/virginia-politics/blue-summer-red
-fall-virginia-republicans-change-colors-with-the-season-stepping-up-attacks
-on-democrats/2019/10/30/0115f352-fb26-11e9-8190-6be4deb56e01_story
.html.

58 *a woman speaker, Democrat Eileen Filler-Corn*: Max Smith, "Women Take
Charge of Virginia House as Historic Assembly Session Convenes," WTOP
News, January 8, 2020, https://wtop.com/virginia/2020/01/women-take
-charge-of-virginia-house-as-historic-assembly-session-convenes/.

58 *an African American female majority leader, Charniele Herring*: Lauren
Francis, "Women Selected to Lead House of Delegates for the First Time in
History," 6 News Richmond, November 9, 2019, https://wtvr.com/2019/11/09
/eilen-filler-corn-elected-speaker/.

58 *Suzette Denslow was unanimously elected the chamber's first female clerk*:
Robert McCartney, "Virginia's Year of the Woman Produces Historic Package
of Liberal Legislation," *Washington Post*, March 2, 2020, https://www.washing
tonpost.com/local/virginia-politics/virginias-year-of-the-woman-produces
-historic-package-of-liberal-legislation/2020/03/01/4d1177da-599b-11ea
-ab68-101ecfec2532_story.html.

CHAPTER 5: BLUE-COLLAR BETRAYAL

59   *defeated John McCain there by 3 percent in 2008*: "Election Results 2008" *New York Times*, December 9, 2008, https://www.nytimes.com/elections/2008 /results/states/florida.html.

59   *and edged out Mitt Romney in 2012 by a single, vital percentage point*: Robert Pear, "State Highlights: Florida. Election 2012," *New York Times*, https://www .nytimes.com/elections/2012/results/states/florida.html.

60   *Bill Clinton carried Volusia County twice*: For 1992, see: Dave Leip, "1992 Presidential General Election Data Graphs—Florida," *Dave Leip's Atlas of U.S. Presidential Elections*, https://uselectionatlas.org/RESULTS/datagraph .php?year=1992&fips=12&f=0&off=0&elect=0; for 1996, see Dave Leip, "1996 Presidential General Election Data Graphs—Florida," *Dave Leip's Atlas of U.S. Presidential Elections*, https://uselectionatlas.org/RESULTS/datagraph .php?year=1996&fips=12&f=0&off=0&elect=0.

60   *Barack Obama carried Volusia County handily in 2008*: "Election Results 2008, Florida: Presidential County Results," *New York Times*, December 9, 2008, https://www.nytimes.com/elections/2008/results/states/president/florida .html.

60   *Obama lost Volusia County by 2,742 votes—less than 1 percent*: Dave Leip, "2012 Presidential General Election Results—Volusia County, FL, *Dave Leip's Atlas of U.S. Presidential Elections*, https://uselectionatlas.org/RESULTS /statesub.php?year=2012&fips=12127&f=0&off=0&elect=0.

60   *she lost it by nearly 34,000 votes*: Dave Leip, "2016 Presidential General Election Results—Volusia County, FL," *Dave Leip's Atlas of U.S. Presidential Elections*, https://uselectionatlas.org/RESULTS/statesub.php?year=2016&fips= 12127&f=0&off=0&elect=0.

61   *Obama carried Luzerne by a solid 9 points in 2008*: Dave Leip, "2008 Presidential General Election Results—Luzerne County, PA," *Dave Leip's Atlas of U.S. Presidential Elections*, https://uselectionatlas.org/RESULTS/statesub.php?year =2008&fips=42079&f=0&off=0&elect=0.

61   *and by 5 percent in 2012*: Dave Leip, "2012 Presidential General Election Results—Luzerne County, PA," *Dave Leip's Atlas of U.S. Presidential Elections*, https://uselectionatlas.org/RESULTS/statesub.php?year=2012&fips=42079&f =0&off=0&elect=0.

61   *a far cry from the 14-point landslide Bill Clinton won there in 1996*: Dave Leip, "1996 Presidential General Election Data Graphs—Pennsylvania," *Dave Leip's Atlas of U.S. Presidential Elections*, https://uselectionatlas.org/RESULTS /datagraph.php?year=1996&fips=42&f=0&off=0&elect=0.

61　*"I think she has Scranton's back and hopefully we can have hers, so, I'm excited for today"*: Stacy Lange, "Hillary Clinton Visits Scranton," WNEP, July 29, 2015, https://wnep.com/2015/07/29/hillary-clinton-visits-scranton/.

61　*She lost this formerly reliable Democratic county by a staggering 24,237 votes*: Dave Leip, "2016 Presidential General Election Results—Luzerne County, PA, *Dave Leip's Atlas of U.S. Presidential Elections*, https://uselectionatlas.org /RESULTS/statesub.php?year=2016&fips=42079&f=0&off=0&elect=0.

61　*victory in the Keystone State by less than 1 percent*: Dave Leip, "2016 Presidential General Election Results—Pennsylvania," *Dave Leip's Atlas of U.S. Presidential Elections*, https://uselectionatlas.org/RESULTS/state.php?year=20 16&fips=42&off=0&elect=0.

62　*any of the twenty-two counties in Wisconsin that flipped from Obama to Trump*: Jessica Taylor and Katie Park, "The Counties That Flipped from Obama to Trump, in 3 Charts," NPR, November 15, 2016, https://www.wbez .org/shows/npr/counties-that-flipped-from-obama-to-trump-in-3-charts /9be8c083-a93b-451d-bf70-d4936b08b7e3/amp.

62　*Bill Clinton carried forty-two of them*: Dave Leip, "1992 Presidential General Election Data Graphs—West Virginia," *Dave Leip's Atlas of U.S. Presidential Elections*, https://uselectionatlas.org/RESULTS/datagraph.php?year=1992&fip s=54&f=0&off=0&elect=0.

62　*Kennedy traveled there at least three times to shine a light on rural poverty*: Rick Hampton, "When W. Va. Lost Its Voice: JFK's Death Still Resonates," *USA Today*, October 29, 2013, https://www.usatoday.com/story/news/nation/2013 /10/27/jfk-west-virginia-coalfields/3235311/.

62　*They gave him 74.8 percent of the vote against Richard Nixon*: Office of the Secretary of State of West Virginia, "Official Election Results: President of the United States, 1960"; Dave Leip, "1960 Presidential General Election Data Graphs—West Virginia," *Dave Leip's Atlas of U.S. Presidential Elections*, https://uselectionatlas.org/RESULTS/datagraph.php?year=1960&fips=54&f=0 &off=0&elect=0.

63　*carried McDowell County with 71.8 percent of the vote*: Leip, "1992 Presidential General Election Data Graph—West Virginia."

63　*35,000 when Clinton carried it*: "Population of McDowell County," Population. US, https://population.us/county/wv/mcdowell-county/.

63　*Just 2,068 of them have a job*: "Quick Facts: McDowell County, West Virginia," United States Census Bureau, https://www.census.gov/quickfacts/fact/table /mcdowellcountywestvirginia/PST045218.

63　*at or near the bottom in life expectancy*: "COUNTY PROFILE: McDowell County, West Virginia," Institute for Health Metrics and Evaluation,

University of Washington, http://www.healthdata.org/sites/default/files
/files/county_profiles/US/2015/County_Report_McDowell_County_West
_Virginia.pdf.

63   *racking up 68.5 percent of the vote*: Mac Warner, West Virginia Secretary
of State, "McDowell County Results, General Election, November 8, 2016.
Official Results, West Virginia Secretary of State—Online Data Services, http:/
/services.sos.wv.gov/apps/elections/results/results.aspx?year=2016&eid=
23&county=McDowell&type=Official.

65   *"I wish to God," Stimson said, "that I were young enough to face it with you"*:
Jean Edward Smith, *George Bush's War* (New York: Henry Holt, 1992),
136–37.

66   *"as a way to explain their frustrations"*: Ben Smith, "Obama on Small-Town
Pa: Clinging to Religion, Guns, Xenophobia," *Politico*, April 11, 2008, https://
www.politico.com/blogs/ben-smith/2008/04/obama-on-small-town-pa
-clinging-to-religion-guns-xenophobia-007737.

67   *"depth of condescension the far left wing of the Democrat party has for the folks
out here in flyover country"*: David Mikkelson, "Charlie Daniels on Barack
Obama," https://www.snopes.com/fact-check/guns-and-church/

67   *"we have to understand and empathize with as well"*: Katie Reilly, "Read
Hillary Clinton's 'Baskett of Deplorables' Remarks About Donald Trump
Supporters," *Time*, September 10, 2016, https://time.com/4486502/hillary
-clinton-basket-of-deplorables-transcript/.

70   *"his natural and normal condition"*: "'Cornerstone Speech' by Alexander
Stephens in Savannah, Georgia, March 21, 1861," State Historical Society of
Iowa, https://iowaculture.gov/history/education/educator-resources/primary
-source-sets/civil-war/cornerstone-speech-alexander.

70   *"our churches and our places of recreation and amusement"*: "Segregation in
America," Just Mercy, https://segregationinamerica.eji.org/segregationists#full.

70   *"give him somebody to look down on, and he'll empty his pockets for you"*:
David Emery, "Did LBJ Advocate: 'Convince the Lowest White Man He's
Better Than the Best Colored Man?,'" Snopes, August 23, 2016, https://www
.snopes.com/fact-check/lbj-convince-the-lowest-white-man/.

73   *voted Republican in presidential elections for eighty years before Hillary Clinton
carried it in 2016*: Charles Mahtesian, "The GOP's Suburban Nightmare,"
Politico Magazine, June 22, 2017, https://www.politico.com/magazine/story
/2017/06/22/handel-republicans-suburban-nightmare-215289

73   *the Democrats would be 0 for life*: Ronald Brownstein, "The Parties Invert," *The
Atlantic*, May 23, 2016, https://www.theatlantic.com/politics/archive/2016/05
/an-election-in-negative/483905/.

73 *losing college-educated white voters to Mitt Romney by 14 percent*: Ruy Teixeira and John Halpin, "The Obama Coalition in the 2012 Election and Beyond," Center for American Progress, December 4, 2012, https://www.american progress.org/wp-content/uploads/2012/12/ObamaCoalition-5.pdf.

73 *she won college-educated white women by 7 percent*: CNN Politics, "Election 2016: Exit Polls," CNN, November 23, 2016, https://www.cnn.com/election /2016/results/exit-polls.

74 *"the letter was probably enough to change the outcome of the Electoral College"*: Nate Silver, "The Comey Letter Probably Cost Clinton the Election," Five-ThirtyEight, May 3, 2017, https://fivethirtyeight.com/features/the-comey -letter-probably-cost-clinton-the-election/.

74 *the first in history in which the Democratic Party carried college-educated white people*: Alec Tyson, "The 2018 Midterm Vote: Divisions by Race, Gender, Education," Pew Research Center, November 8, 2018, https://www.pew research.org/fact-tank/2018/11/08/the-2018-midterm-vote-divisions-by-race -gender-education/.

75 *A decade ago, it was just 28 percent*: Reid Wilson, "Census: More Americans Have College Degrees than Ever Before," *The Hill*, April 3, 2017, https://thehill .com/homenews/state-watch/326995-census-more-americans-have-college -degrees-than-ever-before.

76 *The central African nation of Chad has the lowest, at 50.6 years*: "Country Comparison: Life Expectancy at Birth," *CIA World Factbook*, https://www.cia .gov/library/publications/the-world-factbook/rankorder/2102rank.html.

77 *For white women without a high school education, it is 73.5 years*: Sabrina Tavernise, "Life Spans Shrinks for Least-Educated Whites in the U.S.," *New York Times*, September 20, 2012, https://www.nytimes.com/2012/09/21/us/life -expectancy-for-less-educated-whites-in-us-is-shrinking.html.

77 *life expectancy for African Americans without a high school diploma actually surpassed that of whites*: Ibid.

77 *"diseases of despair": death by drug and alcohol abuse, and suicide*: Anne Case and Sir Angus Deaton, "Mortality and Morbidity in the 21st Century," *Brook-ings Papers on Economic Activity*, March 23, 2017, https://www.brookings.edu /bpea-articles/mortality-and-morbidity-in-the-21st-century/.

77 *"and social dysfunction in the lives of the white working class . . ."*: Ibid.

78 *67,367 Americans died from drug overdoses, the vast majority of them—46,802—from opioids*: "Drug Overdose Deaths, Centers for Disease Control and Prevention, https://www.cdc.gov/drugoverdose/data/statedeaths.html.

78 *400,000 of the deaths were due to opioids*: Lawrence Scholl, et al., "Drug and Opioid-Involved Overdose Deaths—United States, 2013–2017," Centers for

Disease Control and Prevention, *Morbidity and Mortality Weekly Report*, January 4, 2019, https://www.cdc.gov/mmwr/volumes/67/wr/mm675152e1.htm.

78   *Trump typically won 60 percent of the votes in counties with higher than average rates of chronic opioid prescriptions, the study found*: Paul Chisholm, "Analysis Finds Geographic Overlap in Opioid Use and Trump Support in 2016," NPR, June 23, 2018, https://www.npr.org/sections/health-shots/2018/06/23/622692550/analysis-finds-geographic-overlap-in-opioid-use-and-trump-support-in-2016.

78   *"Trump's campaign was a promise for near-term relief"*: Ibid.

79   *Fifty-seven grand can't save the lives of seventy thousand people*: German Lopez, "Trump Declared an Emergency Over Opioids. A New Report Finds It Led to Very Little," *Vox*, October 23, 2018, https://www.vox.com/policy-and-politics/2018/10/23/18010304/trump-opioid-epidemic-emergency-gao-report.

79   *All told, they spend $11 billion a year*: Joann Donnellan, "Tracking Federal Funding to Combat the Opioid Crisis," Bipartisan Policy Center, March 26, 2019, https://bipartisanpolicy.org/report/tracking-federal-funding-to-combat-the-opioid-crisis/.

80   *farm income plunged 45 percent*: Ibid.

80   *leaving him $82,500 in the hole*: Ibid.

81   *in the bottom quarter of years for farmers since they started keeping the statistics ninety years ago*: "USDA's Early Look at 2019 Farm Income," Market Intel, Farm Bureau Federation, March 6, 2019, https://www.fb.org/market-intel/usdas-early-look-at-2019-farm-income.

81   *Foreclosures were at or above a decade-high in Iowa, Illinois, Kansas, Minnesota, South Dakota, South Carolina, Ohio, as well as Wisconsin*: Kate Gibson, "Farm Bankruptcies Jumped 20% in 2019, Even with Billions in Aid from U.S.," CBS News, January 31, 2020, https://www.cbsnews.com/news/farm-bankruptcies-jumped-20-percent-in-2019-even-with-billions-in-aid-from-u-s-government/.

81   *and two other Atlantic City casinos*: Michelle Lee, "Fact Check: Has Trump Declared Bankruptcy Four or Six Times?" *Washington Post*, September 26, 2016, https://www.washingtonpost.com/politics/2016/live-updates/general-election/real-time-fact-checking-and-analysis-of-the-first-presidential-debate/fact-check-has-trump-declared-bankruptcy-four-or-six-times/.

82   *Ninety-one percent of farmers and farmworkers say financial stress impacts their mental health*: "Rural Stress Polling Presentation," American Farm Bureau Federation, April 16, 2019, https://www.fb.org/files/AFBF_Rural_Stress_Polling_Presentation_04.16.19.pdf.

82 *"a lot more bankruptcies going on, a lot more farmer suicides"*: Benjamin
    Fearnow, "Wisconsin Farmer Tells Fox News Suicides, Bankruptcy Rising in
    Rural U.S. Amid China Trade War," *Newsweek*, May 16, https://www.news
    week.com/farmers-suicide-bankruptcies-rising-fox-news-china-trade-war
    -wisconsin-1428169.

82 *"I think it's actually worse"*: Lois Thielen, "Modern Struggles Large Factor in
    Farmer Suicide Rates," *St. Cloud (MN) Times*, March 4, 2019, https://www
    .sctimes.com/story/opinion/2019/03/04/modern-struggles-large-factor
    -farmer-suicide-rates/3057250002/.

82 *while the opioid crisis was hammering farm country*: Humeyra Pamuk, "Trump
    Budget Proposes Steep Subsidy Cuts to Farmers as They Grapple with Crisis,"
    Reuters, March 11, 2019, https://www.reuters.com/article/us-usa-trump
    -budget-usda-idUSKBN1QS28Z.

83 *pays them just $1.35 a gallon*: Jim Hightower, "Trump to Small Farmers: Get
    Lost," *Madison (WI) Cap Times*, November 6, 2019, https://madison.com
    /ct/opinion/column/jim-hightower-trump-to-small-farmers-get-lost/article
    _4018e754-449e-53ae-83ae-2d85228f50c9.html.

83 *(dairy sales to China dropped 43 percent in 2018, when China hit US dairy
    with tariffs)*: Associated Press, "Trump Agriculture Secretary Says During
    Wisconsin Visit That Family-Run Dairy Farms May Not Survive," *Market-
    Watch*, October 3, 2019, https://www.marketwatch.com/story/trump
    -agriculture-secretary-says-during-wisconsin-visit-that-family-run-dairy
    -farms-may-not-survive-2019-10-03.

83 *551 more in 2019*: Ibid.

83 *the 90 percent of farms that are small got just 27 percent of commodity
    payments*: Rick Smith, "68% of Trump's Farm Bailout Goes to Richest 10%,"
    Iowa Starting Line, December 5, 2018, https://iowastartingline.com/2018/12
    /05/68-of-trumps-farm-bailout-goes-to-richest-10/.

84 *He said he would "make accessibility a priority"*: Joseph Simonds, "How a
    Trump or Hillary Presidency Impacts Fishing—'The Reel Debate,'" Salt
    Strong, August 1, 2016, https://www.saltstrong.com/articles/trump-hillary
    -fishing/.

85 *"the largest rollback of public lands protection in United States history"*: Coral
    Davenport, "Trump Opens National Monument Land to Energy Exploration,"
    New York Times, February 6, 2020, https://www.nytimes.com/2020/02/06
    /climate/trump-grand-staircase-monument.html?smid=nytcore-ios-share.

85 *just 10 percent say they're liberal*: Annie Sneed, "Conservative Hunters and
    Fishers May Help Determine the Fate of National Monuments," *Scientific
    American*, October 30, 2017, https://www.scientificamerican.com/article

/conservative-hunters-and-fishers-may-help-determine-the-fate-of-national
-monuments1/.

85 *"They [the politicians] ignore us at their political peril"*: Ibid.

86 *the Sierra Club and the Wilderness Society*: Ben Winslow, "Native American Tribes Sue Trump over Bears Ears National Monument," Fox 13, Salt Lake City, December 5, 2017, https://fox13now.com/2017/12/05/native-american -tribes-sue-trump-over-bears-ears-national-monument/.

88 *Abraham Lincoln (who 53 percent of today's Republicans think was not as good a president as Trump—seriously)*: Daniele Politi, "A Majority of Republicans Say Trump Is Better Than President Lincoln," *Slate*, November 30, 2019, https://slate.com/news-and-politics/2019/11/majority-republicans-trump -better-president-lincoln-poll.html.

CHAPTER 6: THE RISING AMERICAN ELECTORATE

89 *When Ronald Reagan was elected in 1980, 88 percent of voters were white*: "How Groups Voted," Roper Center, https://ropercenter.cornell.edu/how -groups-voted-1980.

89 *By 2016, that percentage had dropped to 71 percent*: "Election 2016: Exit Polls," CNN, November 23, 2016, https://www.cnn.com/election/2016/results/exit -polls.

90 *African American turnout fell by 4.7 percent in 2016*: Bernard L. Fraga, Sean McElwee, Jesse Rhodes, and Brian F. Schaffner, "Why Did Trump Win? More Whites—and Fewer Blacks—Actually Voted," *Washington Post*, May 8, 2017, https://www.washingtonpost.com/news/monkey-cage/wp/2017/05/08/why -did-trump-win-more-whites-and-fewer-blacks-than-normal-actually-voted/.

90 *and 2.1 percent in Pennsylvania*: Ibid.

91 *six in ten African American voters identify as moderate or conservative*: Scott Clement, Cleve R. Wootson Jr., Dan Balz, and Emily Guskin, "Biden Holds Wide Lead Among Black Voters in Democratic Race, Post-Ipsos Poll Finds," *Washington Post*, January 11, 2020, https://www.washingtonpost.com/politics /biden-holds-wide-lead-among-black-voters-in-democratic-presidential-race -post-ipsos-poll-finds/2020/01/11/76ecff08-3325-11ea-a053-dc6d944ba776 _story.html?utm_campaign=wp_main&utm_medium=social&utm _source=twitter.

91 *most important thing is choosing someone they agree with on all the issues*: Ibid.

91 *Ninety-one percent disapprove*: "Washington Post-Ipsos Poll of Black Americans, Jan. 2–8, 2020," *Washington Post*, January 17, 2020, https://www .washingtonpost.com/context/washington-post-ipsos-poll-of-african-ameri

cans-jan-2-8-2020/a41b5691-e181-4cda-bb88-7b31935103d9/?itid=lk_inline
_manual_2.

91 *creating good jobs with good benefits*: Daniel Strauss, "Poll: Black Voters Favor
Biden, Consumed by Pocketbook Issues Ahead of 2020," *Politico*, June 11,
2019, https://www.politico.com/story/2019/06/11/biden-black-economic
-alliance-poll-2020-1359082.

91 *immigration, education, and gun violence*: News Release: "UnidosUS Releases
State Polling of Latino Voters on Priority Issues, Key Traits in a Presidential Candidate and Party Support," UnidosUS, August 5, 2019, https://www
.unidosus.org/about-us/media/press/releases/080519-state-poll-latino-voters.

92 *these are the issues Latinos want Democrats to address as well*: Ibid.

92 *and unmarried women by 29 percent*: James A. Barnes, "Why Did the
'Marriage Gap' Shrink in 2016?" Ballotpedia, November 10, 2016, https://
ballotpedia.org/Why_did_the_%22marriage_gap%22_shrink_in_2016.

92 *and unmarried women by 35 percent*: CNN Politics, "Exit Polls," CNN, 2018,
https://www.cnn.com/election/2018/exit-polls.

93 *"Social Security and Medicare are truly vital"*: Barnes, "Why Did the 'Marriage
Gap' Shrink in 2016?"

93 *"leading women to feel less connected to other women"*: Christopher T. Stout,
Kelsy Kretschmer, Leah Ruppanner, "Gender Linked Fate, Race/Ethnicity, and
the Marriage Gap in American Politics," *Political Research Quarterly*, April 6,
2017, https://journals.sagepub.com/doi/abs/10.1177/1065912917702499.

93 *while 29 percent are conservative*: Jonathan Chait, "New Survey Shows Young
People Are Staying Liberal and Conservatives Are Dying Off," *New York
Magazine*, March 1, 2018, http://nymag.com/intelligencer/2018/03/new
-survey-young-staying-liberal-conservatives-dying-off.html.

93–4 *Democratic congressional candidates won 67 percent of it in 2018*: Joey
Garrison and Rebecca Morin, "'I Think They Will Decide the Race': Can
Young Voters Again Push Democrats to Victory in 2020?," *USA Today*,
November 4, 2019, https://www.usatoday.com/story/news/politics/elections
/2019/11/04/election-2020-young-voters-key-democrats-path-beating-trump
/2458445001/.

94 *less than half view capitalism favorably*: Frank Newport, "Democrats More
Positive About Socialism than Capitalism," Gallup News, August 13, 2018,
https://news.gallup.com/poll/240725/democrats-positive-socialism-capitalism
.aspx.

94 *other countries are better than the USA as say America is the greatest country
on earth*: Hannah Hartig and Hannah Gilberstadt, "Younger Americans More
Likely Than Older Adults to Say There Are Other Countries That Are Better

Than the U.S.," Pew Research Center Fact Tank, January 8, 2020, https://www
.pewresearch.org/fact-tank/2020/01/08/younger-americans-more-likely-than
-older-adults-to-say-there-are-other-countries-that-are-better-than-the-u-s/ft
_2020-01-08_exceptionalism-2/.

94 *want our country to prioritize renewable energy sources over fossil fuels*: Cary
Funk and Meg Herreron, "U.S. Public Views on Climate and Energy," Pew
Research Center, Science and Society, November 25, 2019, https://www.pew
research.org/science/2019/11/25/u-s-public-views-on-climate-and-energy/.

95 *often called the Silent Generation (9.4 percent)*: Ronald Brownstein, "Brace
for a Voter-Turnout Tsunami," *The Atlantic*, June 13, 2019, https://www.theat
lantic.com/politics/archive/2019/06/2020-election-voter-turnout-could-be
-record-breaking/591607/.

95 *voters under thirty cast a ballot in the 2016 presidential contest*: Ibid.

95 *Those who did overwhelmingly favored Hillary Clinton*: "CNN Politics: Election
2016 Exit Polls," CNN, November 23, 2016, https://www.cnn.com/election
/2016/results/exit-polls.

95 *seniors solidly preferred Trump*: Ibid.

95 *If Democrats reach out to young voters, they will respond*: Garrison and Morin,
"'I Think They Will Decide the Race': Can Young Voters Again Push Democrats to Victory in 2020?"

95 *Nones: people who say they have no religious affiliation*: "America's Changing
Religious Landscape," Pew Research Center Forum on Religion & Public Life,
May 12, 2015, https://www.pewforum.org/2015/05/12/americas-changing
-religious-landscape/.

95 *Sixty-eight million adults in America are Nones*: "In U.S., Decline of Christianity Continues at Rapid Pace," Pew Research Center Forum on Religion &
Public Life, October 17, 2019, https://www.pewforum.org/2019/10/17/in-u-s
-decline-of-christianity-continues-at-rapid-pace/.

96 *the most Republican-leaning faith is to vote GOP*: "The Political Preferences
of U.S. Religious Groups," Pew Research Center, February 23, 2016, https://
www.pewresearch.org/fact-tank/2016/02/23/u-s-religious-groups-and-their
-political-leanings/ft_16-02-22_religionpoliticalaffiliation_640px-2/.

96 *there are three times as many atheists in America as Mormons*: "In U.S.,
Decline of Christianity Continues at Rapid Pace."

96 *30 percent of evangelicals share that view*: "U.S. Becoming Less Religious,"
Chapter 4: "Social and Political Attitudes," Pew Research Center Forum on
Religion & Public Life, November 3, 2015, https://how many black people
voted in the us presidential election in 2932www.pewforum.org/2015/11/03
/chapter-4-social-and-political-attitudes/.

CHAPTER 7: BANANA REPUBLICANS

100   *"You start whining before the game's even over?"*: Matt Wilstein, "Obama to Trump: Stop 'Whining' About 'Rigged' Election," *Daily Beast*, October 13, 2017, https://www.thedailybeast.com/cheats/2016/10/18/obama-to-donald-trump-stop-whining-about-rigged-election.

101   *two million zombies would be lurching to the polls*: Darren Samuelsohn, "A Guide to Donald Trump's 'Rigged' Election," *Politico*, October 25, 2016, https://www.politico.com/story/2016/10/donald-trump-rigged-election-guide-230302.

101   *"We may have people vote 10 times"*: David Weigel, "For Trump, a New 'Rigged' System: The Election Itself," *Washington Post*, August 2, 2016, https://www.washingtonpost.com/politics/for-trump-a-new-rigged-system-the-election-itself/2016/08/02/d9fb33b0-58c4-11e6-9aee-8075993d73a2_story.html.

101   *He formed a group called Stop the Steal*: Samuelsohn, "A Guide to Donald Trump's 'Rigged' Election."

102   *"evidence by which to accuse a major company of election interference"*: Devin Coldeway, "Without Evidence, Trump Accuses Google of Manipulating Millions of Votes," *TechCrunch*, August 19, 2016, https://techcrunch.com/2019/08/19/without-evidence-trump-accuses-google-of-manipulating-millions-of-votes/.

102   *Hillary Clinton won California by 4,269,978 votes*: Secretary of State Alex Padilla, "Statement of Vote, General Election, November 8, 2016," Secretary of State of California, https://elections.cdn.sos.ca.gov/sov/2016-general/sov/2016-complete-sov.pdf.

103   *The* Mercury News *called Trump's claim "preposterous"*: Patrick May, "Trump Says Illegal Votes Cost Him California. Here's Why That's Preposterous," *San Jose Mercury News*, January 26, 2017, https://www.mercurynews.com/2017/01/26/trump-says-illegal-votes-cost-him-california-heres-why-that's-preposterous/.

103   *"I knew where their location was"*: Amy Gardner, "Trump's Revival of Claim of Voting Fraud in New Hampshire Alarms Some State Republicans," *Washington Post*, August 29, 2019, https://www.washingtonpost.com/politics/trumps-revival-of-claim-of-voting-fraud-in-new-hampshire-alarms-some-state-republicans/2019/08/28/0c22107e-c38f-11e9-9986-1fb3e4397be4_story.html.

104   *"there used to be sightings of Bigfoot and aliens all the time"*: Ibid.

104   *"stir up fears and paranoia about our election system"*: Amy B. Wang, "Kris Kobach Couldn't Prove Widespread Voter Fraud. Can He Prove to Voters That He Can 'Make Kansas Great Again?,'" *Washington Post*, July 31, 2018,

https://www.washingtonpost.com/politics/kris-kobach-couldnt-find-wide
spread-voter-fraud-can-he-find-the-votes-to-make-kansas-great-again/2018
/07/30/5ebae0b2-91f5-11e8-8322-b5482bf5e0f5_story.html.

105 *"created by confusion and administrative error"*: Ibid.

105 *the only senator in history to lose his Senate seat to a dead man*: "Republican Senator Loses to Dead Rival in Missouri," CNN, November 8, 2000, https:// www.cnn.com/2000/ALLPOLITICS/stories/11/07/senate.missouri/.

105 *"that's a voter fraud rate of 0.00000013 percent"*: Bob Cesca, "Trump's Outrageous Claims of Voter Fraud Have a Clear Goal: Refusing to Accept Defeat in 2020," *Salon*, August 20, 2019, https://www.salon.com/2019/08/20/trumps -outrageous-claims-of-voter-fraud-are-about-one-thing-invalidating-the -2020-election/.

105 *more likely that an American would be "struck by lightning than that he will impersonate another voter at the polls"*: Justin Levitt, "The Truth About Voter Fraud," The Brennan Center for Justice, November 9, 2007, https://www .brennancenter.org/our-work/research-reports/truth-about-voter-fraud.

106 *Thirty-one in a billion*: Justin Levitt, "A Comprehensive Investigation of Voter Impersonation Finds 31 Credible Incidents Out of One Billion Ballots Cast," *Washington Post*, August 6, 2014, https://www.washingtonpost.com/news /wonk/wp/2014/08/06/a-comprehensive-investigation-of-voter-imperson ation-finds-31-credible-incidents-out-of-one-billion-ballots-cast/.

106 *"The polls are rigged," she said, echoing her hero*: Ibid.

107 *"700,000, or 10 percent, removed from the rolls in the year before the election"*: Glenn Kessler, "Did Racially Motivated Voter Suppression Thwart Stacey Abrams?," *Washington Post*, October 30, 2019, https://www.washingtonpost .com/politics/2019/10/30/did-racially-motivated-voter-suppression-thwart -stacey-abrams/.

107 *"because they had decided not to vote in prior elections"*: Angela Caputo, Geoff Hing, and Johnny Kauffman, "They Didn't Vote . . . Now They Can't," *American Public Media*, October 19, 2018, https://www.apmreports.org/story/2018 /10/19/georgia-voter-purge.

108 *"We're following the process"*: Ibid.

108 *"making sure we have secure, accessible, and fair elections"*: Ibid.

108 *70 percent of the registrations Kemp put on hold were of African American Georgians*: Ben Nadler, "Voting Rights Become a Flashpoint in Georgia Governor's Race," Associated Press, October 9, 2018, https://apnews.com /fb011f39af3b40518b572c8cce6e906c.

109 *they just get frustrated and leave*: Kessler, "Did Racially Motivated Voter Suppression Thwart Stacey Abrams?"

109 *"the goal of federalizing elections under the guise of security"*: Johnny Kauffman, "Election Security Becomes a Political Issue in Georgia Governor's Race," NPR, August 12, 2018, https://www.npr.org/2018/08/12/637163104 /election-security-becomes-a-political-issue-in-georgia-governors-race.

109 *"I don't necessarily believe" that Russia was behind the effort to influence the 2016 election*: Ibid.

110 *the lowest since 2000—down by 91,000*: "Wisconsin Voter ID Law Proved Insurmountable for Many Voters," CBS News, May 9, 2017, https://www .cbsnews.com/news/wisconsin-voter-id-law-turned-voters-estimate/.

110 *Milwaukee County is 49 percent non-white*: "Quick Facts: Milwaukee County, Wisconsin," United States Census Bureau, https://www.census.gov/quickfacts /fact/table/milwaukeecountywisconsin/PST045218.

110 *seventy-two hours to produce the proper ID*: "Wisconsin Voter ID Law Proved Insurmountable for Many Voters."

110–11 *300,000 Wisconsinites who are old enough to vote don't have one of those forms of photo ID*: Ibid.

111 *"I think photo ID is going to make a little bit of a difference as well"*: Ari Berman, "Rigged: How Voter Suppression Threw Wisconsin to Trump," Mother Jones, November/December, 2017, https://www.motherjones.com /politics/2017/10/voter-suppression-wisconsin-election-2016/.

112 *The League of Women Voters is appealing*: Marisa Iati, "A Judge Ordered Up to 234,000 People to Be Tossed from the Registered Voter List in a Swing State," *Washington Post*, December 14, 2019, https://www.washingtonpost.com /politics/2019/12/14/judge-ordered-up-people-be-tossed-registered-voter-list -swing-state/.

112 *60 percent of the people on the list had, in fact, become citizens*: Mimi Swartz, "The Voter Suppression State," *New York Times*, January 31, 2019, https:// www.nytimes.com/2019/01/31/opinion/texas-voter-suppression.html.

113 *"WHITLEY: I do not have an answer for that"*: Alex Ura, "'Someone Did Not Do Their Due Diligence': How an Attempt to Review Texas' Voter Rolls Turned into a Debacle," *Texas Tribune*, February 1, 2019, https://www.texas tribune.org/2019/02/01/texas-citizenship-voter-roll-review-how-it-turned -boondoggle/.

113 *"a plan carefully calibrated to intimidate legitimate registered voters from continuing to participate in the election process"*: Ibid.

113 *"ferret the infinitesimal needles out of the haystack of 15 million Texas voters"*: Devan Cole, "Federal Judge Temporarily Blocks Texas from Purging Voter Rolls," CNN, February 28, 2019, https://www.cnn.com/2019/02/28/politics /texas-voter-rolls-purging/index.html.

113 *Securities fraud. So there's that*: Emma Platoff, "Ken Paxton's Criminal Trial Has Been Pending for Nearly Four Years. Here's a Timeline of His Legal Drama," *Texas Tribune*, June 19, 2019, https://www.texastribune.org/2019/06/19/ken-paxton-criminal-case-timeline-texas-attorney-general-fraud/.

114 *"rural Texans and survivors of natural disasters to cast their ballots"*: Katie Hall and Chuck Lindell, "Texas Democratic Party Challenges Mobile Voting Ban in Lawsuit," *Austin American-Statesman*, October 31, 2019, https://www.statesman.com/news/20191030/texas-democratic-party-challenges-mobile-voting-ban-in-lawsuit.

114 *nothing says "I'm gonna cast a vote to change my government" like packing heat*: W. Gardner Selby, "'If You Want to Vote in' Texas, 'You Can Use a Concealed-Weapon Permit as a Valid Form of Identification, but a Valid Student ID Isn't Good Enough,'" PolitiFact, June 26, 2015, https://www.politifact.com/fact-checks/2015/jun/26/hillary-clinton/hillary-clinton-says-you-can-vote-texas-concealed-/.

116 *Jefferson was made president and Aaron Burr vice president*: John Ferling, "Thomas Jefferson, Aaron Burr and the Election of 1800," *Smithsonian*, November 1, 2004, https://www.smithsonianmag.com/history/thomas-jefferson-aaron-burr-and-the-election-of-1800-131082359/.

117 *sixteen states (with 196 electoral votes) have joined the compact*: National Popular Vote, https://www.nationalpopularvote.com/.

117 *That's what Donald Trump said on July 27, 2016*: Ashley Parker and David E. Sanger, "Donald Trump Calls on Russia to Find Hillary Clinton's Missing Emails," *New York Times*, July 27, 2016, https://www.nytimes.com/2016/07/28/us/politics/donald-trump-russia-clinton-emails.html.

118 *"We'll be looking at that: Yeah, we'll be looking"*: Philip Bump, "Donald Trump's Falsehood-Laden Press Conference, Annotated," *Washington Post*, July 27, 2016, https://www.washingtonpost.com/news/the-fix/wp/2016/07/27/donald-trumps-falsehood-laden-press-conference-annotated/.

118 *Russians started their efforts to hack Hillary Clinton's email*: Dylan Scott, "July 27, 2016: Trump Publicly Asked Russia to Find Hillary's Emails. They Acted Within Hours," *Vox*, July 13, 2018, https://www.vox.com/policy-and-politics/2018/7/13/17569264/mueller-indictment-trump-russia-email-hack.

118 *"two senior former State Department officials told NBC News"*: Ken Dilanian, "Former Diplomats: Trump Team Sought to Lift Sanctions on Russia," NBC News, June 1, 2017, https://www.nbcnews.com/politics/white-house/former-diplomats-trump-team-sought-lift-sanctions-russia-n767406.

118 *backed down when a bipartisan group of senators raised hell*: Damien Sharkov, "Trump Warned Not to Hand Putin Luxury Compounds Back on Advice of

U.S. Senators," *Newsweek*, July 7, 2017, https://www.yahoo.com/news/trump
-warned-not-hand-putin-121050431.html.

118   *in the words of the late senator John McCain, "an act of war"*: Ibid.

119   *it's likely Russia tried to hack into election systems in all fifty states*: Mike
       Levine, "Russia Likely Targeted All 50 States in 2016, but Has Yet to Try
       Again, DHS Cyber Chief Says," ABC News, April 24, 2018, https://abcnews.go
       .com/US/russia-targeted-50-states-2016-dhs-cyber-chief/story?id=54695520.

119   *they still don't have enough funding to replace their voting machines*: Nicole
       Goodkind, "Every State Was Given Funding to Increase Election Security.
       Here's How They Spent It," *Fortune*, November 5, 2019, https://fortune.com
       /2019/11/05/us-election-security-states-funding/.

119   *"they have not adequately faced the election security threat that we've learned
       the severity of"*: Ibid.

119   *in 2018, thirty-six states had one*: Ibid.

120   *Thirty-two states allow some online voting*: Ibid.

120   *It is maddeningly successful*: Ibid.

120   *the Russians may be able to delete voters from the registration rolls*: Report of
       the Senate Select Committee on Intelligence, "Russian Targeting of Election
       Infrastructure During the 2016 Election," May 8, 2018, https://www.burr
       .senate.gov/imo/media/doc/RussRptInstlmt1-%20ElecSec%20Findings,Recs2
       .pdf.

120   *which was precisely what the Russians wanted*: Edward-Isaac Dovere, "Biden:
       McConnell Stopped Obama from Calling Out Russians," *Politico*, January 23,
       2018, https://www.politico.com/story/2018/01/23/mitch-mcconnell-russia
       -obama-joe-biden-359531.

121   *berating him for even briefing Congress in the first place*: David Jackson and
       Nicholas Wu, "'Screaming Red Siren': Trump's Replacement of Spy Chief
       After Russia Briefing Stirs Outcry," *USA Today*, February 21, 2020, https://
       www.usatoday.com/story/news/politics/2020/02/21/trump-replacing-spy
       -chief-maguire-after-russia-briefing-stirs-uproar/4830237002/.

122   *ransomware, which has already crippled cities across America*: Nathaniel
       Popper, "Ransomware Attacks Grow, Crippling Cities and Businesses," *New
       York Times*, February 9, 2020, https://www.nytimes.com/2020/02/09
       /technology/ransomware-attacks.html.

122   *"shall have extensive national security expertise"*: 50 U.S. Code Section §3023
       (a)(1), https://www.law.cornell.edu/uscode/text/50/3023.

122   *Russia was trying to aid Bernie Sanders's 2020 campaign*: Shane Harris, Ellen
       Nakashima, Michael Scherer, and Sean Sullivan, "Bernie Sanders Briefed by
       U.S. Officials That Russia Is Trying to Help His Presidential Campaign,"

Washington Post, February 21, 2020, https://www.washingtonpost.com /national-security/bernie-sanders-briefed-by-us-officials-that-russia-is -trying-to-help-his-presidential-campaign/2020/02/21/5ad396a6-54bd-11ea -929a-64efa7482a77_story.html?utm_campaign=wp_main&utm_medium= social&utm_source=twitter.

123 *Other accounts told people they could vote by text*: Kurt Wagner, "These Are Some of the Tweets and Facebook Ads Russia Used to Try and Influence the 2016 Presidential Election," *Vox*, October 31, 2017, https://www.vox.com /2017/10/31/16587174/fake-ads-news-propaganda-congress-facebook-twitter -google-tech-hearing.

123 *require big digital platforms to disclose the content of political ads, who they are targeted at, and who paid for them*: Senator Mark R. Warner, Press Release, "The Honest Ads Act," May 2019, https://www.warner.senate.gov/public /index.cfm/the-honest-ads-act.

123 *easy-to-read disclaimers telling the audience who paid for them*: Tony Romm, "Here's How U.S. Lawmakers Want to Regulate Political Ads on Facebook, Google and Twitter," *Vox*, October 19, 2017, https://www.vox.com/2017/10/19 /16503006/facebook-google-twitter-russia-senate-political-ads.

123 *"that's what I hear that these platforms do"*: Harper Neidig, "Franken Blasts Facebook for Accepting Rubles for U.S. Election Ads," *The Hill*, October 31, 2017, https://thehill.com/policy/technology/358102-franken-blasts-facebook -for-accepting-rubles-for-us-election-ads.

124 *"fight misinformation aggressively, and trust our eyes a little less every day"*: Kevin Roose, "Here Come the Fake Videos, Too," *New York Times*, March 4, 2018, https://www.nytimes.com/2018/03/04/technology/fake-videos-deep fakes.html.

125 *"it will be impossible to distinguish between the real pictures and the fake pictures"*: Cade Metz, "Inernet Companies Prepare to Fight the 'Deepfake' Future," *New York Times*, November 24, 2019, https://www.nytimes.com/2019 /11/24/technology/tech-companies-deepfakes.html.

125 *Senator Marco Rubio (R-FL) has taken the lead in pushing for efforts to counter deep fakes*: Donie O'Sullivan, "When Seeing Is No Longer Believing," CNN, 2019, https://www.cnn.com/interactive/2019/01/business/pentagons-race -against-deepfakes/.

125 *Trump was telling people, "We don't think that was my voice"*: Maggie Haberman and Jonathan Martin, "Trump Once Said the 'Access Hollywood' Tape Was Real. Now He's Not Sure," *New York Times*, November 28, 2017, https://www.nytimes.com/2017/11/28/us/politics/trump-access-hollywood -tape.html.

126 *when he says that if Trump is defeated in November 2020, he may not leave office*: Tommy Christopher, "Bill Maher Asks Terrifying Question About Trump Refusing to Leave Office: 'Democrats, What's the Plan?'" *Mediaite*, January 25, 2020, https://www.mediaite.com/tv/bill-maher-asks-terrifying -question-about-trump-refusing-to-leave-office-democrats-whats-the-plan/.

127 *Dr. Yphtach Lelkes, an assistant professor at the Annenberg School for Communication at the University of Pennsylvania*: Ariel Malka and Yphtach Lelkes, "In a New Poll, Half of Republicans Say They Would Support Postponing the 2020 Election If Trump Proposed It," *Washington Post*, August 10, 2017, https://www.washingtonpost.com/news/monkey-cage/wp/2017/08/10/in-a -new-poll-half-of-republicans-say-they-would-support-postponing-the-2020 -election-if-trump-proposed-it/.

128 *"having such a high turnout that the barriers to voting have limited effect"*: Nichelle Smith, "'Overwhelm the System' to Thwart Voter Suppression, Stacey Abrams Counsels Blacks," *USA Today*, February 4, 2020, https://www .usatoday.com/story/news/2020/02/04/stacey-abrams-message-black-voters -2020/4490921002/.

129 *Only one Republican did*: Mark Erik Elias, "Voting Rights Are on the Ballot in 2020," *Medium*, December 8, 2019, https://medium.com/@marceelias/voting -rights-are-on-the-ballot-in-2020-37777f4ac976.

129 *"If Republicans control any part of the legislative process, we won't"*: Ibid.

130 *"these kinds of attacks on our very fundamentals of democracy"*: Sergei Karazy and Matthias Williams, "Senator McCain Says Russia Must Pay Price for Hacking," Reuters, December 30, 2016, https://www.reuters.com/article/us -usa-russia-cyber-mccain/senator-mccain-says-russia-must-pay-price-for -hacking-idUSKBN14J1LW.

131 *"the damage done has ravaged our institutions and shaken our belief in our immovability"*: Mark Hertling and Molly K. McKew, "Putin's Attack on the U.S. Is Our Pearl Harbor," *Politico*, July 16, 2018, https://www.politico.com /magazine/story/2018/07/16/putin-russia-trump-2016-pearl-harbor-219015.

CHAPTER 8: THIS CHAPTER WILL BEAT TRUMP. I GUARANTEE.

134 *He told the conservative site the Daily Signal in 2015*: Vishakha Darbha, "6 Times Donald Trump Promised Not to Cut Medicare," *Mother Jones*, December 8, 2017, https://www.motherjones.com/politics/2017/12/donald -trump-paul-ryan-medicare-medicaid/.

134 *"now all of a sudden they wanna be cut"*: Ibid.

135 *"Have to do it"*: Ibid.

135 *"You made a deal a long time ago"*: Ibid.

135 *"we will always protect your Medicare and your Social Security"*: Sanya Mansoor, "Read the Full Transcript of President Trump's 2020 State of the Union Address," *Time*, February 4, 2020, https://time.com/5777857/state-of-the-union-transcript-2020/.

135 *His 2021 budget also includes spending $451 billion less on Medicare*: Anne Flahery and Jordyn Phelps, "3 Things to Know About Trump's Budget Plan for Medicare, Medicaid," ABC News, February 11, 2020, https://abcnews.go.com/Politics/things-trumps-budget-plan-medicare-medicaid/story?id=68913201.

135 *"changing the way doctors are paid and making other changes"*: John Cassidy, "Trump's Reverse-Robin Hood Budget Should be a Gift to the Democrats," *New Yorker*, February 11, 2020, https://www.newyorker.com/news/our-columnists/trumps-reverse-robin-hood-budget-should-be-a-gift-to-the-democrats.

135 *"If 'you don't cut something in entitlements'"*: Hanna Trudo, "Dems Pounce After Trump Says He Intends to Cut Entitlements," *Daily Beast*, March 5, 2020, https://www.thedailybeast.com/dems-pounce-after-president-trump-says-in-fox-news-town-hall-that-he-intends-to-cut-entitlements?ref=scroll.

136 *"The spending plan calls for a cut of nearly $1.5 trillion in Medicaid over 10 years"*: Amy Goldstein and Jeff Stein, "Trump Proposes Big Cuts to Health Programs for Poor, Elderly and Disabled," *Washington Post*, March 11, 2019, https://www.washingtonpost.com/national/health-science/trump-proposes-big-cuts-to-health-programs-for-poor-elderly-and-disabled/2019/03/11/55e42a56-440c-11e9-aaf8-4512a6fe3439_story.html.

136 *brought health insurance to more than 17 million Americans*: "Medicaid Expansion Enrollment, Timeframe FY 2017," Kaiser Family Foundation, https://www.kff.org/health-reform/state-indicator/medicaid-expansion-enrollment/?currentTimeframe=0&sortModel=%7B%22colId%22:%22Location%22,%22sort%22:%22asc%22%7D.

136 *the bottom-line Trump cuts to Medicaid came to $777 billion*: Tara Golshan, "Trump Said He Wouldn't Cut Medicaid, Social Security, and Medicare. His 2020 Budget Cuts All 3," *Vox*, March 12, 2019, https://www.vox.com/policy-and-politics/2019/3/12/18260271/trump-medicaid-social-security-medicare-budget-cuts.

136 *cutting Social Security by $550 billion*: Goldstein and Stein, "Trump Proposes Big Cuts to Health Programs for Poor, Elderly and Disabled."

136 *"The impact for seniors would be devastating"*: Ibid.

137 *his white-trash hellhole, err, country club, in Bedminster, New Jersey*: David A. Fahrenthold, "What President Trump's Company Charges the Secret Service,"

Washington Post, March 5, 2020, https://www.washingtonpost.com/graphics
/2020/politics/trump-secret-service-spending/.

138   *"OK," Trump reportedly replied, "we can fix welfare"*: Matthew Yglesias, "Mick
Mulvaney Brags That He Tricked Trump into Proposing Social Security Cuts,"
Vox, September 1, 2017, https://www.vox.com/policy-and-politics/2017/9/1
/16243288/mick-mulvaney-social-security.

138   *11 million Americans rely on Social Security Disability Insurance*: Michelle
Ye Hee Lee, "White House Budget Director's Claim That Social Security
Disability Is 'Very Wasteful,'" *Washington Post*, April 7, 2017, https://www
.washingtonpost.com/news/fact-checker/wp/2017/04/07/white-house-budget
-directors-claim-that-social-security-disability-is-very-wasteful/.

138   *underpayments made up 0.22 percent*: Ibid.

138   *"You know, that's actually the easiest of all things"*: Michael Collins and David
Jackson, "Trump Says He'd 'Take a Look' at Changing Entitlements Such as
Medicare," *USA Today*, January 22, 2020, https://www.usatoday.com/story
/news/politics/2020/01/22/trump-opens-door-cuts-medicare-other-programs
-davos/4544840002/.

140   *"taking that same $2 trillion out of Medicare, Medicaid, Social Security, and the
Affordable Care Act"*: Senators Martin Heinrich and Chris Van Hollen, *The
Hill*, July 30, 2018, https://thehill.com/blogs/congress-blog/economy-budget
/399575-tax-breaks-for-wealthy-paid-for-with-deep-cuts-to-medicare.

140   *the Trump tax cut for the rich costs $1.9 trillion over ten years*: John Yarmuth,
Chairman, House Committee on the Budget, "CBO Confirms GOP Tax Law
Contributes to Darkening Fiscal Future," https://budget.house.gov/publica
tions/report/cbo-confirms-gop-tax-law-contributes-darkening-fiscal-future.

141   *and in rural counties that number was even higher*: Nate Cohn, "Trump
Supporters Have the Most to Lose in the GOP Repeal Bill," *New York Times*,
March 10, 2017, https://www.nytimes.com/2017/03/10/upshot/why-trump
-supporters-have-the-most-to-lose-with-the-gop-repeal-bill.html.

141   *59.8 million Americans*: "Total Number of Medicare Beneficiaries," Kaiser
Family Foundation, 2018, https://www.kff.org/medicare/state-indicator/total
-medicare-beneficiaries/?currentTimeframe=0&selectedDistributions=to
tal&sortModel=%7B%22colId%22:%22Location%22,%22sort%22:%22as
c%22%7D.

141   *(56 percent, to be exact) had no health insurance at all*: Martin E. Gornick
et al., "Thirty Years of Medicare: Impact on the Covered Population," *Health
Care Financing Review* 18, no. 2 (Winter 1996): 179–237, https://www.ncbi
.nlm.nih.gov/pmc/articles/PMC4193632/.

142   *"what it once was like in America when men were free"*: Eric Zorn, "Ronald

Reagan on Medicare, Circa 1961. Prescient Rhetoric or Familiar Alarmist Claptrap?" *Chicago Tribune*, September 2, 2009, https://blogs.chicagotribune .com/news_columnists_ezorn/2009/09/ronald-reagan-on-medicare-circa -1961-prescient-rhetoric-or-familiar-alarmist-claptrap-.html.

142 *seniors rebelled against the surtax on middle and upper-middle income seniors that funded it*: Steve Daley and Rogers Worthington, "Seniors' Wrath Stings Lobby," *Chicago Tribune*, September 3, 1989, https://www.chicagotribune.com /news/ct-xpm-1989-09-03-8901100068-story.html.

143 *more than 64.5 million Americans get their health insurance through Medicaid*: ObamaCare Facts, "ObamaCare Medicaid Expansion," August 8, 2014, updated March 4, 2020, https://obamacarefacts.com/obamacares-medicaid -expansion/.

143 *(Arizona was the last; it waited until 1982 to join)*: "Program History," Medicaid .gov, https://www.medicaid.gov/about-us/program-history/index.html.

143 *sixteen states have not*: ObamaCare Facts, "ObamaCare Medicaid Expansion."

143 *Children's Health Insurance Program, which was created by President Bill Clinton*: Jon Greenberg, "Medicaid Expansion Drove Health Insurance Coverage Under Health Law, Rand Paul Says," PolitiFact, January 15, 2017, https://www.politifact.com/factchecks/2017/jan/15/rand-paul/medicaid -expansion-drove-health-insurance-coverage/.

143 *Sixty-two percent of all Americans in nursing homes today have their care paid by Medicaid*: "Medicaid's Role in Nursing Home Care," Kaiser Family Foundation, June 20, 2017, https://www.kff.org/infographic/medicaids-role-in -nursing-home-care/.

143 *Sixty-four million Americans receive Social Security benefits*: "Understanding the Benefits," Securing Today and Tomorrow, 2020, Social Security Adminis- tration, https://www.ssa.gov/pubs/EN-05-10024.pdf.

143 *and benefits for the survivors of workers who have died*: Ibid.

143 *"22.1 million more Americans would be poor"*: Kathleen Romig, "Social Secu- rity Lifts More Americans Above Poverty Than Any Other Program," Policy Futures, Center for Budget and Policy Priorities, February 20, 2020, https:// www.cbpp.org/research/social-security/social-security-lifts-more-americans -above-poverty-than-any-other-program.

143 *"39.2 percent of elderly Americans would have incomes below the official poverty line"*: Ibid.

143 *Social Security is 90 percent of it*: Ibid.

144 *he didn't get 48 percent, he won by 48 percent*: "Presidential Election Results: Donald J. Trump Wins," *New York Times*, August 9, 2017, https://www.ny times.com/elections/2016/results/president.

144 *Eleven percent of West Virginia's seniors live in poverty*: Romig, "Social Security Lifts More Americans Above Poverty Than Any Other Program."

144 *far better than the overall poverty rate in West Virginia*: Casey Leins, "States with the Highest Poverty Rates," *U.S. News & World Report*, September 26, 2019, https://www.usnews.com/news/best-states/slideshows/us-states-with -the-highest-poverty-rates?slide=8.

144 *West Virginia seniors living in poverty would skyrocket to more than 48 percent*: Kathleen Romig, "Social Security Lifts More Americans Above Poverty than any Other Program."

144 *87 percent wanted to maintain funding levels or increase them*: John Gramlich, "Few Americans Support Cuts to Most Government Programs, Including Medicaid," Pew Research Center Fact Tank, May 26, 2017, https://www.pew research.org/fact-tank/2017/05/26/few-americans-support-cuts-to-most -government-programs-including-medicaid/.

144 *85 percent of Republicans agreed with them*: Ibid.

144 *Only 10 percent of Republicans and 3 percent of Democrats say they support cutting it*: Ibid.

145 *"Donald Trump will cut it and take it away"*: Trudo, "Dems Pounce After Trump Says He Intends to Cut Entitlements."

145–6 *Seniors voted overwhelmingly for Biden in the Democratic primaries*: Gary Langer, Christine Filer, Sofi Sinozich, and Allison De Jong, "Late Support Lifts Biden; Sanders Keeps His Base: Takeaways from Super Tuesday Exit Polls," ABC News, March 4, 2020, https://abcnews.go.com/Politics/late-support-lifts -biden-sanders-base-takeaways-super/story?id=69381829.

CHAPTER 9: HEALTH CARE

149 *Trump fired the entire NSC pandemic response team in May 2018*: Lena H. Sun, "Top White House Official in Charge of Pandemic Response Exits Abruptly," *Washington Post*, May 10, 2018, https://www.washingtonpost.com/news/to -your-health/wp/2018/05/10/top-white-house-official-in-charge-of-pandemic -response-exits-abruptly/.

149 *He was fired, too—a month before Rear Admiral Ziemer*: Vivian Salama, Ken Dilanian, and Dartunorro Clark, "Tom Bossert, Trump's Homeland Security Adviser, Fired as Bolton Takes Power, Source Says," NBC News, April 10, 2018, https://www.nbcnews.com/politics/politics-news/tom-bossert-trump-s -homeland-security-adviser-resign-n864321.

150 *Only one of them died from it*: Centers for Disease Control and Prevention, "Ebola (Ebola Virus Disease), 2014–2016 Ebola Outbreak in West Africa,"

CDC.gov, March 8, 2019, https://www.cdc.gov/vhf/ebola/history/2014-2016
-outbreak/index.html#anchor_1515001446180.

150 *calling President Obama "stupid" and "incompetent"*: Kurt Bardella, "Trump
Tweets About Obama, Coronavirus and Ebola Reveal Hypocrisy of His Crisis
Response," NBC News, March 10, 2020, https://www.nbcnews.com/think
/opinion/trump-tweets-about-obama-coronavirus-ebola-reveal-hypocrisy-his
-crisis-ncna1153666.

150 *"You've got to fight epidemic diseases where they emerge"*: Lena H. Sun, "CDC
to Cut by 80 Percent Efforts to Prevent Global Disease Outbreak," February 1,
2018, https://www.washingtonpost.com/news/to-your-health/wp/2018/02/01
/cdc-to-cut-by-80-percent-efforts-to-prevent-global-disease-outbreak/.

150 *he called Democrats' concerns about a pandemic "a hoax"*: Gabrielle Bruney,
"Trump Called Coronavirus Response Criticisms a 'New Hoax' from Democrats," *Esquire*, February 29, 2020, https://www.washingtonpost.com/politics
/trump-lashes-out-at-dems-calls-coronavirus-their-new-hoax/2020/02/28
/3dc9582c-5a92-11ea-8efd-0f904bdd8057_story.html.

151 *estimated death rate was "a false number," based on his own "hunch"*: Arthur
Allen and Meridith McGraw, "Trump Gets a Fact Check on Coronavirus
Vaccines—from His Own Officials," *Politico*, March 5, 2020, https://www
.politico.com/news/2020/03/05/coronavirus-trump-vaccine-rhetoric
-121796.

151 *It does not include China, which the OECD still considers "emerging"*: D. L.
Davis, "Universal Health Care Diagnosis Is on the Mark," PolitiFact, June 21,
2019, https://www.politifact.com/factchecks/2019/jun/21/mark-pocan
/universal-health-care-diagnosis-mark/.

151–2 *Johnson claiming that leaving the EU could bring a windfall of 350 million
pounds per week (about $455 million) to the NHS*: Rob Merrick, "Boris
Johnson Lambasted for Claiming Brexit Can Deliver Even More Than 350M
Pounds a Week to NHS," *The Independent*, January 16, 2018, https://www
.independent.co.uk/news/uk/politics/claiming-brexit-can-deliver-even-more
-than-350m-a-week-to-nhs-a8161316.html.

152 *Their name for that single payer: Medicare*: Danielle Martin, et al., "Canada's
Universal Health-Care System: Achieving Its Potential," *The Lancet*, February
22, 2018, https://www.thelancet.com/journals/lancet/article/PIIS0140
-6736(18)30181-8/fulltext.

153 *and with that, control of both chambers*: "Election 2010, House Map," *New
York Times*, https://www.nytimes.com/elections/2010/results/house.html.

154 *"I like people who weren't captured"*: Jonathan Martin and Alan Rappeport,
"Donald Trump Says John McCain Is No War Hero, Setting Off Another

Storm," *New York Times*, July 18, 2016, https://www.nytimes.com/2015/07/19
/us/politics/trump-belittles-mccains-war-record.html.

154 "*Wait for the show*": Dylan Scott, "I'll Never Forget Watching John McCain
Vote Down Obamacare Repeal," *Vox*, August 27, 2018, https://www.vox.com
/policy-and-politics/2018/8/25/17782664/john-mccain-legacy-obamacare
-repeal-thumbs-down.

154 "*dour*" *during the conversation*: Ibid.

154 *preserved the rights of tens of millions of Americans to get health care if they
have a preexisting condition*: Ibid.

155 *the whole law must go—including protection for people with preexisting conditions*: Shefali Luthra, "Trump's Talk on Preexisting Conditions Doesn't Match
His Administration's Actions," *Kaiser Health News*, May 16, 2019, https://khn
.org/news/trumps-talk-on-preexisting-conditions-doesnt-match-his-admin
istrations-actions/.

155 *129 million non-elderly Americans have some sort of preexisting health condition*: The Center for Consumer Information & Insurance Oversight, "At Risk:
Pre-Existing Conditions Could Affect 1 in 2 Americans," Centers for Medicare & Medicaid Services, https://www.cms.gov/CCIIO/Resources/Forms
-Reports-and-Other-Resources/preexisting.

155 *denied health insurance altogether*: Ibid.

155 *will develop a preexisting condition before they reach sixty-five, when they can
go on Medicare*: Ibid.

155 "*just being a woman could be considered a preexisting condition*": Brandie
Temple, "Worst TBT Ever: When Being a Woman Was a Pre-Existing Condition," National Woman's Law Center, January 19, 2017, https://nwlc.org/blog
/worst-tbt-ever-when-being-a-woman-was-a-pre-existing-condition/.

155 "*denied women coverage for having a cesarean delivery or for seeking medical
treatment for domestic or sexual violence*": Ibid.

156 *a high of 55 percent in February 2020*: Ashley Kirzinger, Audrey Kearney, and
Mollyann Brodie, "KFF Health Tracking Poll—February 2020: Health Care
in the 2020 Election," Kaiser Family Foundation, February 21, 2020, https://
www.kff.org/health-reform/poll-finding/kff-health-tracking-poll-february-2020/.

156 *20 million Americans have health insurance today because of Obamacare*:
Rachel Garfield, Kendal Orgera, and Anthony Damico, "The Uninsured and
the ACA: A Primer—Key Facts About Health Insurance and the Uninsured
Amidst Changes to the Affordable Care Act," January 25, 2019, https://www
.kff.org/report-section/the-uninsured-and-the-aca-a-primer-key-facts-about
-health-insurance-and-the-uninsured-amidst-changes-to-the-affordable-care
-act-how-many-people-are-uninsured/.

157 *I mean 90 percent*: Berkeley Lovelace Jr., "Here's How Trump Hobbled Obamacare and Drove Enrollment Down This Year," CNBC, December 15, 2018, https://www.cnbc.com/2018/12/15/heres-how-trump-hobbled -obamacare-and-drove-enrollment-down.html.

157 *"Lung disease patients need access to treatment to be able to breathe"*: Amy Goldstein, "Trump Administration Widens Availability of Skimpy, Short -Term Health Plans," *Washington Post*, August 1, 2018, https://www.wash ingtonpost.com/national/health-science/trump-administration-widens-avail ability-of-skimpy-short-term-health-plans/2018/07/31/a5cf2bc2-94d2-11e8 -810c-5fa705927d54_story.html?arc404=true.

157 *God help you if you have an expensive accident or illness*: Dylan Scott, "Trump's Audacious New Plan to Cut Medicaid, Explained," *Vox*, January 30, 2020, https://www.vox.com/policy-and-politics/2020/1/30/21113436/trump-health -care-policy-medicaid-cuts.

157 *number of uninsured jumped up by about a half-million people*: Garfield, Orgera, and Damico, "The Uninsured and the ACA: A Primer—Key Facts About Health Insurance and the Uninsured Amidst Changes to the Afford- able Care Act."

158 *just punished people for being poor and sick*: Dylan Scott, "How Republican Medicaid Proposals Restrict Access, in One Chart," *Vox*, June 22, 2018, https://www.vox.com/policy-and-politics/2018/6/22/17494744/voxcare -medicaid-expansion.

158 *the Affordable Care Act had not taken effect*: Dylan Scott, "The Uninsured Rate Had Been Steadily Declining for a Decade. But Now It's Rising Again," *Vox*, September 10, 2019, https://www.vox.com/policy-and-politics/2019/9/10 /20858938/health-insurance-census-bureau-data-trump.

158 *17.8 percent for Hispanics*: Ibid.

158 *2,626, to just 487 for Hillary*: "How Many Counties Did Hillary Clinton Win? 487, Not 57, as Fake News Story Claims," Associated Press/*Columbus Dispatch*, December 6, 2016, https://www.dispatch.com/content/stories /national_world/2016/12/06/1206-clinton-won-487-counties.html.

158 *Montana, Nebraska, and South Dakota, in case it comes up on Trivia Night*: Sara Clarke, "You're More Likely to See Cows Here Than People," *U.S. News & World Report*, November 13, 2018, https://www.usnews.com/news/best-states /slideshows/9-states-with-more-cattle-than-humans?slide=3.

158 *the 60–34 drubbing he took in urban areas*: "CNN Politics, Election 2016: Exit Polls," CNN, November 23, 2016, https://www.cnn.com/election/2016/results /exit-polls.

159 *two ambulances to cover a 3,800-square-mile area*: Emily Ramshaw, "No Country

for Health Care, Part 2: The Trauma Hole," *Texas Tribune*, January 4, 2010, https://www.texastribune.org/2010/01/05/little-trauma-care-in-rural-texas/.

159   *more than one-third of all the rural hospitals in America would be gone*: National Rural Health Association, "NHRA Save Rural Hospitals Action Center," https://www.ruralhealthweb.org/advocate/save-rural-hospitals.

159   *19 going under*: Ibid.

159   *"nine percent have no physicians at all"*: Ibid.

160   *not one word about the 11.7 million facing the prospect of losing their lifeline*: Amber Phillips and Kristina Orrego, "President Trump's 2020 State of the Union Address, Annotated," *Washington Post*, February 4, 2020, https://www .washingtonpost.com/politics/2020/02/04/transcript-president-trumps-2020 -state-union-address/.

160   *a 62 percent greater likelihood of surviving*: Dylan Scott, "1 in 4 Rural Hospitals Is Vulnerable to Closure, a New Report Finds," *Vox*, February 18, 2020, https://www.vox.com/policy-and-politics/2020/2/18/21142650/rural-hospi tals-closing-medicaid-expansion-states.

160   *what the propeller-heads call poor people who can't pay their hospital bills*: Ibid.

160   *cuts in Medicare, which they note hurt rural hospitals*: "NRHA Endorses Reintroduction of Save Rural Hospitals Act to New Congress," *National Rural Health Association*, June 20, 2017, https://www.ruralhealthweb.org/NRHA /media/Emerge_NRHA/Press%20releases/NRHA-Release-2017-Save-Rural -Hospitals-Act.pdf.

161   *his allowance was $1 million a year*: Susanne Craig, Russ Buettner, David Barstow, and Gabriel J. X. Dance, "4 Ways Fred Trump Made Donald Trump and His Siblings Rich," *New York Times*, October 2, 2018, https://www .nytimes.com/interactive/2018/10/02/us/politics/trump-family-wealth.html.

161   *is extremely or very important to them*: Adam Cancryn, "Politico-Harvard Poll: Health Care Costs Are Top Priority Heading into Elections," *Politico*, February 2, 2020, https://www.politico.com/news/2020/02/19/poll-health -care-election-115866.

161   *76 percent of Republicans agree with them*: Ibid.

161   *cost of prescription drugs is rated as important by 75 percent of voters*: Ibid.

161   *This buy-in option, by the way, earns the support of 43 percent of Republicans*: Ibid.

161   *37 percent overall support for his attack on ACA is pretty low*: Press Release, "Health Care a Minefield for Republicans: Many Trump Voters in Denial on Russia," Public Policy Polling, July 18, 2017, https://www.publicpolicypolling .com/wp-content/uploads/2017/09/PPP_Release_National_71817.pdf.

162   *"at least for a moment, that I could breathe again"*: Laura Packard, "Op-Ed: We

Must Stop Trump, Gardner from Dismantling the ACA," *Westword*, July 28, 2019, https://www.westword.com/news/op-ed-we-must-stop-trump-gardner -from-dismantling-the-aca-11425841.

162   *that single vote—cast by a warrior fighting his own battle with cancer—saved her life*: Ibid.

164   *"they are shutting the doors of the hospital in the faces of kids like my daughter"*: Protect Our Care, Facebook, September 27, 2018, https://www.facebook.com /ProtectOurCare/videos/2086824054868494/.

164   *if it had not have been for that law, he would be dead*: Jim Nintzel, "The Skinny: A Sick Debate," *Tucson Weekly*, October 25, 2018, https://www.tucson weekly.com/tucson/the-skinny/Content?oid=21584888.

167   *Trump has made this claim or one like it 260 times*: Glenn Kessler, Salvador Rizzo, and Sarah Cahlan, "Fact-Checking President Trump's 2020 State of the Union Address," *Washington Post*, February 4, 2020, https://www.washington post.com/politics/2020/02/04/fact-checking-president-trumps-2020-state -union-address/.

167   *which was during the high-tax Eisenhower era*: Ibid.

167   *4.5 percent in 1998, and 4.7 percent in 1999*: Ibid.

168   *191,000 per month under Trump*: Ibid.

168   *transportation, and other classic blue-collar industries*: Ibid.

168   *the 4 percent they rose under President Obama*: Lori Robertson, "Are Wages Rising or Flat?," FactCheck.org, June 28, 2019, https://www.factcheck.org /2019/06/are-wages-rising-or-flat/.

168   *"Never have corporate profits outgrown employee compensation so clearly and for so long"*: "Corporate Profits Versus Labor Income," *The Fred Blog*, Economic Research, Federal Reserve Bank of St. Louis, August 9, 2018, https:// fredblog.stlouisfed.org/2018/08/corporate-profits-versus-labor-income/.

168   *"The most excited group out there are big CEOs"*: Peter Cary and Allan Holmes, "Workers Barely Benefited from Trump's Sweeping Tax Cut, Investigation Shows," *The Guardian*, April 30, 2019, https://www.theguardian.com/us-news /2019/apr/30/trump-tax-cut-law-investigation-worker-benefits.

169   *the ten-year cost of the Trump tax cut is $1.9 trillion*: John McLelland and Jeffrey Werling, "How the 2017 Tax Act Affects CBO's Projections," *Congressional Budget Office*, April 20, 2018, https://www.cbo.gov/publication/53787.

169   *subsidized broadband internet, especially in rural areas*: Editorial Board, "What the Stimulus Accomplished," *New York Times*, February 22, 2014, https://

www.nytimes.com/2014/02/23/opinion/sunday/what-the-stimulus-accom
plished.html.

170 *700,000 lost per month*: Paul Waldman, "Guess What: Barack Obama Has
Been a Great President for Job Creation," *Washington Post*, January 8, 2016,
https://www.washingtonpost.com/blogs/plum-line/wp/2016/01/08/guess
-what-barack-obama-has-been-a-great-president-for-job-creation/.

170 *created 15.6 million jobs in the private sector alone*: Ben White, "Trump
Inherits Obama Boom," *Politico*, December 2, 2016, https://www.politico.com
/story/2016/12/trump-obama-economic-success-232120.

170 *Luke Bartholomew of Aberdeen Asset Management told* Politico: Ibid.

171 *pulled out of the Great Recession and was finally booming again*: Matt Egan,
"Corporate America's Big, Fat Profitable Year," CNN Business, December 22,
2017, https://money.cnn.com/2017/12/22/investing/corporate-profits-2017
-wall-street/index.html.

171 *After the Trump tax cut, they fell a bit: to 0.77 percent*: Lydia DePillis, "4 Ways
Trump's Tax Cuts Changed the American Economy," CNN Business, April
15, 2019, https://www.cnn.com/2019/04/15/economy/trump-tax-cuts-impact
-economy/index.html.

171 *"These are guys that shift paper around and they get lucky"*: Brad Tuttle, "10
Times Donald Trump Bad-Mouthed People for Not Paying Taxes," *Money*,
October 3, 2016, https://www.cnn.com/2019/04/15/economy/trump-tax-cuts
-impact-economy/index.html.

172 *they pay around 20 percent in taxes*: Chris Isidore and Jill Disis, "Tax Break
for Hedge Fund Managers Survives in GOP Bill," CNN Money, December 21,
2017, https://money.cnn.com/2017/12/21/news/trump-carried-interest-tax
-plan/index.html.

172 *Oh, and real estate managers*: Ibid.

172 *$129 million more*: Andrew Davis, "Why Amazon Paid No 2018 U.S. Federal
Income Tax," CNBC, April 4, 2019, https://www.cnbc.com/2019/04/03/why
-amazon-paid-no-federal-income-tax.html.

173 *they should trouble you nonetheless*: Seth A. Donovan and David H. Bradley,
"Real Wage Trends, 1979–2018," *Congressional Research Service*, July 23, 2019,
https://fas.org/sgp/crs/misc/R45090.pdf.

173 *and Jimmy Carter was in the White House*: Ibid.

173 *"the hardworking Americans who make up our forgotten middle class"*:
William Jefferson Clinton, "Democratic Presidential Nomination Acceptance
Address," *American Rhetoric*, July 16, 1992, https://americanrhetoric.com
/speeches/wjclinton1992dnc.htm.

173 *71 percent of them voted for their blue-collar billionaire*: CNN Politics, Election

2016, "Exit Polls," CNN, November 23, 2016, https://www.cnn.com/election /2016/results/exit-polls.

176 *"think big and look up, beyond the horizon of what is possible in America"*: Dan Merica, "Basking in Union Support, Clinton Rolls Out Infrastructure Plan," CNN, November 29, 2015, https://www.cnn.com/2015/11/29/politics/hillary -clinton-infrastructure-spending/index.html.

176 *a half-trillion-dollar investment*: Matthew Yglesias, "Hillary Clinton's Infra- structure Plan, Explained," *Vox*, December 1, 2015, https://www.vox.com /2015/12/1/9826668/clinton-infrastructure-plan-explained.

176 *"to create the next generation of good-paying jobs"*: Hillary Rodham Clinton, "Fixing America's Infrastructure," The Office of Hillary Rodham Clinton, https://www.hillaryclinton.com/issues/fixing-americas-infrastructure/.

177 *it preferred tolls as a means of paying for roads and bridges*: Yglesias, "Hillary Clinton's Infrastructure Plan, Explained."

177 *"Comey's testimony" on Capitol Hill as part of the Russia investigation*: Katie Rogers, "How 'Infrastructure Weak' Became a Long-Running Joke," *New York Times*, May 22, 2019, https://www.nytimes.com/2019/05/22/us/politics/trump -infrastructure-week.html.

177 *She called it "little more than a Trojan horse"*: Press Release, "Pelosi Statement on Trump's Trojan Horse Infrastructure Plan," Nancy Pelosi, Speaker of the House, June 5, 2017, https://www.speaker.gov/newsroom/6517.

178 *American Society of Civil Engineers gives our infrastructure a D+*: American Society of Civil Engineers, "America's Infrastructure Scores a D+," 2017 Infra- structure Report Card, https://www.infrastructurereportcard.org/.

178 *by 2016 that percentage had dwindled to just 2.5 percent*: Liz Carey, "U.S. Infrastructure Needs Exceed $2 Trillion, American Society of Civil Engineers Says," *Transportation Today*, February 18, 2020, https://transportationtoday news.com/news/17049-u-s-infrastructure-needs-exceed-2-trillion-american -society-of-civil-engineers-says/.

178 *Eight hundred fifty water mains rupture every day*: Ibid.

178 *9.1 percent of bridges are structurally deficient*: American Society of Civil Engi- neers, "America's Infrastructure Scores a D+."

178 *Forty-four percent of the major roads in this country are in poor or mediocre condition*: Carey, "U.S. Infrastructure Needs Exceed $2 Trillion, American Society of Civil Engineers Says.

178 *Drivers spend $129 billion a year on car repairs that they would not need . . .*: Ibid.

178 *"'Thanksgiving-peak traffic volume' at least one day every week"*: American Society of Civil Engineers, "America's Infrastructure Scores a D+."

178 *2,170 dams as "deficient high-hazard potential"*: Ibid.

178 *It was built to last fifty years. Do the math*: Ibid.

179 *we need at least $271 billion invested in wastewater systems to avoid disaster*: Ibid.

179 *0.7 percent of GDP*: Kimberly Amadeo, "U.S. Budget Deficit by Year Compared to GDP, Debt Increase, and Events," *The Balance*, March 2, 2020, https://www.thebalance.com/us-deficit-by-year-3306306.

179 *about 5 percent of GDP*: Jeff Stein and Erica Werner, "Trump Proposes $4.8 Trillion Election-Year Budget with Big Domestic Cuts," *Washington Post*, February 10, 2020, https://www.washingtonpost.com/business/2020/02/09 /trump-budget-plan-would-fail-eliminate-deficit-over-10-years-briefing -document-shows/.

179 *left his successor with a debt-to-GDP ratio of just 54 percent*: Robert Reich, "How Democrats Clean Up the Messes Left by Republicans," RobertReich.org, February 18, 2020, https://robertreich.org/ post/190905737165.

180 *"Yeah, but I won't be here," he said*: Aswain Suebsaeng and Lachlan Markay, "Trump on Coming Debt Crisis: 'I Won't Be Here' When It Blows Up," *Daily Beast*, March 14, 2019, https://www.thedailybeast.com/trump-on-coming -debt-crisis-i-wont-be-here-when-it-blows-up.

181 *32 percent say it will be worse*: Ruth Igielnik and Kim Parker, "Most Americans Say the Current Economy Is Helping the Rich, Hurting the Poor and Middle Class," Pew Research Center, Social & Demographic Trends, December 11, 2019, https://www.pewsocialtrends.org/2019/12/11/most-americans-say-the -current-economy-is-helping-the-rich-hurting-the-poor-and-middle-class/.

183 *Yes, Tucker Fox News Carlson*: Tucker Carlson, "Mitt Romney Supports the Status Quo. But for Everyone Else, It's Infuriating," Fox News, January 3, 2019, https://www.foxnews.com/opinion/tucker-carlson-mitt-romney-supports -the-status-quo-but-for-everyone-else-its-infuriating. Used with the author's permission.

CHAPTER 11: CLIMATE CHANGE

185 *"no party-wide view like this anywhere in the world that I am aware of"*: Max Fisher, "Why Republicans Deny Climate Change," *The Atlantic*, October 18, 2010, https://www.theatlantic.com/technology/archive/2010/10/why-republi cans-deny-climate-change/343790/.

185 *"something that threatens us so directly as a species"*: David Scharfenberg, "The Flat Earth Society Weighs in on Climate Change," *Boston Globe*, September 7,

2018, https://www.bostonglobe.com/ideas/2018/09/07/the-flat-earth-society -weighs-climate-change/pyRLW25ksFUvzsxQ5iDuHO/story.html.

185 *lying about graduating first in your class*: Justin Elliott, "Just What Kind of Student Was Donald Trump?," *Salon*, May 3, 2011, https://www.salon.com /2011/05/03/donald_trump_wharton/.

186 *"in order to make U.S. manufacturing non-competitive"*: Louis Jacobson, "Yes, Donald Trump Did Call Climate Change a Chinese Hoax," PolitiFact, June 3, 2016, https://www.politifact.com/factchecks/2016/jun/03/hillary-clinton/yes -donald-trump-did-call-climate-change-chinese-h/.

186 *"They burn everything you could burn; they couldn't care less"*: Ibid.

186 *a charge PolitiFact rated as "Pants on Fire"*: Ibid.

186 *"It's a hoax, a lot of it"*: Ibid.

187 *Here are a few tweets that PolitiFact cited*: Ibid.

188 *in cities, suburbs, and rural areas all agree*: Dante Chinni and Sally Bronston, "Polling: Consensus Emerges in Climate Change Debate," NBC News, December 21, 2018, https://www.nbcnews.com/politics/meet-the-press /consensus-emerges-climate-change-debate-n950646.

188 *"up 22 points since 1999"*: Ibid.

188 *"unchanged since the same question was asked in 1999"*: Ibid.

189 *"other leaders to laugh at us anymore"*: Kevin Liptak and Jim Acosta, "Trump on Paris Accord: 'We're Getting Out,'" CNN, June 2, 2017, https://www.cnn .com/2017/06/01/politics/trump-paris-climate-decision/index.html.

189 *where he had a jazz band perform*: Ibid.

189 *"very unfair, at the highest level, to the United States"*: "Statement by President Trump on the Paris Climate Accord," The White House, June 1, 2017, https:// www.whitehouse.gov/briefings-statements/statement-president-trump-paris -climate-accord/.

189 *"nationally determined contributions"*: United Nations Climate Change, "What Is the Paris Agreement?," https://unfccc.int/process-and-meetings/the-paris -agreement/what-is-the-paris-agreement.

190 *"With continued growth in emissions at historic rates"*: "Trump on Climate Change Report: 'I Don't Believe It,'" BBC, https://www.bbc.com/news/world -us-canada-46351940.

190 *climbing up three flights of stairs to make a delivery*: Interview with Peggy Howard, March 5, 2020.

191 *"straying onto perilously thin ice and tumbling into the frigid water"*: Steven Mufson, Chris Mooney, Juliet Eilperin, and John Muyskens, "2°C: Beyond the Limit: Extreme Climate Change Has Arrived in America," *Washington Post*,

August 13, 2019, https://www.washingtonpost.com/graphics/2019/national /climate-environment/climate-change-america/.

191 *"already crossed the 2-degree Celsius mark"*: Ibid.

191 *Connecticut, Maine, Massachusetts, New Jersey, and elsewhere*: Ibid.

191 *She fondly remembers hot summer afternoons swimming in the cool lake water*: Text from Peggy Howard (how great is it that she texts?), March 5, 2020.

191 *the bacteria can cause liver and neurological damage*: Michele S. Byers, "How Blue-Green Algae Blooms Stole New Jersey's Summer," North Jersey.com, August 5, 2019, https://www.northjersey.com/story/opinion/2019/08/05/lake -hopatcong-algae-bloom-how-blue-green-algae-stole-nj-summer/1921662001/.

191 *Neither can your dog, because it can kill him or her*: Christine Hauser, "Algae Can Poison Your Dog," *New York Times*, August 12, 2019, https://www.ny times.com/2019/08/12/us/blue-green-algae-dogs.html.

192 *"it only bought us 10 years"*: Mufson, Mooney, Eilperin and Muyskens, "2°C: Beyond the Limit: Extreme Climate Change Has Arrived in America."

192 *a 3.6 degree rise has been called "irreversible and apocalyptic"*: Alessandra Potenza, "Here's How Climate Change Is Already Affecting the U.S.," *The Verge*, August 9, 2017, https://www.theverge.com/2017/8/9/16116198/climate -change-report-extreme-weather-co2-donald-trump.

192 *Heat waves that are dangerous for your health*: Ibid.

192 *Crops dying in fields from the heat*: Ibid.

192 *Power outages from too much heat-related demand*: Ibid.

192 *Extreme rain, causing flash floods*: Ibid.

192 *toxic algae blooms, harming water quality, killing dogs and fish*: Ibid.

192 *a longer tornado season, and more intense twisters*: Ibid.

192 *Forest fires like we saw in Australia, which will hit the United States*: Ibid.

193 *gun policy, education, the economy, and immigration*: Zach Hrynowski, "Several Issues Tie as Most Important in 2020 Election," Gallup News, January 13, 2020, https://news.gallup.com/poll/276932/several-issues-tie-important -2020-election.aspx.

193 *whose dog, Ollie, died just one hour after he went for a swim in Lady Bird Lake*: Pattrik Perez and Abigail Arredondo, " 'I Love You for All of Time': Woman Sends Warning When Dog Dies After Swimming in Lady Bird Lake," KVUE, August 7, 2019, https://www.kvue.com/article/news/local/i-love-you-for-all -of-time-woman-sends-warning-when-dog-dies-after-swimming-in-lady -bird-lake/269-978e420e-b095-4b71-9e0f-78ad40a5adcd.

193 *dubbing the powerful US Chamber of Commerce the "Chamber of Carbon"*: Sen. Sheldon Whitehouse (@SenWhitehouse), Twitter, May 24, 2019, 4:48 p.m., https://twitter.com/SenWhitehouse/status/1132025613936660480?ref_src=

twsrc%5Etfw%7Ctwcamp%5Etweetembed%7Ctwterm%5E11320256139366
60480&ref_url=https%3A%2F%2Fwww.vox.com%2Fenergy-and-environ
ment%2F2019%2F6%2F7%2F18654957%2Fclimate-change-lobbying
-chamber-of-commerce.

193 *He says that this "is a fissure we want to expose and exploit"*: David Roberts,
"These Senators Are Going After the Biggest Climate Villains in Washington,"
Vox, November 18, 2019, https://www.vox.com/energy-and-environment
/2019/6/7/18654957/climate-change-lobbying-chamber-of-commerce.

193 *Hewlett-Packard, Mattel, Kraft Heinz, Mars, and others*: Dominic Rushe,
"Disney, the Gap and Pepsi Urged to Quit US Chamber of Commerce," *The
Guardian*, April 24, 2017, https://www.theguardian.com/business/2017/apr
/24/disney-the-gap-and-pepsi-urged-to-quit-us-chamber-of-commerce.

194 *a family of four would receive about $2,000; the amount will increase as the
carbon fee increases*: Climate Leadership Council, "The Four Pillars of Our
Carbon Dividends Plan," September 2019, https://clcouncil.org/our-plan/.

195 *universal health care, a guaranteed job, and more*: Zachary B. Wolf, "Here's
What the Green New Deal Actually Says," CNN, March 2, 2020, https://www
.cnn.com/2019/02/14/politics/green-new-deal-proposal-breakdown/index.html.

195 *photovoltaic and other renewable sources of energy*: Mark Muro, Jonathan
Rothwell, and Devashree Saha, "Sizing the Clean Economy: A National
and Regional Green Jobs Assessment," Brookings Institution, July 13, 2011,
https://www.brookings.edu/research/sizing-the-clean-economy-a-national
-and-regional-green-jobs-assessment/.

195 *13 percent higher than median wages in the rest of the economy*: Ibid.

CHAPTER 12: THE TRUMP COURTS

197 *"no agenda. I have no platform"*: John Roberts, "Opening Statement to Senate
Committee on the Judiciary," CNN, September 12, 2005, https://www.cnn
.com/2005/POLITICS/09/12/roberts.statement/.

198 *"More common was 'Hillary Clinton age' "*: Philip Bump, "A Quarter of
Republicans Voted for Trump to Get Supreme Court Picks—And It Paid
Off," *Washington Post*, June 26, 2018, https://www.washingtonpost.com/news
/politics/wp/2018/06/26/a-quarter-of-republicans-voted-for-trump-to-get
-supreme-court-picks-and-it-paid-off/.

198 *"The fact of the matter is that it's been standard practice"*: Steve Benen, "Justice
Kennedy's Confirmation Debunks Key GOP Talking Point," MSNBC, http:
//www.msnbc.com/rachel-maddow-show/justice-kennedys-confirmation
-debunks-key-gop-talking-point.

198   *He himself voted to confirm Anthony Kennedy nine months before the 1988*
      presidential election: Senate Vote #436 in 1988, "To Confirm the Nomination
      of Anthony B. Kennedy of California to Be an Associate Justice of the United
      States Supreme Court," February 3, 1988, https://www.govtrack.us/congress
      /votes/100-1988/s436.

198   *Kennedy was nominated on November 12, 1987*: Linda Greenhouse, "Reagan
      Nominates Anthony Kennedy to Supreme Court," *New York Times*, November
      12, 1987, https://www.nytimes.com/1987/11/12/us/reagan-nominates
      -anthony-kennedy-to-supreme-court.html.

198   *The first day of the Judiciary Committee hearings was December 14*: "Kennedy
      Nomination Day 1, Part 2," C-SPAN, December 14, 1987, https://www.c-span
      .org/video/?10492-1/kennedy-nomination-day-1-part-2.

198–9   *confirmed by the Democratically controlled Senate on February 4, 1988, by*
      a vote of 97–0: Linda Greenhouse, "Senate, 97–0, Confirms Kennedy to High
      Court," *New York Times*, February 4, 1988, https://www.nytimes.com/1988/02
      /04/us/senate-97-to-0-confirms-kennedy-to-high-court.html.

199   *Grassley publicly thanked Biden for "expediting this vote"*: "User Clip: Grassley
      Supports Kennedy," C-SPAN, January 27, 1988, https://www.c-span.org/video
      /?c4580671/user-clip-grassley-supports-kennedy.

199   *"the American people will know what's up"*: Greenhouse, "Reagan Nominates
      Anthony Kennedy to Supreme Court."

199   *Merrick Garland, a widely respected moderate sixty-three-year-old who had*
      served presidents of both parties: Juliet Eilperin and Mike DeBonis, "President
      Obama Nominates Merrick Garland to the Supreme Court," *Washington Post*,
      March 16, 2016, https://www.washingtonpost.com/world/national-security
      /president-obama-to-nominate-merrick-garland-to-the-supreme-court
      -sources-say/2016/03/16/3bc90bc8-eb7c-11e5-a6f3-21ccdbc5f74e_story.html.

199   *"deny Garland a hearing and a vote after he has been the subject of effusive*
      bipartisan accolades for years": Ibid.

200   *John McCain, of Arizona; and Pat Roberts, of Kansas*: Ibid.

200   *"but in order to politicize it for the purposes of election"*: Ibid.

200   *urged Obama to put him on the high court in 2010*: Thomas Burr, "White
      House Notes Hatch Called Supreme Court Nominee a 'Consensus Pick' in
      2020," *Salt Lake Tribune*, March 16, 2016, https://archive.sltrib.com/article
      .php?id=3670228&itype=CMSID.

200   *" 'no question' Merrick would be confirmed with bipartisan support"*: Ibid.

200–1   *much less confirming Garland, his "consensus nominee"*: Seung Min Kim,
      "Hatch Repeats: No Hearings for Garland Before Election," *Politico*, May 26,

2016, https://www.politico.com/story/2016/05/orrin-hatch-merrick-garland
-meeting-223626.

201 *op-ed was written, filed, and run before the meeting ever took place*: Eliza
Collins, "In Op-Ed, Hatch Mentions Meeting with Garland That Hadn't
Happened," *USA Today*, May 26, 2016, https://www.usatoday.com/story/news
/politics/onpolitics/2016/05/26/hatch-garland-op-ed/84981478/.

201 *61 percent thought they were wrong*: Irin Carmon, "Poll: Majority of Americans Want Senate to Vote on Garland Nomination," MSNBC, March 18, 2016,
http://www.msnbc.com/msnbc/poll-majority-americans-want-senate-vote
-garland-nomination.

201 *"1.7 million of them thought that the court was the most important reason to
cast that vote"*: Bump, "A Quarter of Republicans Voted for Trump to Get
Supreme Court Picks—And It Paid Off."

203 *give him a list of potential Supreme Court nominees*: Lawrence Baum and
Neal Devins, "Federalist Court: How the Federalist Society Became the de
Facto Selector of Republican Supreme Court Justices," *Slate*, January 31,
2017, https://slate.com/news-and-politics/2017/01/how-the-federalist-society
-became-the-de-facto-selector-of-republican-supreme-court-justices.html.

203 *"from Supreme Court Justices to big-name politicians to renowned legal
scholars"*: Senator Sheldon Whitehouse, "The Third Federalist Society," March
27, 2019, https://www.whitehouse.senate.gov/news/speeches/the-third-feder
alist-society.

204 *"willing to go to drastic lengths to secure that power"*: Ibid.

204 *dark as a barrel of Koch Industries oil*: Ibid.

204 *like bedbugs at a Trump Hotel*: Leonard Greene, "Trump International Hotel
in Las Vegas Teeming with Bed Bugs, Some Guests Claim," *New York Daily
News*, May 24, 2017, https://www.nydailynews.com/news/national/trump
-international-hotel-vegas-bed-bugs-guests-claim-article-1.3193510; Jose
Lambiet, "Trump Doral Settles Lawsuit over Biting Bedbugs," *Miami Herald*,
January 30, 2017, https://www.miamiherald.com/entertainment/ent-columns
-blogs/jose-lambiet/article129651494.html.

204 *"Guess whose interests she's had conveyed on to the D.C. Court of Appeals to
protect?"*: Whitehouse, "The Third Federalist Society."

205 *lowering the cost of prescription drugs, to cleaning up corruption in Washington*:
Ella Nilsen, "House Democrats Have Passed Nearly 400 Bills. Trump and
Republicans Are Ignoring Them," *Vox*, November 29, 2019, https://www.vox
.com/2019/11/29/20977735/how-many-bills-passed-house-democrats-trump.

205 *Trump has named fifty*: Ian Millhiser, "What Trump Has Done to the Courts,

Explained," *Vox*, February 4, 2020, https://www.vox.com/policy-and-politics /2019/12/9/20962980/trump-supreme-court-federal-judges.

205 *And one was for a technical court that deals with patents and other geekizoid stuff*: Ibid.

205 *Harry Reid (D-NV) confirmed ten appeals court judges Bush sent him*: Ibid.

206 *Trump's executive order barring refugees and other people from several Muslim -dominated countries*: Michael D. Shear, Mark Landler, Matt Apuzzo and Eric Lichtblau, "Trump Fires Acting Attorney General Who Defied Him," *New York Times*, January 30, 2017, https://www.nytimes.com/2017/01/30/us /politics/trump-immigration-ban-memo.html.

206 *he was a Federalist Society member and regularly spoke at Federalist Society events*: Baum and Devins, "Federalist Court: How the Federalist Society Became the de Facto Selector of Republican Supreme Court Justices."

206 *The arched ceiling rises 96 feet and is decorated with 22-karat gold leaf*: "10 Fun Facts About Washington DC's Union Station: Things to See and Do in the Washington, D.C., Area," May 23, 2016, https://washingtondcmetroarea .blogspot.com/2016/05/10-fun-facts-about-union-station-DC.html.

206 *guarded by thirty-six giant Roman legionnaires hand-carved by Louis Saint- Gaudens*: John Canning, "Preserving the Guardians: The Legionnaire Statues of Union Station," John Canning: Perfecting Preservation, https://johncanning co.com/blog/legionnaire-statues-union-station/.

207 *"It's not a shadowy cabal in need of Joe McCarthy"*: Josh Gerstein, "Gorsuch Takes Victory Lap at Federalist Dinner," *Politico*, November 16, 2017, https:// www.politico.com/story/2017/11/16/neil-gorsuch-federalist-society-speech -scotus-246538.

204 *a trucking company was within its rights to fire Al Maddin for the offense of not dying on the job*: United States Court of Appeals, Tenth Circuit, *Trans Am Trucking, Inc., Petitioner, v. Administrative Review Board, United States Department of Labor, Respondent Alphonse Maddin, Intervenor*, No. 15-9504, August 8, 2016, 833 F.3d 1206 (2016), https://caselaw.findlaw.com/us-10th -circuit/1745686.html.

208 *The company told Al to "hang in there"*: Ibid.

208 *Al refused*: Ibid.

208 *The company fired Al for abandoning his load*: Ibid.

209 *the law only empowers a driver to "refuse to operate" a truck*: Ibid.

209 *despite his ruling that a truck driver should have been fired for refusing to freeze to death*: Audrey Carlsen and Wilson Andrews, "How Senators Voted on the Gorsuch Confirmation," *New York Times*, April 7, 2017, https://www.nytimes .com/interactive/2017/04/07/us/politics/gorsuch-confirmation-vote.html.

209 *"He was trying to attack me and remove my clothing"*: Emma Brown, "California Professor, Writer of Confidential Letter, Speaks Out About Her Allegation of Sexual Assault," *Washington Post*, September 16, 2018, https://www.washingtonpost.com/investigations/california-professor-writer-of-confidential-brett-kavanaugh-letter-speaks-out-about-her-allegation-of-sexual-assault/2018/09/16/46982194-b846-11e8-94eb-3bd52dfe917b_story.html.

210 *"Brett Kavanaugh just put his penis in Debbie's face"*: Ronan Farrow and Jane Mayer, "Senate Democrats Investigate a New Allegation of Sexual Misconduct, from Brett Kavanaugh's College Years," *New Yorker*, September 23, 2018, https://www.newyorker.com/news/news-desk/senate-democrats-investigate-a-new-allegation-of-sexual-misconduct-from-the-supreme-court-nominee-brett-kavanaughs-college-years-deborah-ramirez.

210 *"he was distressed to the degree that he took his own life"*: Glenn Kessler, "No, Donald Trump, There's Nothing 'Fishy' About Vince Foster's Suicide," *Washington Post*, May 25, 2016, https://www.washingtonpost.com/news/fact-checker/wp/2016/05/25/no-donald-trump-theres-nothing-fishy-about-vince-fosters-suicide/.

211 *the FBI, and the Park Police all joined in that conclusion*: Robert O'Harrow Jr. and Michael Kranish, "After Investigating Clinton White House and Vincent Foster's Death, Brett Kavanaugh Had a Change of Heart," *Washington Post*, August 2, 2018, https://www.washingtonpost.com/investigations/after-investigating-clinton-white-house-and-vincent-fosters-death-brett-kavanaugh-had-change-of-heart/2018/08/02/66ee2b2c-91f5-11e8-9b0d-749fb254bc3d_story.html.

211 *"there is no evidence to the contrary"*: Kessler, "No, Donald Trump, There's Nothing 'Fishy' About Vince Foster's Suicide."

211 *"Vincent W. Foster, Jr. took his own life in Fort March Park, Virginia on July 20, 1993"*: Ibid.

211 *"Vincent Foster took his own life in Fort Marcy Park"*: Ibid.

212 *The Foster family was outraged and issued a statement to that effect*: O'Harrow Jr. and Kranish, "After Investigating Clinton White House and Vincent Foster's Death, Brett Kavanaugh Had a Change of Heart."

212 *business dealings Starr was investigating*: Ibid.

212 *Kavanaugh decided to ask Clinton personally*: Ibid.

212 *blond hairs were found on Foster's body*: Ibid.

213 *"I have to say that I fear for the future"*: CBS/Associated Press, "Brett Kavanaugh's Attack on Democrats Could Pose Risk to Supreme Court," CBS News, September 29, 2019, https://www.cbsnews.com/news/brett-kavanaugh-attack-on-democrats-poses-risk-to-supreme-court/.

213 *"I am pro-choice in every respect, as far as it goes. But I just hate it"*: "Trump in 1999: 'I Am Very Pro-Choice,'" *Meet the Press*/NBC News, October 24, 1999, https://www.nbcnews.com/meet-the-press/video/trump-in-1999-i-am-very -pro-choice-480297539914.

214 *"through the Supreme Court and putting people in the court"*: Steve Benen, "Trump's Promise: 'I Will Appoint Judges That Will Be Pro-Life,'" MSNBC, May 11, 2016, http://www.msnbc.com/rachel-maddow-show/trumps-promise -i-will-appoint-judges-will-be-pro-life.

214 *"the firewall for abortion rights"*: Julie Hirschfeld Davis, "Departure of Kennedy, 'Firewall for Abortion Rights,' Could End *Roe v. Wade*," *New York Times*, June 27, 2018, https://www.nytimes.com/2018/06/27/us/politics /kennedy-abortion-roe-v-wade.html.

214 *Kennedy's retirement "would leave the* Roe v. Wade *decision very vulnerable"*: Karen Turner, "The Woman Who Argued *Roe v. Wade* on Kennedy Retiring: 'We Thought We Had Won This,'" *Vox*, June 29, 2018, https://www.vox.com /conversations/2018/6/29/17515690/anthony-kennedy-retirement-justice-roe -vs-wade.

214 *"a sordid business, this divvying us up by race"*: Linda Greenhouse, "The Chief Justice on the Spot," *New York Times*, January 8, 2009, https://www.nytimes .com/2009/01/09/opinion/09greenhouse.html.

215 *Apparently, your corporate overlords have the final word*: Bill Mears and Tom Cohen, "Supreme Court Rules Against Obama in Contraception Case," CNN, June 30, 2014, https://www.cnn.com/2014/06/30/politics/scotus-obamacare -contraception/index.html.

216 *"including the belief that women should not be in the workforce"*: Sarah McCammon, "Supreme Court Takes Up Birth-Control Conscience Case," NPR, January 17, 2020, https://www.npr.org/2020/01/17/795342900/supreme -court-takes-up-birth-control-conscience-case.

216 *"dismantling clean air and water protections"*: Lisa Friedman, "Trump's Move Against Landmark Environmental Law Caps a Relentless Agenda," *New York Times*, January 9, 2020, https://www.nytimes.com/2020/01/09/climate/trump -nepa-environment.html.

216 *oil tanker spilled 3 million gallons of crude oil on the California coast at Santa Barbara*: Ibid.

CHAPTER 13: SWAMP MONSTER TRUMP

218 *Trump clocked in at a third-grade level*: Jack Shafer, "Donald Trump Talks Like a Third-Grader," August 13, 2015, https://www.politico.com/magazine/story /2015/08/donald-trump-talks-like-a-third-grader-121340.

218 *half of the voters in the last presidential election did not have a college education*: CNN Politics, Election 2016, "Exit Polls," CNN, November 23, 2016, https://www.cnn.com/election/2016/results/exit-polls.

219 *his disapproval rating was 51.8 percent*: "How Popular Is Donald Trump?," FiveThirtyEight, https://projects.fivethirtyeight.com/trump-approval-ratings/.

220 *he had given a secret sweetheart plea deal to Jeffrey Epstein*: Richard Lardner, "Trump Outpaces Obama, Bush in Naming Ex-Lobbyists to Cabinet," Associated Press, September 17, 2019, https://apnews.com/08dce0f5f9c24a6aa355cd 0aab3747d9.

220 *187 lobbyists in the Trump Administration*: Ben Mathis-Lilley, "Swamp -Draining Trump Administration Has Hired 187 Lobbyists, New Report Finds," *Slate*, March 7, 2018, https://slate.com/news-and-politics/2018/03 /trump-administration-has-hired-187-lobbyists-propublic-finds-swamp -much.html.

220 *allowing his people to cash in quicker*: Isaac Arnsdorf, "Trump Lobbying Ban Weakens Obama Rules," *Politico*, January 28, 2017, https://www.politico.com /story/2017/01/trump-lobbying-ban-weakens-obama-ethics-rules-234318.

220 *A former lobbyist for British Petroleum has a top job at the EPA*: Mathis-Lilley, "Swamp-Draining Trump Administration Has Hired 187 Lobbyists, New Report Finds."

220 *A former pharmaceutical lobbyist was named counsel at the FDA*: Ibid.

221 *A former lobbyist for the health insurance industry is now at the Department of Health and Human Services*: Ibid.

221 *Oh, look, there's another health insurance lobbyist at HHS*: Ibid.

221 *removes protection from wetlands and streams across the country*: Bill Chappell, "EPA Makes Rollback of Clean Water Rules Official, Repealing 2015 Protections," NPR, September 12, 2019, https://www.npr.org/2019/09/12 /760203456/epa-makes-rollback-of-clean-water-rules-official-repealing-2015 -protections.

221 *as well as all the other provisions of the Affordable Care Act*: Lori Robertson, "Trump Misleads on Preexisting Conditions," FactCheck.org, October 2, 2018, https://www.factcheck.org/2018/10/trump-misleads-on-preexisting -conditions/.

221 *36 percent of people who tried to buy health insurance faced this kind of*

discrimination: Centers for Medicare and Medicaid Services, "At Risk: Pre-Existing Conditions Could Affect 1 in 2 Americans," CMS.gov, https://www.cms.gov/CCIIO/Resources/Forms-Reports-and-Other-Resources/preexisting.

221 *or sought treatment for domestic abuse or sexual violence*: Brandie Temple, "Worst TBT Ever: When Being a Woman Was a Pre-Existing Condition," National Women's Law Center, January 19, 2017, https://nwlc.org/blog/worst -tbt-ever-when-being-a-woman-was-a-pre-existing-condition/.

221 *with nine more in the pipeline*: Nadia Popovich, Livia Albeck-Ripka, and Kendra Pierre-Louis, "95 Environmental Rules Being Rolled Back Under Trump," *New York Times*, December 21, 2019, https://www.nytimes.com /interactive/2019/climate/trump-environment-rollbacks.html.

222 *"reduce regulatory burden for industries and the states"*: Umair Irfan, "The Trump Administration Is Lifting Key Controls on Toxic Air Pollution," *Vox*, January 26, 2018, https://www.vox.com/energy-and-environment/2018/1/26 /16936104/epa-trump-toxic-air-pollution.

222 *Oh, and the American Chemistry Council*: Ibid.

222 *"priced access to our nation's resources at $30 million and counting"*: Rebecca Leber, "Energy Companies Have a Great Friend at Trump's Interior Department: Their Former Lobbyist," *Mother Jones*, January 16, 2020, https://www .motherjones.com/environment/2020/01/energy-companies-have-a-great -friend-at-trumps-interior-department-their-former-lobbyist/.

223 *gutted safety rules for offshore drilling that were put in place after the Deepwater Horizon debacle of 2010*: Carol Davenport, "Interior Dept. Loosens Offshore-Drilling Safety Rules Dating from Deepwater Horizon," *New York Times*, May 2, 2019, https://www.nytimes.com/2019/05/02/climate/offshore-drilling -safety-rollback-deepwater-horizon.html.

223 *eleven hardworking family men whose lives were briefly profiled in* USA Today: "Short Portraits of 11 Who Died on the Deepwater Horizon," *Jackson (MS) Clarion-Ledger/USA Today*, April 18, 2015, https://www.clarionledger.com /story/news/2015/04/18/short-portraits-died-deepwater-horizon/26007421/.

225 *Here's what this massive, sweeping anticorruption bill does*: Ella Nilsen, "House Democrats Officially Unveil Their First Bill in the Majority: A Sweeping Anti-Corruption Proposal," *Vox*, January 4, 2019, https://www.vox.com/policy-and -politics/2018/11/30/18118158/house-democrats-anti-corruption-bill-hr-1 -pelosi.

225 *publicly disclose ten years of tax returns*: Ibid.

225 *code of ethics for the Supreme Court, which right now has fewer rules than a Nevada bordello*: Ibid.

225 *using taxpayers funds to settle sexual harassment claims*: Ibid.

226 *Prohibit members of Congress from serving on the boards of for-profit corporations*: "H.R. 1—For the People Act of 2019," Congress.gov, https://www .congress.gov/bill/116th-congress/house-bill/1.

226 *more oversight for foreign agents*: Nilsen, "House Democrats Officially Unveil Their First Bill in the Majority: A Sweeping Anti-Corruption Proposal."

226 *Makes Election Day a federal holiday*: Ibid.

226 *automatic voter registration*: Amy Sherman, "House Democrats and HR 1: Voting Rights Expansion or Federal Power Grab?" PolitiFact, February 8, 2019, https://www.politifact.com/article/2019/feb/08/democrats-seek-expand -voting-access-2020-election-/.

226 *same-day registration for federal elections*: Ibid.

226 *online voter registration*: Ibid.

226 *Makes colleges and universities voter registration agencies (the way the Department of Motor Vehicles is now)*: Nilsen, "House Democrats Officially Unveil Their First Bill in the Majority."

226 *Restores voting rights to felons who have completed their prison sentences*: Ibid.

226 *banning the use of non-forwardable mail to remove people from the voter rolls*: Ibid.

226 *Require fifteen days of early voting*: Ibid.

226 *Requires states to have paper ballots*: Press Release, "Chairman Thompson Lauds Election Security Inclusion in H.R. 1," House Committee on Homeland Security, January 4, 2019, https://homeland.house.gov/news/press-releases /chairman-thompson-lauds-election-security-inclusion-hr-1.

226 *Sets cybersecurity standards for voting machines*: Ibid.

226 *Requires the director of national intelligence to assess threats six months before an election*: Ibid.

226 *creates a National Commission to Protect Democratic Institutions*: Ibid.

227 *encourage low-donor fund-raising*: Nilsen, "House Democrats Officially Unveil Their First Bill in the Majority: A Sweeping Anti-Corruption Proposal."

227 *Requires super PACs and "dark money" groups to make all their donors public*: Ibid.

227 *disclose how much money was spent*: Ibid.

227 *Discloses political spending by government contractors*: Ibid.

227 *targeting shell corporations*: Ibid.

228 *threw out the century-old ban on corporate spending in elections*: John Dunbar, "The 'Citizens United' Decision and Why It Matters," Center for Public Integrity, March 10, 2018, https://publicintegrity.org/politics/the-citizens-united -decision-and-why-it-matters/.

228 *shook his head vigorously and mouthed the words "Not true"*: Tiffany Muller,

"Obama Was Right, Alito Wrong: Citizens United Has Corrupted American Politics, *USA Today,* January 20, 2020, https://www.usatoday.com/story /opinion/2020/01/20/citizens-united-money-talks-on-guns-climate-drug -prices-column/4509987002/.

229 *"the candidates combined for less than $50 million"*: Ibid.

230 *"For the love of money is the root of all evil"*: 1 Timothy 6:10.

CHAPTER 14: AMERICA LAST

231 *business interests in 144 companies in at least twenty-five countries*: Curt Devine, "Trump's Foreign Business Interests: 144 Companies in 25 Countries," CNN, November 28, 2016, https://www.cnn.com/2016/11/28/politics /trump-foreign-businesses/index.html.

231 *condos in Mumbai*: "Trump Tower Mumbai," The Trump Organization, https://www.trump.com/residential-real-estate-portfolio/trump-tower -mumbai-india.

231 *use of his name in Uruguay*: *Time* Staff, "Donald Trump's Many, Many Business Dealings in 1 Map," *Time*, January 10, 2017, https://time.com/4629308 /donald-trump-business-deals-world-map/.

232 *"gas station masquerading as a country"*: Gabe Lamonica, "McCain Calls Russia a 'Gas Station,'" Political Ticker, April 22, 2014, https://politicalticker .blogs.cnn.com/2014/04/22/mccain-calls-russia-a-gas-station/.

232 *down to $1.65 trillion in 2018*: "Russian Federation GDP 2018," World Bank, https://data.worldbank.org/country/russian-federation?view=chart.

233 *although you have 141.7 million people*, "The World Factbook: Russia," Central Intelligence Agency, February 28, 2020 https://www.cia.gov/library/publica tions/the-world-factbook/geos/rs.html.

233 *"not be a major military power"*: Ibid.

233 *is less than Japan or France or the Brits or the Saudis spend*: Ibid.

233 *2020 US Defense budget is $718.3 billion*: "DOD Releases Fiscal Year 2020 Budget Proposal," Department of Defense, March 12, 2019, https://www .defense.gov/Newsroom/Releases/Release/Article/1782623/dod-releases-fiscal -year-2020-budget-proposal/.

233 *national security at $989 billion*: Kimberly Amadeo, "US Military Budget, Its Components, Challenges, and Growth," The Balance, March 3, 2020, https:// www.thebalance.com/u-s-military-budget-components-challenges-growth -3306320.

233 *On fire*: Kyle Mizokami, "Russia's Only Aircraft Carrier Is on Fire," *Popular*

Mechanics, December 12, 2019, https://www.popularmechanics.com/military/navy-ships/a30211682/admiral-kuznetsov-fire/.

233 *"All roads with you lead to Putin"*: Katie Rogers, "Inside the Derailed White House Meeting," *New York Times*, October 16, 2019, https://www.nytimes.com/2019/10/16/us/politics/trump-pelosi-meeting.html.

234 *"if so, will he become my new best friend?"*: Tom Porter, "How Do I Love Thee? A Short History of Trump's Praise for Putin," *Newsweek*, November 11, 2017, https://www.newsweek.com/heres-all-times-trump-has-praised-putin-708859.

234 *"their world prestige is very strong"*: Christopher Massie and Andrew Kaczynski, "Trump Called Russia's Invasion of Ukraine 'So Smart' in 2014," *BuzzFeed*, August 1, 2016, https://www.buzzfeednews.com/article/christophermassie/trump-called-russias-invasion-of-ukraine-so-smart-in-2014.

234 *"who could not have been nicer"*: Sara Jerde, "Trump Now Says He Never Met with Putin After Bragging About Chats with Him," *Talking Points Memo*, July 27, 2016, https://talkingpointsmemo.com/livewire/trump-never-met-putin-fact-check.

234 *not even on the same continent*: Ibid.

235 *using chemical weapons in Britain*: Porter, "How Do I Love Thee? A Short History of Trump's Praise for Putin."

235 *previous tough-on-Russia language*: Josh Rogin "Trump Campaign Guts GOP's Anti-Russia Stance on Ukraine," *Washington Post*, July 18, 2016, https://www.washingtonpost.com/opinions/global-opinions/trump-campaign-guts-gops-anti-russia-stance-on-ukraine/2016/07/18/98adb3b0-4cf3-11e6-a7d8-13d06b37f256_story.html.

235 *"in a certain way"*: Ibid.

235 *"know what he looks like"*: Alexander Mallin, "Trump: Crimea's People Prefer Russia, But If He's Elected Putin Is 'Not going into Ukraine,'" ABC News, July 31, 2016, https://abcnews.go.com/ThisWeek/trump-crimeas-people-prefer-russia-elected-putin-ukraine/story?id=41029437.

236 *that hothead was me*: Jeva Lange, "Clinton Ally Paul Begala Thinks Trump Should Consider Bombing Russia's Intelligence Headquarters," *The Week*, July 14, 2017, https://theweek.com/speedreads/712015/clinton-ally-paul-begala-thinks-trump-should-consider-bombing-russias-intelligence-headquarters.

236 *as a result of his request*: Eugene Kiely, "Michael Flynn's Russia Timeline," FactCheck.org, December 1, 2017, https://www.factcheck.org/2017/12/michael-flynns-russia-timeline/.

236 *"top spy and recruiter of spies"*: Tom Lister, "Who Is Sergey Kislyak, the Russian Ambassador to the United States?," CNN, March 2, 2017, https://

www.cnn.com/2017/03/02/world/sergey-kislyak-russian-ambassador-us
-profile/index.html.

236 *smuggle in espionage devices*: Carol Morello and Greg Miller, "Presence of
Russian Photographer in Oval Office Raises Alarms," *Washington Post*, March
10, 2017, https://www.washingtonpost.com/world/national-security/trump
-to-meet-russian-foreign-minister-at-the-white-house-as-moscows-alleged
-election-interference-is-back-in-spotlight/2017/05/10/c6717e4c-34f3-11e7
-b412-62beef8121f7_story.html.

236 *"That's taken off"*: Matt Apuzzo, Maggie Haberman, and Matthew Rosenberg,
"Trump Told Russians That Firing 'Nut Job' Comey Eased Pressure from
Investigation," *New York Times*, May 19, 2017, https://www.nytimes.com/2017
/05/19/us/politics/trump-russia-comey.html.

237 *"intelligence on the Islamic State"*: Greg Miller and Greg Jaffe, "Trump
Revealed Highly Classified Information to Russian Foreign Minister and
Ambassador," *Washington Post*, May 15, 2017, https://www.washingtonpost
.com/world/national-security/trump-revealed-highly-classified-information
-to-russian-foreign-minister-and-ambassador/2017/05/15/530c172a-3960
-11e7-9e48-c4f199710b69_story.html.

237 *"with our own allies"*: Ibid.

237 *"our meeting will yield concrete results"*: Patrick Wintour, " 'It Is an Honour to
Meet with You'—Trump and Putin Meet at G20 Summit in Hamburg," *The
Guardian*, July 7, 2017, https://www.theguardian.com/world/2017/jul/07
/donald-trump-and-putin-exchange-handshake-at-g20-summit-in-hamburg.

237 *two hours and fifteen minutes*: Paul Roderick Gregory, "What Really
Happened at the Trump-Putin Meeting in Hamburg, Germany," *Forbes*,
July 7, 2017, https://www.forbes.com/sites/paulroderickgregory/2017/07/07
/what-really-happened-at-the-trump-putin-meeting-in-hamburg-germany
/#3f262c07428f.

238 *Trump replied, "I believe you"*: Greg Miller, "Trump Has Concealed Details of
His Face-to-Face Encounters with Putin from Senior Officials in Administration," *Washington Post*, January 12, 2019, https://www.washingtonpost.com
/world/national-security/trump-has-concealed-details-of-his-face-to-face
-encounters-with-putin-from-senior-officials-in-administration/2019/01/12
/65f6686c-1434-11e9-b6ad-9cfd62dbb0a8_story.html.

238 *"Not good"*: Eli Watkins and Jeremy Diamond, "Trump, Putin Met for Nearly
an Hour in Second G20 Meeting," CNN, July 18, 2017, https://www.cnn.com
/2017/07/18/politics/trump-putin-g20/index.html.

239 *scope to manipulate Trump*: Miller, "Trump Has Concealed Details of His Face
-to-Face Encounters with Putin from Senior Officials in Administration."

239 *"any reason why it would be"*: Ron Elvin, "Trump's Helsinki Bow to Putin Leaves World Wondering: Why?," NPR, July 17, 2018, https://www.npr .org/2018/07/17/629601233/trumps-helsinki-bow-to-putin-leaves-world -wondering-whats-up.

239 *"Putin was extremely strong and powerful in his denial today"*: Elvin, "Trump's Helsinki Bow to Putin Leaves World Wondering: Why?"

239 *allow an American interpreter in*: Adam Taylor, "Trump Met Putin in Helsinki. More Than 200 Days Later, Will We Ever Find Out What They Said?," *Washington Post*, March 5, 2019, https://www.washingtonpost.com /world/2019/03/05/trump-met-putin-helsinki-more-than-days-later-will-we -ever-find-out-what-they-said/.

240 *"Where are you???"*: Jeremy Diamond, "Trump Sides with Putin over US Intelligence," CNN, July 16, 2018, https://m.cnn.com/en/article/h_4e330b37337 a8790a12dcc1aea8c0203.

240 *"in support of our national security"*: Ibid.

240 *"made us look like a pushover"*: Ibid.

240 *"A sad day for the world"*: Ibid.

240 *"with nothing in return at a meeting"*: "Former Intel Chiefs Condemn Trump's News Conference with Putin," CNN, July 17, 2018, http://lite.cnn.com/en /article/h_8d38e5d3a43918785d86f23c92ba3fc4.

241 *"that they had on Trump"*: Adam Entous, "House Majority Leader to Colleagues in 2016: 'I Think Putin Pays' Trump," *Washington Post*, May 17, 2017, https://www.washingtonpost.com/world/national-security/house -majority-leader-to-colleagues-in-2016-i-think-putin-pays-trump/2017/05 /17/515f6f8a-3aff-11e7-8854-21f359183e8c_story.html.

241 *calling the EU "a foe"?*: Jeff Glor, "'I Think the European Union Is a Foe,' Trump Says Ahead of Meeting Putin in Helsinki," CBS News, July 15, 2018, https://www.cbsnews.com/news/donald-trump-interview-cbs-news-european -union-is-a-foe-ahead-of-putin-meeting-in-helsinki-jeff-glor/.

241 *Trump says Crimea is part of Russia?*: Grace Panetta, "Trump Reportedly Claimed to Leaders at the G7 That Crimea Is Part of Russia Because Everyone There Speaks Russian," *Business Insider*, June 14, 2018, https://www.business insider.com/trump-claims-crimea-is-part-of-russia-since-people-speak -russian-g7-summit-2018-6?op=1.

242 *which would then go back to being called the "G8"?*: "US President Trump Reiterates Calls for Russia to Rejoin 'G8,'" France 24, August 20, 2019, https:// www.france24.com/en/20190820-usa-trump-letting-russia-join-g7-appro priate-g8-industrialised-nations-france-putin.

242 *enshrines press freedom in our First Amendment?*: "Trump Defends Putin

Killing Journalists: US Kills People, Too," *Daily Beast*, December 18, 2015, https://www.thedailybeast.com/cheats/2015/12/18/trump-defends-putin-u-s-kills-too.

242　*"Well, you think our country is so innocent?"*: Abby Phillip, "O'Reilly Told Trump That Putin Is a Killer. Trump's Reply: 'You Think Our Country Is So Innocent?,'" *Washington Post*, February 4, 2017, https://www.washingtonpost.com/news/post-politics/wp/2017/02/04/oreilly-told-trump-that-putin-is-a-killer-trumps-reply-you-think-our-countrys-so-innocent/.

242　*and his daughter in England?*: Josh Lederman, "Skripal Poisoning: Trump Admin Yet to Impose New Russia Sanctions Required by Law," NBC News, January 24, 2019, https://www.nbcnews.com/politics/national-security/trump-admin-has-not-imposed-new-sanctions-russia-required-law-n962216.

242　*sanctions imposed to punish Russia for the 2016 cyberattack?*: Kevin Bohn, "Treasury Department Lifts Sanctions on Three Russian Firms with Ties to Oleg Deripaska," CNN, January 27, 2019, https://www.cnn.com/2019/01/27/politics/trump-admin-lifts-sanctions-oleg-deripaska/index.html.

242　*thus legitimizing the fraudulent Putin victory?*: Carol Leonnig, David Nakamura, and Josh Dawsey, "Trump's National Security Advisers Warned Him Not to Congratulate Putin. He Did It Anyway," *Washington Post*, March 20, 2018, https://www.washingtonpost.com/politics/trumps-national-security-advisers-warned-him-not-to-congratulate-putin-he-did-it-anyway/2018/03/20/22738ebc-2c68-11e8-8ad6-fbc50284fce8_story.html.

242　*"code-word classified intel to an alleged Russian spy in the Oval Office?"*: Miller and Jaffe, "Trump Revealed Highly Classified Information to Russian Foreign Minister and Ambassador."

243　*US cancel military exercises with South Korea?*: John Marshall, "Trump Says He Got Korea Idea from Putin," *Talking Points Memo*, June 13, 2018, https://talkingpointsmemo.com/edblog/its-almost-like-a-pattern.

243　*Soviet invasion of Afghanistan was in response to terrorism?*: David Frum, "Why Is Trump Spouting Russian Propaganda?," *Atlantic*, January 3, 2019, https://www.theatlantic.com/ideas/archive/2019/01/trump-just-endorsed-ussrs-invasion-afghanistan/579361/.

242　*Russian influence in the region?*: Liz Sly, "In the Middle East, Russia Is Back," *Washington Post*, December 4, 2018, https://www.washingtonpost.com/world/in-the-middle-east-russia-is-back/2018/12/04/e899df30-aaf1-11e8-9a7d-cd30504ff902_story.html.

243　*"Far more than our president has been a leader"*: "Trump: Putin Is Better Leader Than Obama," *Daily Beast*, April 13, 2017, https://www.thedailybeast.com/cheats/2016/09/07/trump-putin-is-better-leader-than-obama.

243 *His girlfriend watched in horror*: Joshua Yaffa, "The Unaccountable Death of Boris Nemtsov," *New Yorker*, February 26, 2016, https://www.newyorker.com /news/news-desk/the-unaccountable-death-of-boris-nemtsov.

244 *"The evidence . . . indicates that the defendants were not guilty and the murder was organized by the regime"*: David Satter, "The U.S. Must Speak Out on Russian Terror," *National Review*, March 6, 2018, https://www.nationalreview .com/2018/03/vladimir-putin-russian-human-rights-violations-united-states -must-speak-out/.

244 *Putin responded, "We also have. It's the same"*: Julian Borger, "Trump Jokes to Putin They Should 'Get Rid' of Journalists," *The Guardian*, June 28, 2019, https://www.theguardian.com/us-news/2019/jun/28/smirking-trump-jokes -to-putin-dont-meddle-in-us-election-g20.

244 *"Well, I think our country does plenty of killing also, Joe"*: Phillip, "O'Reilly Told Trump That Putin Is a Killer. Trump's Reply: 'You Think Our Country Is So Innocent?'"

245 *Erdogan threw him in jail*: Ozgur Ozgret, "Turkey Crackdown Chronicle: Week of September 17, 2017," Committee to Protect Journalists, September 18, 2017, https://cpj.org/blog/2017/09/turkey-crackdown-chronicle-week-of -september-17-20.php.

245 *"he's getting very high marks"*: Ibid.

245 *"Not a peep from Trump or the White House"*: Ibid.

246 *with Erdogan in attendance*: Eric Levitz, "Trump's (Insane) Conflict of Interest in the Turkey-Syria Dispute," *New York Magazine*, October 8, 2019, https:// nymag.com/intelligencer/2019/10/trump-turkey-kurds-syria-conflict-of -interest-istanbul-towers.html.

246 *"that brand on their building should immediately remove it"*: "Erdogan Calls For Removal of 'Trump' from Tower in Istanbul," PressTV, June 25, 2016, https://www.presstv.com/Detail/2016/06/25/472171/erdogan-trump-tower -istanbul.

246 *and reportedly stunned our close allies in places like Israel and the United Kingdom*: Mark Landler, Helene Cooper, and Eric Schmitt, "Trump to With-draw US from Syria, Declaring 'We Have Won Against Isis,'" *New York Times*, December 19, 2018, https://www.nytimes.com/2018/12/19/us/politics/trump -syria-turkey-troop-withdrawal.html.

247 *and to Syrian leader Bashar al-Assad*: Ibid.

247 *Mattis was so outraged he resigned*: Paul Sonne, Josh Dawsey, and Missy Ryan, "Mattis Resigns After Clash with Trump over Troop Withdrawal from Syria and Afghanistan," *Washington Post*, December 20, 2018, https://www.wash ingtonpost.com/world/national-security/trump-announces-mattis-will-leave

-as-defense-secretary-at-the-end-of-february/2018/12/20/e1a846ee-e147
-11e8-ab2c-b31dcd53ca6b_story.html.

247   *the victory over ISIS could be reversed if the United States pulled out*: "Trump's
      Call with Turkish Leader Led to US Pullout from Syria," Associated Press/*LA
      Times*, December 21, 2018, https://www.latimes.com/nation/nationnow/la-na
      -pol-syria-withdraw-erdogan-trump-20181221-story.html.

247   *and hung up without offering any more specifics*: Ibid.

248   *"reports of attacks on schools by government forces"*: "Philippines: Duterte's
      'Drug War' Claims 12000 Lives," Human Rights Watch, January 18, 2018,
      https://www.hrw.org/news/2018/01/18/philippines-dutertes-drug-war-claims
      -12000-lives#.

248   *"a way of speaking for him"*: Charlie Campbell, "Obama Plays It Cool on
      Duterte's 'Son of a Whore' Slur at ASEAN Summit," *Time*, September 8, 2016,
      https://time.com/4483650/obama-duterte-son-of-a-whore-asean/.

249   *"neither will he accept any official invitation to visit the United States"*: Karen
      Lima, Martin Petty, and Phil Stewart, "Duterte Eliminates Philippines Troop
      Pact; US Calls Move 'Unfortunate,'" Reuters, February 11, 2020, https://www
      .reuters.com/article/us-philippines-usa-defence-idUSKBN2050E9.

249   *"a serious step with significant implications"*: "The Philippines Tears Up a
      Defence Pact with America," *The Economist*, February 13, 2020, https://www
      .economist.com/asia/2020/02/13/the-philippines-tears-up-a-defence-pact
      -with-america.

249   *licensing his name and receiving royalties*: Carolyn Kenney and John Norris,
      "Trump's Conflicts of Interest in the Philippines," American Progress, June
      14, 2017, https://www.americanprogress.org/issues/security/news/2017/06/14
      /433950/trumps-conflicts-interest-philippines/.

249   *they didn't constitute a majority of either chamber of Congress*: Dareh
      Gregorian, "Democrats Lack Legal Standing to Sue Trump over Alleged
      Emoluments Violations, Appeals Court Rules," NBC News, February 7, 2020,
      https://www.nbcnews.com/politics/donald-trump/federal-appeals-court
      -dismisses-trump-emoluments-case-n1132441.

250   *according to a debt prospectus* Forbes *obtained*: Dan Alexander, "Trump's
      Biggest Conflict of Interest Is Hiding in Plain Sight," *Forbes*, February
      13, 2018, https://www.forbes.com/sites/danalexander/2018/02/13/trump
      -conflicts-of-interest-tenants-donald-business-organization-real-estate-assets
      -pay/#f629c2148f97.

250   *reduce its Trump Tower presence to just one floor*: "China's Biggest Bank to
      Reduce Its Space at Trump Tower," *Bloomberg*, January 9, 2019, https://www

.bnnbloomberg.ca/china-s-biggest-bank-to-reduce-its-space-at-trump-tower
-1.1195744.

250 *"the world's principal IP infringer"*: Sherisse Pham, "How Much Has the US
Lost from China's IP Theft," CNN, March 23, 2o18, https://money.cnn.com
/2018/03/23/technology/china-us-trump-tariffs-ip-theft/index.html.

250 *"charitable fundraising and art valuation services"*: "Ivanka Trump Receives 5
Trademarks from China Amid Trade Talks," CBS News, January 21, 21019,
https://www.cbsnews.com/news/ivanka-trump-receives-5-trademarks-from
-china-amid-trade-talks/.

250 *And, of course, voting machines*: Ibid.

251 *several of the trademarks will remain viable until 2028*: Caroline Zhang,
"Ivanka Trump's Business Wins Approval for 16 New Chinese Trademarks
Despite Shutting Down," Citizens for Responsibility and Ethics in Washington, November 5, 2018, https://www.citizensforethics.org/ivanka-trump
-trademarks/.

251 *"fire and fury like the world has never seen"*: Peter Baker and Choe Sang-Hun,
"Trump Threatens 'Fire and Fury' Against North Korea If It Endangers US,"
New York Times, August 8, 2017, https://www.nytimes.com/2017/08/08/world
/asia/north-korea-un-sanctions-nuclear-missile-united-nations.html.

251 *"And we fell in love"*: " 'He Wrote Me Beautiful Letters and We Fell in Love':
Donald Trump on Kim Jong-un," *The Guardian*, September 30, 2018, https://
www.theguardian.com/us-news/video/2018/sep/30/he-wrote-me-beautiful
-letters-and-we-fell-in-love-donald-trump-on-kim-jong-un-video.

251 *"from everything we're seeing"*: Quint Forgey, "Trump Praises Kim Jong Un as
'Very Honorable,' " *Politico*, April 24, 2018, https://www.politico.com/story
/2018/04/24/trump-praise-kim-jong-un-547610; "Otto Warmbier's Parents
Open Up About Son's Torture by North Korea: 'They Are Terrorists,' " Fox
News, September 26, 2017, https://www.foxnews.com/us/otto-warmbiers
-parents-open-up-about-sons-torture-by-north-korea-they-are-terrorists.

252 *Days later, Otto was dead*: Susan Svrluga and Anna Fifield, "Otto Warmbier
Dies Days After Release from North Korean Detainment," *Washington Post*,
June 19, 2017, https://www.washingtonpost.com/news/grade-point/wp/2017
/06/19/otto-warmbier-dies-days-after-release-from-north-korean-detainment/.

252 *"No excuse or lavish praise can change that"*: David Nakamura and Susan
Svrluga, "Otto Warmbier's Family Rebukes Trump's Defense of Kim Jong Un:
Kim and His Evil Regime Are Responsible for Unimaginable Cruelty," *Chicago
Tribune*, March 1, 2019, https://www.chicagotribune.com/nation-world/ct
-otto-warmbier-family-trump-20190301-story.html.

252 *"That's attractive to Trump"*: Philip Rucker, " 'Dictator Envy': Trump Praise of Kim Jong Un Widens His Embrace of Totalitarian Leaders," *Washington Post*, June 15, 2018, https://www.washingtonpost.com/politics/dictator-envy -trumps-praise-of-kim-jong-un-marks-embrace-of-totalitarian-leaders/2018 /06/15/b9a8bbc8-70af-11e8-afd5-778aca903bbe_story.html.

252 *She could bait Trump*: Alex Pereene, "How We Fooled Donald Trump into Retweeting Benito Mussolini," *Gawker*, February 28, 2016, https://gawker.com /how-we-fooled-donald-trump-into-retweeting-benito-musso-1761795039.

253 *"he'd be convicted in 30 minutes"*: Alex Ward, "US Senators Say Saudi Crown Prince Is 'Complicit' in Khashoggi Murder," *Vox*, December 4, 2018, https:// www.vox.com/policy-and-politics/2018/12/4/18125821/jamal-khashoggi -saudi-arabia-mbs-corker-graham-trump.

253 *"very good control"*: Josh Dawsey, "In Post Interview, Trump Calls Saudi Prince Mohammed a 'Strong Person' Who 'Truly Loves His Country,' " *Washington Post*, November 20, 2018, https://www.washingtonpost.com/politics /in-post-interview-trump-calls-saudi-crown-prince-mohammed-a-strong -person-who-truly-loves-his-country/2018/10/20/1eda48c0-d4d5-11e8-b2d2 -f397227b43f0_story.html?noredirect=on.

253 *"maybe he did and maybe he didn't!"* Donald Trump, "Statement from President Donald J. Trump on Standing with Saudi Arabia," The White House, November 20, 2018, https://www.whitehouse.gov/briefings-statements/state ment-president-donald-j-trump-standing-saudi-arabia/.

253 *"And really took control of it"*: Cristiano Lima, "Trump Praises Egypt's al-Sisi: 'He's a Fantastic Guy,' " *Politico*, November 22, 2016, https://www.politico.com /story/2016/09/trump-praises-egypts-al-sisi-hes-a-fantastic-guy-228560.

253 *to describe the massacre of 817 protestors*: Patrick Kinsley, "Egypt's Rabaa Massacre: One Year On," *The Guardian*, August 16, 2014, https://www.the guardian.com/world/2014/aug/16/rabaa-massacre-egypt-human-rights-watch.

253 *"Where's my favorite dictator?"* Nancy A. Youseff, Vivian Salama, and Michael C. Bender, "Trump, Awaiting Egyptian Counterpart at Summit, Called Out for 'My Favorite Dictator,' " *Wall Street Journal*, September 13, 2019, https:// www.wsj.com/articles/trump-awaiting-egyptian-counterpart-at-summit -called-out-for-my-favorite-dictator-11568403645.

254 *"Doral, yes, in Miami"*: Michael Birnbaum, Philip Rucker, and Ashley Parker, "NATO Summit Ends with Trump calling Trudeau 'Two-Faced' After Video of World Leaders Apparently Mocking the President," *Washington Post*, December 4, 2019, https://www.washingtonpost.com/world/europe/nato -braces-for-contentious-summit-as-trump-other-leaders-gather-near-london /2019/12/04/5994d97c-0fc0-11ea-924c-b34d09bbc948_story.html.

255 *give himself a big fat government contract*: Philip Rucker and David A. Fahrenthold, "Trump Says His Doral Golf Resort Will No Longer Host Next Year's G-7 Summit, Bowing to Criticism," *Washington Post*, October 20, 2019, https://www.washingtonpost.com/politics/trump-announces-that-his-doral-golf-resort-in-miami-will-no-longer-host-next-years-g-7-summit-after-criticism/2019/10/19/857361d0-f2dd-11e9-8693-f487e46784aa_story.html.

255 *"and even scorned by other nations are long behind us"*: Nicole Narea and Catherine Kim, "Read the Full Text of Trump's State of the Union Speech," *Vox*, February 4, 2020, https://www.vox.com/2020/2/4/21123394/state-of-the-union-full-transcript-trump.

255 *to 49 percent in Trump's first year in office*: Richard Wike, "9 Charts on How the World Sees Trump" Pew Research Center Fact Tank, July 17, 2017. https://www.pewresearch.org/fact-tank/2017/07/17/9-charts-on-how-the-world-sees-trump/.

255 *62 percent say he is dangerous*: Ibid.

255 *sitting pretty in Russia, with 53 percent approval*: Ibid.

256 *the autocratic leaders of China (28 percent) and Russia (27 percent)*: Ibid.

256 *"from Tel Aviv to Jerusalem"*: Maria Sheahan, "Germany Must Stop Relying on US Foreign Policy: Foreign Minister," Reuters, December 4, 2017, https://www.reuters.com/article/us-germany-foreign/germany-must-stop-relying-on-u-s-for-foreign-policy-foreign-minister-idUSKBN1DY2U1.

256 *"authoritarian leaders in North Korea, Russia, or Turkey"*: Ibid.

257 *"four or five years hasn't gone there"*: Alissa J. Rubin, "France's President Criticizes Trump over Paris Remarks, *New York Times*, February 25, 2017, https://www.nytimes.com/2017/02/25/world/europe/frances-president-criticizes-trump-over-paris-remarks.html.

257 *The terrorist attack in Nice was in 2016*: Ibid.

257 *"not do that with regard to France"*: Ibid.

258 *by saving us from climate change*: Sophie Tatum, "Macron's Call to 'Make Our Planet Great Again' Attracts Six More US-Based Scientists," CNN, May 2, 2018, https://www.cnn.com/2018/05/02/politics/make-our-planet-great-again-macron/index.html.

258 *"and the middle class will have to pay for it"*: Ibid.

258 *"a bigger market taken together than the American market"*: Jean-Baptiste Vey and Michel Rose, "No Leader Is Forever, Macron Says, as 'G6' Gears Up to Confront Trump," Reuters, June 7, 2018, https://www.reuters.com/article/us-g7-summit-macron/no-leader-is-forever-macron-says-as-g6-gears-up-to-confront-trump-idUSKCN1J329V.

258 *"represent a real force at the international level today"*: Ibid.

CHAPTER 15: YA GOTTA SERVE SOMEBODY

261 *"Do you see?"*: Khaled Hosseini, *The Kite Runner* (New York: Riverhead Books, 2013), 18.

261 *"what self-centered men have torn down, other-centered men can build up"*: Dr. Martin Luther King Jr., "Acceptance Speech on the Occasion of the Award of the Nobel Peace Prize in Oslo," December 10, 1964, https://www.nobelprize.org/prizes/peace/1964/king/26142-martin-luther-king-jr-acceptance-speech-1964/.

262 *"helping spread the word about volunteerism in cities all over the country"*: Richard Dunham, "Q&A: President George H. W. Bush Talks about Volunteerism, His Family and Friendship with Bill Clinton," *Houston Chronicle*, March 21, 2011, https://blog.chron.com/txpotomac/2011/03/qa-president-george-h-w-bush-talks-about-volunteerism-his-family-and-his-friendship-with-bill-clinton/.

263 *"giving us all a sense of new hope and limitless possibilities"*: Bill Clinton, "In Their Own Words; Transcript of Speech by Clinton Accepting Democratic Nomination," *New York Times*, July 17, 1992, https://www.nytimes.com/1992/07/17/news/their-own-words-transcript-speech-clinton-accepting-democratic-nomination.html.

263 *and in 2009 signed the Edward M. Kennedy Serve America Act*: Samantha Joe Warfield, "President Obama Signs Landmark National Service Legislation," Corporation for National and Community Service, April 21, 2009, https://www.nationalservice.gov/newsroom/press-releases/2009/president-obama-signs-landmark-national-service-legislation.

264 *so, too, should today's young people*: Paul Begala, "Thank Bill Clinton for AmeriCorps," CNN Opinion, September 11, 2014, https://stories.clintonfoundation.org/thank-bill-clinton-for-americorps-30c1de468365. Used with the permission of CNN.

266 *"I think I have an answer to that question"*: Michael Brown, "A Message from the Co-Founder/CEO of City Year," Wind Walking, January 18, 2009, https://windwalking.blogspot.com/2009/01/.

266 *they have a 75 percent chance of graduating*: "Our Impact," Service Year, https://serviceyear.org/cityyear/.

266 *"but is not defined by your existence alone"*: John Eades, "With 1 Quote John McCain Taught 3 Vital Lessons on What It Means to Be a Leader," *Inc.*, August 27, 2018, https://www.inc.com/john-eades/with-1-quote-john-mccain-taught-3-vital-lessons-on-what-it-means-to-be-a-leader.html.

267 *Think of a sumo wrestler sitting on your chest*: Stephen A. Nelson,

"Earthquakes and the Earth's Interior," Tulane University, September 24, 2015, https://www.tulane.edu/~sanelson/eens1110/earthint.htm.

267   *you'd have to have a car that held more than 160 million people*: Tom Kertscher, "Bernie Sanders on Target Saying 3 Richest Have as Much Wealth as Bottom Half of All Americans," PolitiFact, July 3, 2019, https://www.politifact.com /factchecks/2019/jul/03/bernie-sanders/bernie-sanders-target-saying-3 -richest-have-much-w/.

268   *from a meager 4 percent in 1989 to just 1 percent today*: Pedro Nicolaci da Costa, "America's Humongous Wealth Gap Is Widening Further," *Forbes*, May 29, 2019, https://www.forbes.com/sites/pedrodacosta/2019/05/29/americas -humungous-wealth-gap-is-widening-further/#43cf612a42ee.

268   *the rock splits and the earth quakes*: Nelson, "Earthquakes and the Earth's Interior."

268   *"I don't know anybody who voted for him"*: James Wolcott, "The Fraudulent Factoid That Refuses to Die," *Vanity Fair*, October 23, 2012, https://www .vanityfair.com/culture/2012/10/The-Fraudulent-Factoid-That-Refuses-to-Die.

269   *"But sometimes when I'm in a theater I can feel them"*: Ibid.

269   *"can barely conceive of 'those people' who live just a few miles away"*: Billy Bishop with Robert G. Cushing, "Why the Clustering of Like-Minded Americans Is Tearing Us Apart," *The Big Sort* (New York: Houghton Mifflin, 2008), http://www.thebigsort.com/home.php.

270   *The number of people currently serving in AmeriCorps is 75,000*: "Current Members," AmeriCorps, https://www.nationalservice.gov/newsroom/commu nication-resources/fact-sheets.

270   *The Peace Corps currently has about 7,400 volunteers*: "The Peace Corps: Overview and Issues," Congressional Research Service, June 26, 2019, https:// fas.org/sgp/crs/misc/RS21168.pdf.

270   *currently serving on active duty in our military*: George Reynolds and Amanda Shendruk, "Demographics of the US Military," Council on Foreign Relations, April 24, 2018, https://www.cfr.org/article/demographics-us-military.

270   *are more than 45 million Americans between the ages of twenty and thirty*: Erin Duffin, "Recent Population of the United States by Sex and Age as of July 1, 2018," *Statista*, August 9, 2019, https://www.statista.com/statistics/241488 /population-of-the-us-by-sex-and-age/.

INDEX